MICROECONOMICS

MICROECONOMICS
IDEAS AND ANALYSIS

By

V. P. Raghavan

GYAN

Microeconomics Ideas and Analysis

ISBN : 978-81-212-0188-9

First Published 1988, reprint 2014 in India by
Gyan Publishing House
23, Main Ansari Road, Daryaganj,
New Delhi - 110002
Phones : 23282060, 23261060
Fax : (011) 23285914
E-mail: books@gyanbooks.com
website: gyanbooks.com

Printed at : Sagar Color Scan, New Delhi.

PREFACE

The study of economic theories is an essential part of a systematic study of the science of economics. Economic theories which form the real foundations of economics science generalise economic ideas. The science of economics analyses the basic problems of man and society and find solutions to them.

The study of economic theories has been conveniently divided into Micro Economic Theories and Macro Economic Theories after Ragnar Frisch who has redesigned the approach to the study of modern economics. The present work highlights the basic principles of Micro-economics in simple language and lucid in style, and intelligible even to the beginners.

The book is designed primarily to meet the requirements of the undergraduate students of economics in Indian Universities. I hope this will serve as a useful textbook for them. The treatment, it is hoped, should also find favour with the general readers who are deeply interested in the subject.

I owe a great deal to authorities in economics from whom I have freely drawn up on. I take the opportunity to express my profound gratitude to M/s. Gian Publishing House, Delhi who have rendered every possible assistance in bringing out this book with atmost expedition.

V. P. RAGHAVAN

Department of Economics
Nehru Arts & Science College,
Kanhangad. (Kerala)

CONTENTS

1

THE ANALYTICAL FRAME WORK

THE CENTRAL THEME OF ECONOMICS

Economics is the Science which studies how an economy functions. An economy exists because of economic problems. Economic problem arises from the fundamental fact that human wants are numerous and the means with which we satisfy them are limited or scarce. Economic studies necessarily concentrate on and revolves around the specific area of human endeavour—the efforts to satisfy his needs and desires. In other words, economics is concerned with most of men's activities that are intended to satisfy their many and varied wants.

It is a fact that we are unable to meet all our wants and desires, for resources need to satisfy them are invariably insufficient. Human wants and desires which go so far beyond the capacity of our productive resources pose the fundamental problem to human existence. Economic problems, thus, arise from insufficiency of resources in relation to our needs. This problem of scarcity necessitates the need to allocate resources. Thus, wants, scarcity and choice form the central theme of economics.

Economics as a scholarly discipline is a relatively new subject. Though the earlier treatise on economics was Kautilya's 'Arthasastra', the real beginning of economics as a pure science may be traced to the appearance of 'Wealth of Nations' (1776) of Adam Smith.

Prior to the publication of 'Wealth of Nations' economics was only a handmaid of politics or theology. The word 'economics' itself has been derived from the Greek 'Oconomicus' which implies the science of household management. It was Alfred Marshall who used the term 'economics' in place of 'political economy' when a systematic treatise on which modern developm ent of the science of economics appeared.

Defining Economics

Defining economics is a delicate task. Much dust has been created about the nature and scope of economics since the definitions of economics are numerous and conflicting. J.N. Keynes was right when he stated, "Political Economy is said to have strangled itself with definitions."[1] Many definitions have been suggested from time to time and a few of them may briefly be examined.

The earlier definitions of economics were in terms of wealth. Classical economists like Adam Smith and J.S. Mill considered economics as the science of wealth. Adam Smith, the Father of modern economics, named his work as 'An inquiry into the nature and causes of wealth of Nations' and according to him economics "proposes to enrich both the people and the Sovereign." To J.S. Mill, economics is "the practical science of the production and distribution of wealth." Nassau Senior opines that the subject treated by political economists "is not happiness, but wealth" and F.A. Walker defines economics as "that body of knowledge which relates to wealth." The wealth definition was criticised by later writers as unsatisfactory on the ground that it has given undue importance to wealth ignoring man and his welfare. They narrowed the scope of economics, by excluding all economic activities that are related to the production of non-material goods and services. The exphasis has then shifted from wealth to man and his welfare. Alfred Marshall rightly points out that economics is 'on the one side a study of wealth, and on the other, and more important side a part of the study of man.

Accordingly, until recently the definition given by Alfred Marshall was accepted as the best working basis for the study of economics. In his words, "Political Economy or Economics is a study of mankind in the ordinary business of life; it examines that part of individual and social action which is most closely connected with the use of the material requisites of well-being."[2]

The logical inferences that can be drawn from the above definition are (i) Economics examines economic activities of man. It deals with man's "efforts to satisfy his wants, insofar as the efforts and wants are capable of being measured in terms of wealth or its representative, i.e., money."[3] (ii) Economics is a "study of men as they live and move and think in the ordinary business of life."[4] Economics is a Social science that considers man as a member of society. It is concerned with the economic aspects of men's social life. (iii) Economics is the study of economic activities which promote material welfare. Non-economic activities and activities with ignoble ends are excluded from the purview of economics.

Marshall's treatment of economics as a study of material welfare was followed by other thinkers as well. According to E. Cannan, "the aim of political Economy is the explanation of the general causes on which the material welfare of human beings depends."[5] Beveridge defines economics as "the study of the general methods by which men co-operate to meet their material needs"[6] "the subject-matter of economic science" in the words of A.C. Pigou, is "economic welfare."[7]

Prof. Lionel Robbins of the London School of Economics challenged the traditional view point of the nature of economic science. He made a frontal attack on Marshallian definition of economics as the study of the causes of the material welfare. He rejected the definition as classificatory in the sense that it implied a distinction between material and non-material welfare. He emphasised the fact that modern economics is based on the concept of scarcity and choice.

In his treatise, 'Nature and Significance of Economic Science' Lionel Robbins attempted to define economics in a new fashion. He states—"Economics is the science which studies human behaviour as a relationship between ends and scarce means which have alternative uses."[8] Economics is concerned with the fundamental aspect of human behaviour which arises from the fact of the disposal of limited means to achieve given ends. We have multiple wants, but to secure their satisfaction resources provided by nature are definitely limited. No doubt, in few cases, resources such as air, sunlight or water are available to us in plenty. But barring such exceptions, limitness of means to satisfy our desires is almost universal. Thus the need for economising scarce means forms the basis of economic science.

Means are not only scarce but many of them are capable of using in alternative ways to satisfy our competing ends. "Thus, the limitations of our resources and their ability to satisfy different wants creates a problem, the problem of choosing how to dispose of these resources, which wants to satisfy since they cannot all be satisfied. The economic problem is, therefore, essentially a problem arising from the necessity of choice—choice of the manner in which limited resources with alternative uses are disposed of."[9]

After having examined the traditional definitions of economics, we are in a position to formulate a simplest form of definition highlighting the basic theme of the subject. The shortest sketch of it may be formed as—'Economics is the study of the way we choose among alternative use of scarce resources.'

ALLOCATION OF ECONOMIC RESOURCES

The dilemma of human existence is confined to the basic fact that our desires are limitless and economic resources with which we satisfy our desires are scarce. Faced with the problem of scarce resources and many desires, people usually try as best as possible to get the maximum satisfaction from the smallest amount of resources. The problem is thus that of getting the most from the least. How does it possible ? With the desires of the entire economy to consider, how can we know when we may have maximised satisfaction ? Which goods do we desire to get more, and which are we have to sacrifice ? It is hardly possible to get the 750 million people of India to agree unanimously on the answers to these questions. Yet, somehow or the other, these decisions are to be made and to be carried out. This chapter provides an attempt to analyse the underlying forces of the decision making process.

Limitless Desires

As just noted above, people have an unlimited desires for consumer goods. In economics, consumer goods are those things—material or otherwise—that satisfy a human want. Thus, services such as having your shirts tailored or your pen repaired are also consumer goods since they satisfy human desires.

It may be helpful to distinguish among different types of human desires, such as desire for necessaries and the desire for luxuries. We all need food and water to stay alive and clothes and shelter to protect from hostile environment. These are the physical necessities or absolute necessaries of human beings. Since they form the most basic economic desire, these are to be satisfied in the first instance. We may now point out that human desire for physical necessities will reach its limitation at some level. As income increases people requires nutritional food, better house and stylish clothes. But they won't demand more food than their physical requirements or more clothes than their wearing needs. When people's desires for necessities are satisfied, they will prefer to use their excess money, income or productive resources to satisfy other kinds of desires—desires for comforts and luxuries.

Scarce Resources

Another basic assumption of economic studies is that productive resources—the things which are used to create goods and services that we want—are limited or scarce. They are scarce in the sense that they are incapable of producing everything we want.

Thus most of our economic problems are the results of this fact to scarcity and the need to make effective use of our limited economic resources to satisfy our multiple wants. If there were abundant supply of everything for us without working or paying for it, there would be no economy and no economic problems. But there is hardly any State in the world so ideal accomplishing such paraphernelias. Thus, we need to economise our resources—we must choose among alternative ways of using them to satisfy our largest possible desires. We need to economise time, money, other resources and anything scarce to best fulfill our largest possible wants. The money you spend to buy a wrist-watch can't buy a new radio set. You can go to the movies or play tennis in a fine afternoon, but you can't do them all at the same time. If we use land for cultivating wheat, we can't use it for a shopping centre. The steel we use for railway coaches can't use for ship building. Economic life, thus, itself is a series of trade-offs.

MAXIMISING OUTPUT—THE END OF THE ECONOMY

The starting point of the economic problems in any society is the existence of the insufficient resources. Since scarcity is the villain of the piece, it logically follows that to provide as many goods as possible to the living community, an economy must fully employ its available productive resources with most efficient methods of production. In order to maintain full-employment, an economy must provide employment to all employment seekers, it must fully exploit all available natural resources and must utilise the available capital most efficiently and effectively. That means, an economy must ensure that no productive resources of the economy are involuntarily unemployed.

Besides, in order to ensure full-employment, an economy must avoid all kinds of under-employment situations. Under-employment leads to wastage of economic resources by mis-allocating them. Under-employment relates to the inefficient use of productive apparatus which results in waste of resources. If unsuited resources are employed for a job or productive apparatuses are employed less effectively, inefficiency will be the end result. For example, a geologist employed to undertake a construction work well represents an inefficient allocation of labour resource. In such a case, it would be worthwhile to reallocate productive resources so as to produce more of one commodity that society wants most without sacrificing the output of another. Thus, if the geologist's labour were transferred to a mineral explorating unit or employed in Geological Survey talents would contribute to a considerable increase in society's mineral outputs.

Under-employment of capital equipments can also be occurred, for example, when tools or implements are used in a task for which they are unsuited. Digging a well with a drilling machine is more productive and efficient than it is done with a hand shovel. Thus, we see that we can increase efficiency of production by reallocating labour or capital in a more economical way. Productive activities can also be made more efficient by reducing cost of production. Production can be made less costly through economics of scale. Economics of scale relates to the reduction in costs of production by increasing the scale of production. This occurs when the firm increases its size.

As the firm increases its size, it is able to increase its productivity by increasing the level of specialisation of labour and management. Managers skilled in one area can exclusively be employed in that area rather than having entrusted with many other functions. Large-sized firms can also make use of more efficient method of production. Further, they can make use of by-products in one way or other than are small units.

Problem of Choice

If an economy is producing at full-employment level of not, it can hardly satisfy all the desires of all its members. Since resources are scarce the economy needs to make choices. Producing more of one commodity that people wants necessarily means giving up certain other products. The amounts of other goods that are sacrificed to obtain more of any one good is called opportunity cost of that good.

A simple example will provide us a better understanding of opportunity cost. Suppose you have an amount of Rs. 5 in your pocket to spend, since your resources are limited to the extent of Rs. 5 you cannot buy many things you desire. If you decide to spend it on seeing a filmshow, of course, it gains satisfaction, but it forgoes the satisfaction that could have been obtained by purchasing, say, a magazine.

This simple example illuminates a fundamental economic truth : since our means are scarce we must make choices between alternative goods that will satisfy our desires.

Production Possibilities

Like individual house holds, an economy makes economic choices from among alternatives. Even if an economy uses all of its resources, its production possibilities are constrained by the limitations of economic resources which produces a choice between alternative and relatively scarce commodities. To explain this economic problem, the concept of "Production possibilities" is devised. Production possibilities refer to the various output combinations that an economy can produce when it is fully and efficiently employing its productive resources.

We may now illustrate the concept of production possibilities. To simplify our analysis let us make the following few assumptions. First, the economy employs fully its productive resources as efficiently as possible, regardless of goods it chooses to produce. Second, the supply of available quantity of resources is more or less fixed and the state of technological knowhow is constant. Third, the economy chooses to produce only two commodities, say, shoes and soaps.

The production possibilities schedule given in Table 1.1 briefly summarizes the various output combinations of shoes and soaps that an economy produces when all of its resources are fully employed and techniques of production are efficiently used. The list of combinations of goods given in the schedule are some of the possible choices available to an economy. If all the available productive resources are utilised to produce soaps we can produce 100 million units a year. Or, if we use all the resources to produce shoes we can produce 30 million units a year. These are two extremes. In between these two extreme possibilities, various combinations are possible, for example, 80 million units of soaps and 10 million units of shoes, or 60 million units of soaps and 15 million units of shoes, and so on.

TABLE 1.1

Production Possibilities Schedule for Shoes and Soaps

Possibility	*Units of Soaps per year (In millions)*	*Units of Shoes per year (In millions)*
A	100	0
B	80	10
C	60	15
D	40	20
E	20	25
F	0	30

Of course, soaps and shoes are arbitrary examples. We might have used houses and bridges or any other pair of goods to illustrate the same.

The production possibilities can be made more clear when we transfer these data to a graph. This is done in Figure 1.1. Amount of shoes goes on horizontal axis, and amount of soaps goes on vertical axis. Each dot plots one of the production possibility combinations from Table 1.1. By connecting all these plotted dots we get the production possibility curve. At the ends of the curve the possible extremes of production are seen. Each point on the production possibilities curve indicates some possible combination of soaps and shoes that an economy which employs its resources fully and efficiently could produce. As we move along the curve from one extreme to the other, we see how much of one good is to be sacrificed to get successive units of the other.

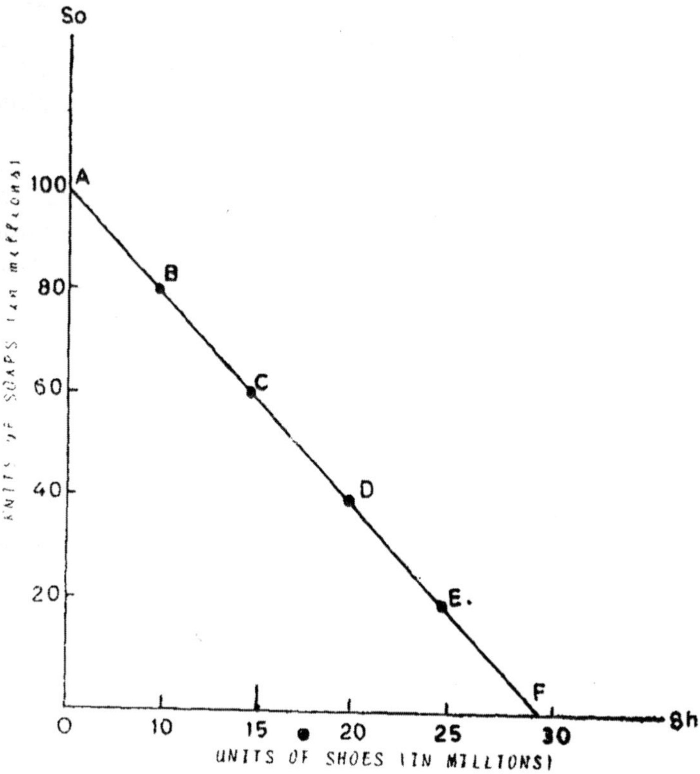

Figure 1.1 : Production Possibilities Curve : Economy's Choices of Goods

The curve that we have, thus, represents the fundamental truth. We can have more of one commodity only by giving up something of another. We may note that there is a 'trade-off' between two or more commodities. If we are willing to give up some amount of soaps, we can have some shoes. Thus, the more resources we use to build public parks, the less will be left to produce private houses, the more we choose to consume of food, the less we are able to get clothing, the more the economy decides to consume today, the less it can produce capital goods to turn out more consumption goods next year. The production possibilities frontier, thus, illustrates many familiar economic processes. Figure 1.2 is self explanatory. It illustrates how an economy consumes much food when it is poor, but shifts towards comforts and luxuries when it develops. Figure 1.2 a shows that since the economy is so poor, it devotes more of its

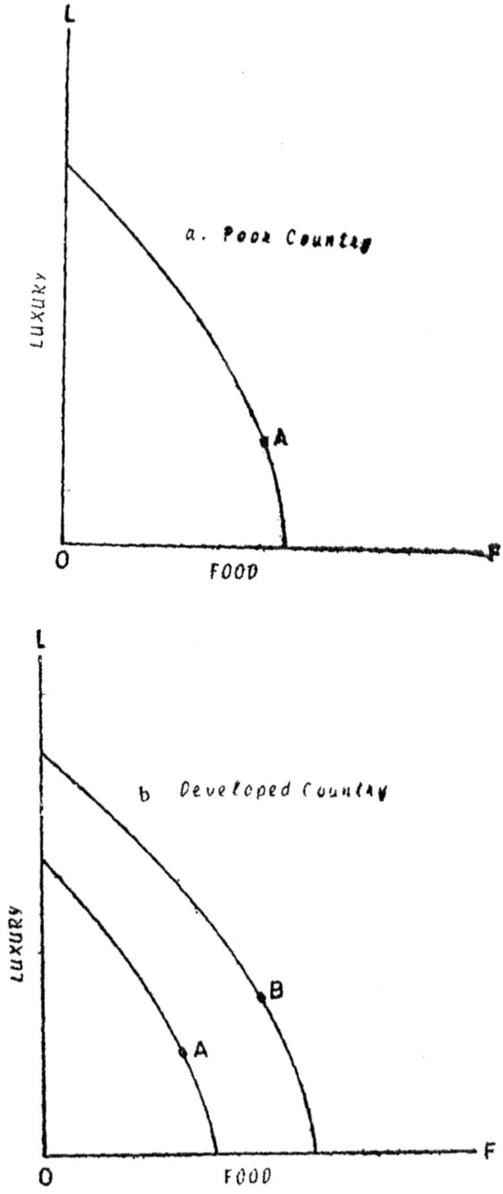

Figure 1.2 : Development shifts production possibilities frontier outward.

productive resources to food, enjoying only very few comforts or luxuries and the production possibility has come to rest at Point A. Figure 1.2b, on the other hand, illustrates that as the nation develops it moves from Point A to B expanding its food consumption comparatively very little against its increased consumption of luxuries.

If the economic resources are not fully employed or employed inefficiently an economy cannot produce the combination of goods with maximum possible extent. If in our given example, the economy produces 40 million units of soaps and 15 million units of shoes, an economy hardly reaches its goal of maximum output. Such a situation is indicated by Point P in Figure 1.3. By producing more

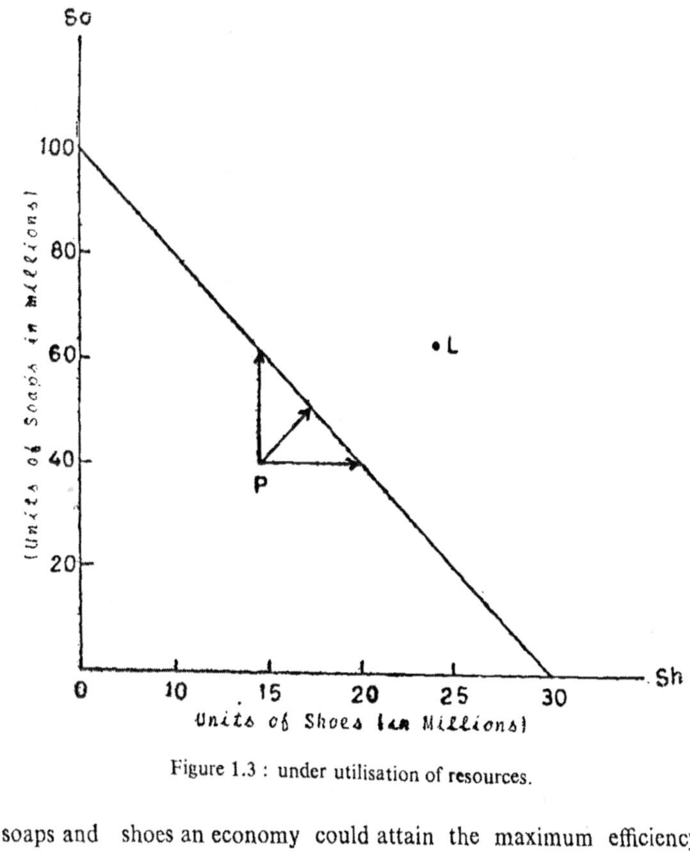

Figure 1.3 : under utilisation of resources.

soaps and shoes an economy could attain the maximum efficiency position on its production possibilities curve. The broken lines indicate some of the ways to reach the maximum efficiency point. A point outside the production possibilities curve points out a level of production which is beyond the production capacity of the economy. Such a situation is indicated by Point L in Figure 1.3. We may note that at the existing resource position and the present state of technical knowhow, it is impossible for an economy to produce beyond the existing production possibilities frontier.

CENTRAL PROBLEMS OF ECONOMIC SYSTEMS

All kinds of economic systems confront the very basic economic problem—the problem of choice. This problem exists because of existence of multiple wants and scarce means. If all our desires are satisfied without any reservation, there would be no economic problems and there exists no economic systems. An economic system, thus, "consists of those institutions which a given people or nation or group of nations has chosen or accepted as the means through which their resources are utilised for the satisfaction of human wants."[10]

Any society, whether it is capitalistic, communistic or of mixed system must somehow or the other solve the basic and inter-dependent problems ofwhat, how, how much and for whom to produce goods and services. These can be summarised in three aspects :

1. What Goods shall be produced and in What Quantities ?

An economy must decide how much and which of alternative goods and services shall be produced, wheat or rice? Much wheat or little rice or *vice versa* ? How much wheat or how much rice ? How much public roads or how much railway tracks? Tubewells or bombers ? Cocacola or drinking water ?

2. How shall Goods be produced ?

After having decided the goods and services to be produced the society must decide by whom and with what resources and in what technique of production that goods shall be produced. The society must decide who will teach and who will fight? Electricity from hydel project or from thermal project ? Large scale or small scale production ? Mass production or production by masses ? Labour-intensive or capital intensive method ?

3. For whom shall goods be produced ?

The society must then decide who is to enjoy and get the benefits of the goods and services produced ? or, in economic jargon, how the total national product is to be distributed ?

The society must also decide, more rich or less poor? Or many in modest comfort? High reward for skill or intelligence ?

These problems, though fundamental, are common to all economic systems. But different economic systems solve these central problems in different ways.

Economic Decisions in A Free-Enterprise System

Let us now focus on free-enterprise market oriented system of the economy and how it allocates productive resources. Free-enterprise capitalistic economy is a system in which property is privately owned and economic decisions are privately taken. Being an advanced edition of *laissez faire* system, there hardly exists any visible means of co-ordinating individual decisions. Without such a concrete co-ordinating mechanism how the system can work ?

A competitive system is an elaborate mechanism of unconscious co-ordination through a system of prices and markets.[11] Before we proceed to examine the operational mechanism of such an economy, we may enunciate certain principles of co-operation and competition, specialisation and competition, specialisation and division of labour, signals and incentives, and the role of prices and markets :

Co-operation and Competition

Members of a volleybal team co-operate with one another in order to compete with another team. Students may co-operate in studying for examinations, and then they themselves compete with each other for getting higher grades in the examination. These are the two veritable examples of indescribably complex net work of competition and co-operation which pervades every aspect of economic life.

We live by co-operating with our fellow citizen. We dress in clothes which we did not make, we eat food which we did not grow. We are all hardly self-sufficient in one way or other. All are interdependent. We go to the grocery shop expecting foodgrains to be waiting there and it is there always. We go to the textile shop where we could find our suitable suitings which are already made and in stock. If we want to buy a radio set, the problem is not of finding one to buy—but of selecting from the vast array of different makes or brands. In short in a free market system, no one is consciously concerned with the triad of economic problems. To paraphrase an example, let us consider Delhi, teeming with hundreds of thousands of people crowded into a few sq. km. without the constant flow of goods and services, it would be on the verge of starvation. But everything is running without much chaos and confusion. Hundreds of millions of commodities are flowed in and out of the city. As the noted French Economist, Frederik Bastiat wrote about Paris, some hundred years ago, that there lived millions of people, each of them would starve in a few days if there was lack of constant flow of provisions into the metropolis. Paris, like any other city in the world, required constant inflow of goods and services, no one planned the inflow, but Paris survived. Bastiat wrote, "imagination is baffled when it tries to appreciate the vast multiplicity of commodities which must enter tomorrow in order to preserve the inhabitants from falting prey to the convulsions of famine, rebellion and pillage. Yet all sleep, and their slumbers are not disturbed for a single minute by the prospect of such a frightful catastrophe."

Specialisation and Division of Lobour

The network of co-operation necessitates division of labour and the consequent specialisation. Division of labour into different tasks and the specialisation of various workers in each of these tasks necessarily increases productivity. It was Adam Smith who first described the advantages of division and specialisation of labour. He visited a pin factory in his nearby town and was struck by the tremendous achievement in productivity that resulted from specialisation. Though the factory was primitive by modern standards, it was well advanced so far as the 18th century England was concerned. He wrote an account of the productive activity in the pin factory and it became a classic in the economic literature. He himseif described the process of pin-making that he could find there as : "One man draws out the wire, another straights it, a third cuts it, a fourth points it, a fifth grinds it at the top for receiving the head, to make the head requires two or three distinct operations, to put it on is a peculiar business, to whiten it is another, it is even a trade by itself to put them into paper."[12]

Competition

Businessmen undertake business activities to earn profit.

Those who undertake productive activities on the same line are to compete with one another to seek maximum possible profits. The competition among business community guarantees the availability of goods and services that are most desired by the households in the market. The profit motive and the competition for profit assures that the goods and services available in the market are those for which the people are most willing and able to pay.

In sum, there lies a two-edged principle of co-operation and competition. Co-operation permits division of labour and specialisation increases productivity. Competition, further, assures each of the participants that he will benefit from specialisation.

Incentives

We have pointed out that the desire for profit causes the businessmen to compete with one another in an attempt to produce those commodities which are most desired by the households. Thus profit motive acts as an important incentive for businessmen and they attempt to maximise profit in their business activities. In the case of individual households it is assumed that the economic behaviour of them is motivated by the desire for money income. Similarly, we select our occupations, to a certain extent, on the basis of money income that we expect to receive from it. That is, we may attempt to maximise our money income and as such the greatest incentive for us is the desire to obtain maximum possible money income.

Signals

When the price of one commodity increases in relation to the prices of other commodities, the bussinesses receive a signal that the consumers want more of that commodity. Since business are motivated by the desire for getting profit, they begin to produce that commodity whose price rises or they begin to increase the present level of production of that commodity. Similarly, if the starting salary of college lecturers were generally higher than the salary of civil servants, more graduate students would be stimulated to pursue their post graduate studies.

Thus there is the principle of signals and incentives to accompany the principle of co-operation and competition. Business men and workers are furnished with the signals of relative prices and wages.

Operational Mechanism of Market System

After having discussed the principles of competition and

co-operation and of signals and incentives, we may now proceed to describe the way in which a free market oriented system, reaches the fundamental decisions. In this analysis we may bear in mind that the economy operates through a price system and that all these fundamental decisions are taken simultaneously. Let us analyse one by one and then proceed to look at the process of simultaneous functioning.

Deciding What to Produce ?

Under a free, competitive and market oriented system, consumers play a decisive role in determining the nature and quantum of output. Price system works in such an economy through the decentralised actions of millions of households and businesses. The central problems of what and how much to produce are solved by the independent decisions of a multitude of buyers and sellers in the market. Since consumers are the final decision makers in the economy, consumer's sovereignty is said to be the fundamental characteristics of the free market economy.

Each individual or household obtains money income by any means. When we spend a rupee on a particular commodity, we cast a vote for the production of that commodity. In essence, those goods that receive the highest number of rupee votes are the ones produced.

Another basic feature of this economic decision is that each consuming unit itself decides what goods it wishes to buy within the limitations of its purchasing power. Whenever we purchase a particular commodity, we register our preferences by the amount of money we spend on that commodity. The more we want something, the more we will spend on it and we will be willing to pay a higher price for it. This is how the price system decides which goods are to be produced in a market system.

Deciding How to Produce ?

We have seen that consumers' choices dominate production decisions and have some consequences on 'What' decision. The businessmen, on the other hand, takes the responsibility for the 'how'. The goods that we want get produced by the businesses. Businessmen are in search of profits and profits will be made maximum when they produce commodities whose prices exceed costs of production. The profit seeking businesses will have an incentive to produce more of anything when the consumers' demand bids up the price of it. They also have an incentive to lower cost of production since that too will increase their profit margins.

Thus the businesemen or entrepreneurs, as we usually call them, perform the most important social function—organisation of productive processes resources are channelled into producing those commodities that are most wanted by the households. Since the businesses are guided by the profit motive, they produce commodities as efficiently as possible. And we note that efficiency can be made possible with least-cost combination of production.

Deciding How to Provide

Finally, let us see how a free-enterprise system decides up on the distribution of its products—who gets the goods that are produced by the businesses? We may note that the price system allocates the goods and services to the consumers according to their desire and purchasing power to buy them. We will approach this in two steps.

The first step involves the distribution of money incomes. Most of us earn incomes either by way of working for business or on profession or by being businessmen or professionals. We also earn incomes on properties. Businessmen earn incomes by offering commodities that enjoys profit. Employees earn their incomes by way of offering their labour services to the businesses. We are able to buy commodities with the money incomes earned for our services. Likewise the entrepreneurs are able to buy the required materials in the form of inputs with the incomes they receive by setting their products.

Secondly, goods and services are distributed to those who desire and are able to purchase. Each consumer must pay a price for goods and services he wants. Those who are having larger amount of money incomes can afford more, while poor people buy streaks. Here again, prices play a vital role by rationing the final products among consumers on the basis of ability to pay for each product. Those who are unwilling and unable to pay are hardly getting any commodity.

Solving All Problems Simultaneously

We have discussed the three basic problems separately. The economic system is not having a separate entity. It consists of large and inter-connected set of markets, each with numerous buyers and sellers. The fundamental economic decisions are, thus, taken simultaneously and interdependently. It can be explained with a

"Circular flow" of economic activity, which is schematically represented in Figure 1.4.

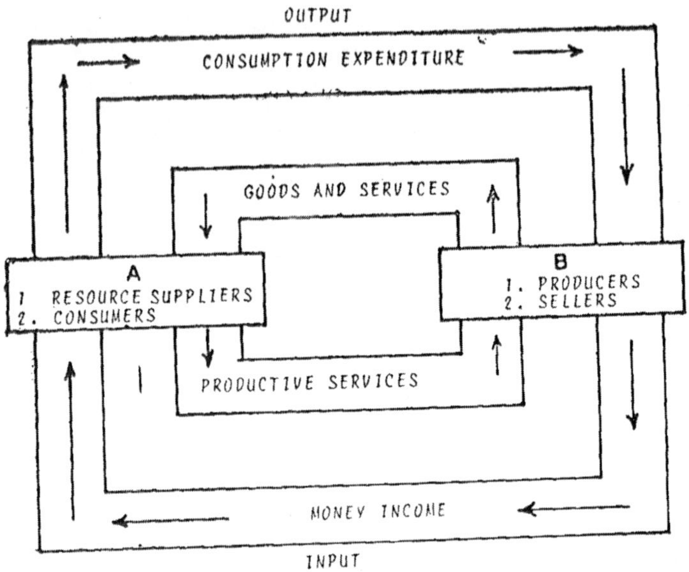

Figure 1.4. Circular Flow of Economic Activity.

In an economy there are two sets of economic objects : households act as the resource suppliers and businessmen, on the otherhand, are the organisers of production. Businessmen employ productive resources in order to produce goods. In return for their productive resources, households get money income from businesses in the form of rent, wages and interest. These two flows labelled "input" are depicted in the lower segment of the diagram.

Again, households are consumers who spend their money incomes to buy commodities produced by businessmen. In return for their consumption expenditures, they receive goods from businessmen. These two flows are depicted in the upper segment of the diagram and are labelled as "output".

We have already seen how a free enterprise system decides what to produce, how to produce and how to distribute national product among the participating members of the society. Adam Smith in his 'Wealth of Nations' proclaimed his notion of invisible hand influencing the basic problems in a free market economy. Economic activities are directed by the invisible hand, he asserts. The price mechanism translated the individual economic actions into an orderly form. Each individual acts to promote his own self-interest as if led by an invisible hand, which in turn promotes the interest of the society as a whole.

Decisions in a Planned Economy

We have just noted how the basic economic problems are solved in a free market economy. It is seen that the major economic decisions are taken through a price-system which is influenced by the impersonal forces of invisible hand.

Let us now discuss how a centrally planned economy takes major economic decisions. In Soviet Russia, a pioneer in command economy, 'What to produce' decision is taken by the State operating through its central planning authority called Gosplan. It is not decided by the price signals or incentives since there is absence of private businesses. The decision regarding 'what to produce' and 'how much' is taken by the central planning agency authoritatively. The Gosplan prepares the national plan that governs the operation of the Russian economy. The goods produced are grouped into three sectors—consumer goods, industrial goods and agricultural goods. Within the broad framework of the national plan specific plans for each sector are prepared alongwith the statement of items of goods produced and its quantities.

The decision regarding how to produce is also contained in the plan. The plan stipulates the location and the pattern of new plants. In addition, the Gosplan maintains 'balances' concerned with the nature and availability of raw materials and labour between number of jobs created and the job-seekers and between the requirements and production of goods and services.

The problem of distribution, the 'for whom' decision, is also handled by the State. Immediately after the Revolution workers were paid a uniform amount as wages irrespective of productivity. But later it was abolished and the extra-productive workers—commonly referred to as stakhanovites, were paid monetary and non-monetary rewards as incentives—in excess of their ordinary wages. But now-a-days large differentials are seen in Soviet Russia, even. However, as just noted, the 'for whom to produce' decision is in the hands of the State authority.

Mixed Economy : Imperfections

Ours is a mixed economy in which both public and private institutions control the economic activity. A free market economy achieves the economic goals of the society through a freely determined market mechanism. Adam Smith thought that this would be the result of the guidance of the invisible hand and that for the smooth functioning of the system there must prevail pure competition.

Mixed economy is an admixture of competitive and monopolistic elements. Monopoly elements are seemed to be the most serious source of imperfections. There may be one or few producers controlling the productive activities. When they undertake production of a commodity, the price may be fixed too high by competitive standards. There may not be many sellers to compete with one another, prices may not be driven down and output may not be as much as it could be otherwise. Resources may, probably, be misallocated and wastefully used.

Freely and competitively determined prices are considered the signals to indicate what to produce and how much. If, on the other hand, prices are monopolistically determined, there arises the possibility for false signals. Thus, even if the production is efficiently undertaken, it may be misdirected. And in the absence of competitive pressure, costs may not be kept minimum and resources may be used inefficiently.

TOOLS OF ANALYSIS

The introductory remarks have laid out the basic problems of economics and suggested the broad outlines of the way the different economics solve these problems. We may now turn to a look at how economists analyse economics problems of the economy.

Straight thinking is much more difficult in economics because, as a social science, economics is mixed up with our everyday life. Every day life of every one has accummulated opinions, ideas, hearsay, semi-truth and all that subtly dominate our minds when economic problems arise.

Economics is an empirical study based on real world data. Like any other sciences, it has to develop theories about the economic world. Any theory, if it is useful, must be rested on empirical facts and relationships about which it is analysing. Economic theories also rest on validated facts and their relationships.

Complexity is apparent fact about the economic world and reality. Hundreds of millions of businesses and households are there in an economy. Numerous products are seen there with multiple stages in the production of each product. In view of this overwhelming complexity, we need to simplify things to manageable proportions.

Theory Models

In order to simplify the complexity of the economy, we begin to develop an analytical framework of the economic reality. These are often referred to as "theories" or "models" in economics. The theory can be illustrated with the help of a non-economic example. Suppose we want to understand how an electric motor works—a theory of its operation—we could study every detail of a single motor examining each and every part of it. If, instead, we get a simple diagram or the working model of an electric motor, we could grasp the essentials more quickly. This diagram may not be concerned with all the details of frame, style and so on. Instead, it would help us to understand the fundamental ideas of an electric motor. Many times and its predictions have been thoroughly validated by empirical evidence. The theory works in the case of electric motor and so in economics.

A model is, thus, defined as a simplified diagram consisting the main elements and their interactions. And a many diagrams is used to explain many of the economic aspects of the complexed real world.

Ceteris Paribus

Since the real world is far more complex, economists use the concept of holding "ceteris paribus" to analyse the economic problems.

In physical sciences we hold 'other things being equal' through controlled experiments. Let us cite an example from Chemistry. If two molecules of hydrogen and one molecule of oxygen are combined water will be formed. If the proportions change we would not get water. Here, other things are made equal by putting 2 molecules of hydrogen and 1 molecule of oxygen.

This is also true in the case of economics as well. One of the fundamental theories in economics states that people will buy more of any commodity at a low price than at a higher price, if other things are held constant. If the price of tea, for example, goes up consumers will buy less tea. But this prediction is safe only if other things are being equal. Suppose at the same time the income of the consumers increases they will buy more tea even at the higher price. Of course, the *ceteris paribus* assumption is critical. In the real world other things seldom stay equal, but by assuming temporarily that they do we can analytically isolate the effects of the higher price of tea.

Equilibrium

The effects of higher price for tea is closely related to the concept of 'equilibrium'. In our given example in Chemistry after we have combined hydrogen and oxygen molecules to form water, this equilibrium is maintained until the condition is disturbed by something else. Like that economists generally think of the economic system as tending towards a new equilibrium state whenever the disturbing changes occur.

Consider a simple example. In economics, it is theorized that people spend their money incomes to get maximum possible satisfaction from all their expenditures. If people are allocating their resources in such a way as to maximise their satisfactions, we may say that they are in "equilibrium". If the businessmen allocate their productive activities in such a way to get greatest possible money profits we may say that the businesses are in "equilibrium". Thus by "equilbrium" we mean "a situation in which those involved are satisfied to keep on doing what they are doing".[13] In equilibrium no changes occur in the economic behaviour under consideration.

Functional Relationships

As already discussed, theories or models are the main tools of economic analysis. Many theories are consisting of an inter-linked series of functional relationships between two or more variables.

If we examine the functional relationship between two variables, we may plot them against each other on a graph. One example is the relationship between price and quantities demanded of any given commodity. It is known that demand for a commodity and its price are closely related. And the fact that demand depends upon price, may easily be deduced to an algebaric form in economics.

$$d=f\ (p)$$

where 'd' denotes for demand for the commodity, 'p' stands for price of the commodity and 'f' means "function of" or "depends on" Suppose we want to show the functional relationship between price of a commodity, say, lemon and its quantities demanded in market we may draw that

$$dL=f\ (PL)$$

where dL stands for quantities demanded of lemon, pL stands for price of lemon in the market and 'f' for 'function of'. The relationship between quantities demanded of lemon at various prices in a market place can be easily drawn in a table, though hypothetically. Other things being equal, we theorize that, people will buy more lemon at lower price than at a higher price. The schedule given in Table 1.2 shows such a relationship.

TABLE 1.2

Weekly Demand for Lemon at Local Vegetable Shop (hypothetical data)

Price per lemon (Rs.)	*Number of lemon bought*
0.60	100
0.50	200
0.40	300
0.30	400
0.20	500

The tabular statement given above can readily be shown on a graph as in Figure 1.5 where price of lemon goes on vertical axis and

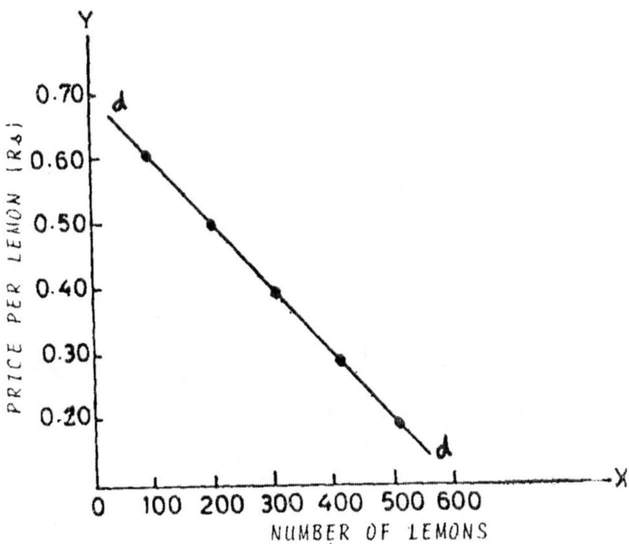

Figure 1.5 Weekly Demand for Lemon.

the number of lemons bought goes on the horizontal axis. Each dot plotted denotes the number of lemons demanded by the consumers at each price. The curve connecting the dots is called demand curve which shows how much lemons are demanded at each price, if other things are held constant.

The data in our given example are, obviously, hypothetical. If we want to determine this functional relationship in the real world, we should try to get 'the weekly sales data for vegetable shop at different prices. Because of the difficulty of holding all other things constant, such a data may be had to come and hence we may contend with a rough approximation.

ANALYSIS OF ECONOMIC PROBLEMS : MICRO AND MACRO APPROACH

The modern approach to the study of economic problems and analysis is a matter of academic interest. Micro and macro economics are the two branches, more specifically, two approaches to the study of economic theory. Micro economics relates to the study of individual economic units while macro economics studies the economy as a whole. It was Ragnar Frisch who first coined and used the terms "macro" and "micro" in economics and now these are widely used and adopted by the economists all the world over. Micro economics is concerned with the analysis of individual units of the economy such as individual consumers, individual firms or farms or a group of individual units. On the other hand, macro economics deals with the analysis of aggregates. It examines the economy as a whole and analyses the aggregative variables such as national income, employment, total consumption and total investment. K.E. Boulding describes micro economics as "the study of particular firms, particular households, individual industries, particular commodities."[14] Macro economics, on the other hand, according to him, deals not only with individual quantities as such but with aggregates of these quantities, not with individual incomes but with the national income, not with individual prices but with the price levels, not with individual outputs but with the national output."[15]

Micro Economics

Micro economics,[16] as already noted, studies the activities of individual units and small group of individual units. It analyses how prices are determined and resources are allocated. In other words it explains the way in which prices of individual commodities or services are determined. The determination of prices of particular commodities like wheat or rice, determination of equilibrium output of a firm or industry, thus, form the subject-matter of micro economics.

Micro economics, in short, is the microscopic examination of the economy. It is like looking at the economy through a microscope, as it were to see how the millions of cells in the body--economic the individuals or households as consumers, and the individuals or firms as producers—play their part in the working of the whole economic organisation.[17] Professor Ackley asserts that 'Price and value theory, the theory of the household, the firms and the industry, most production and welfare theory are of the micro economic variety.[18] To repeat once again, micro economics explains the way in which resources are allocated to the production of particular things or services, how the goods and services are distributed among the people and how efficiently and effectively they are distributed. When we examine the conditions in which the price of a particular thing is determined, it is assumed that total quantity of resources is given and it seeks to explain their allocation to the production of that commodity. The determination of prices of a particular thing depends upon the prices of other things and on factors with which they are produced. It is the relative prices of commodities and services that determine allocation of resources. Micro economics forms the domain of price theory. Micro economic theory, in the words of Watson, "explains the composition or allocation of total production, why more of some things are produced than of others."[19].

The theory of price consists of the theory of product pricing and the theory of factor pricing. The theory of product pricing explains how the prices of commodities or services are determined while the theory of factor pricing studies the manner in which the prices of factors of production are determined or how the national product is shared among resource-owners.

We may note that the pricing of products and of factors as well as the theory of allocation of resources are based on price mechanism. The theory of allocation of resources not only explains what to produce, how to produce and to whom to distribute but also explains how efficiently and effectively the resources are allocated.

Economic resources are efficiently allocated when the satisfaction of the people is maximised. In sum, the theory of pricing and economic welfare constitute the subject-matter of micro economics. The theory of pricing, as already noted, involves the theory of product pricing, the theory of demand and the theory of production and cost. The theory of factor pricing, also called the theory of distribution, examines the determination of prices of factors of production such as rent, wages, interest and profit.

The subject-matter of micro economics in nutshell is given in the following chart :

- Micro Economic Theory
  - →Theory of Product Pricing
    - →Theory of Demand
    - →Theory of Production and Cost
  - →Theory of Factor Pricing
    - →Theory of Rent
    - →Theory of Wages
    - →Theory of Interest
    - →Theory of Profit
  - →Theory of Economic Welfare

Macro Economics*

Macro economics studies the aggregates. It examines the economy as a whole. We may study in marco analysis the large aggregates such as total employment, national output or the general price levels. Also called aggregative economics, it analyses the inter-relationships among various aggregates. Prof. Ackley explains the nature of macro economics thus : "Macro economics deals with economic affairs 'in large', it concerns the over all dimensions of economic life. It looks at the total size and shape and functioning of the "elephant" of economic experience, rather than working of articulation or dimensions of the individual parts. It studies the character of forest, independently of trees."[20]

Macro economics, being general studies of economic problems, is concerned with employment, economic fluctuations, changes in price level, international trade and economic growth. It analyses the causes of employment and economic fluctuations, it explains the determinants of the level of national income and employment, and examines the process of economic growth. Since it studies the determination of the level, fluctuations and trends in the economic

*The term is derived from the Greek "markros" which means large.

sphere of an economy. Macro economics is populary known as the theory of Income and employment.

MECHANISM OF DEMAND AND SUPPLY

We have seen that the basic economic issue in any society is that of choosing among alternative use of scarce resources. An economy, then, makes decisions about what goods to produce, how and how much to produce and which resources are to utilise in production. An individual, as on the same line, must make the parallel decisions some how or the other. We have available resources such as ability to work, acquired consumer goods, ownership of economic resources and the money we obtain from many means. We may decide how to utilise these available, though limited, resources to get the maximum possible satisfactions with them.

The way that the individuals decide to use their resources determines the demand for and supply of goods and services an economy can produce. This is the mechanism of demand and supply—the market mechanism—with which a free enterprise economy tries to solve the basic problems of what, how, how much and for whom to produce.

Let us now analyse demand and supply and their functional relationship with market prices.

Generally businessmen make profits by producing those goods that people want to buy. If there is no consumer who is willing and able to buy, the businesses will become out of gear.

We have already pointed out that the consumers direct productive activities by spending their money incomes on various goods and services. If we demand polyster shirts, the textile mills will produce more polysters. If we want to have folding umbrellas, the umbrella mart will prosper. If we develop a taste for instant coffee the coffee, producers will shift to produce more instant coffee. Consumers' demand is thus the main spring of productive activities. But remember, it is the consumer with ability and willingness to spend who directs the productive activity. Many of us like to have a Vespa PL 170 or a Godrej store-well. But unless we have the ability to buy and are willing to spend it on these products, our desires have little significance for the Andhra Pradesh Scooters or Godrej Company. Thus our demand for any commodity is largely determined by our money income and our willingness to spend it.

Demand

The consumer's behaviour in the market for a goods or service is conveniently summed up in the term 'demand'. Demand is defined as the amount of a goods that the consumers are willing and able to buy at each possible price during a given period of time. It forms the schedule of quantities at different prices during some specified period of time.

In any market, demand becomes effective when the desire for a commodity couples with the ability and willingness to pay. We can say that most American industrial workers show effective demand for television sets. They want television, they also have the ability to pay for it. But we cannot say that most Indian workers have the same demand. Of course, they may have the willingness to own a television, but their desire may not be backed by the ability to pay its price. Their wages are too low to be able to pay for a television set. Since the number of television sets the Indian workers are willing and able to buy is zero at the existing market price, the demand of them for television sets is not effective.

Law of Demand

Economists have propounded the law of demand from the common observations of the decisions of individual consumers. It is a common observance that the quantity of any commodity that the people will buy at any one time depends on price. The higher the price charged for a good, the lesser amount of it will be purchased by the households, and if other things are equal, the lower the price charged, the more of it will be demanded by them. The Law thus states that as the price of any commodity falls, the amount of that commodity the consumers are willing and able to buy will increase. As price rises, on the other hand, smaller quatity of the commodity will be demanded.

Technically, there exists an inverse relationship between price and quantity demanded. To verify this assertion, we may turn to everyday experience of households. From examining our own habitual experience, it is clear that if the price of any commodity rises in the market, we may buy less of it, and in the normal case, if the price is reduced, we buy more.

Demand Schedule

In any market, as already seen, there exists a definite relation between price of a good and its quantity demanded. This relation can, easily, be drawn in a statement. The tabular statement of the quantity demanded of a goods at a variety of prices is known as demand schedule. A demand schedule, thus, focuses the relationship between volume of a product and its price. It expresses the functional relationship between price and quantity demanded.

It is possible to compile an individual's hypothetical demand schedule for any commodity. Demand schedule, which shows the amount demanded at a variety of prices, of an individual consumer for a specific goods is called individual demand schedule.

An individual consumer's demand schedule for eggs during a specified period of time might be as follows. It shows how many eggs our hypothetical buyer would buy every week at each price in a series of possible prices. If the price is 70Ps. per egg, the consumer will purchase only one egg a week. If the price drops to 60 Ps. he will purchase two eggs, at 50 Ps. he will demand three eggs and so on.

TABLE 1.3

Individual Demand Schedule for Eggs
(hypothetical data)

Price per egg *Rs.*	*Quantity demanded* *(per week)*
0.70	1
0.60	2
0.50	3
0.40	4
0.30	5

We may note that, as the law of demand asserts, the buyer will buy more eggs at lower prices than at a higher price. The demand schedule merely indicates the range of many possibilities of purchase and it does not tell us what the actual market price is.

The given numerical data can be shown graphically, as in Figure 1.6.

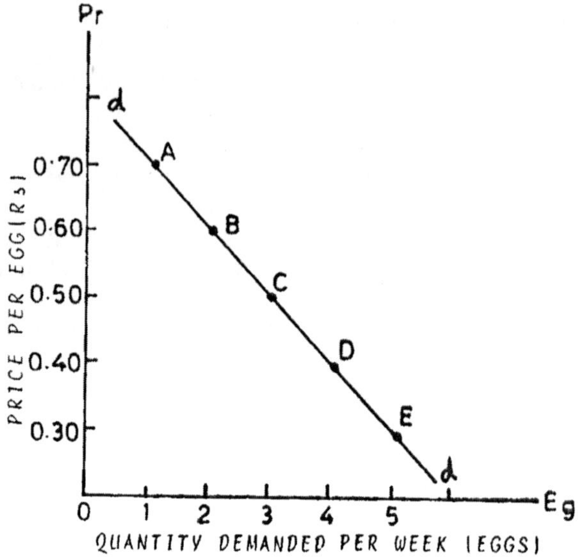

Figure 1.6 Individual Demand Curve for Eggs.

The vertical scale represents the various alternative prices of eggs measured in rupees per egg. The horizontal scale represents the number of eggs demanded by the consumer. To plot a point on this diagram we have two ordinate numbers : a price and quantity. Point A corresponds to one egg demanded at Re. 0.70. At Point B, two eggs are demanded at Re. 0.60, and so on. Through the Points A, B, C, D and E a diagonal line 'dd' is drawn. It is demand curve which is the picturization of demand schedule. A demand curve, thus, conveys the same information as demand schedule, not arithmetically but graphically.

Market Demand

Hundreds of millions of consumers provide the basic signals to the producers through their demand conveying what they want produced. The local milk marketing store isn't much concerned with your personal demand for milk. But it is very much concerned with the aggregate market demand for milk in that area. Market, or aggregate demand, is the sum of all individual consumers' demand in each market.

Consider the market demand for milk at the cross roads milk marketing society of an isolated village that has only three families.

If we know each family's demand schedule for milk, we can derive the demand schedules of all the families buying milk. The demand schedule of all the families can thus, be combined to form a composite demand schedule representing the total demand for milk in the market.

TABLE 1.4

Market Demand Schedule for Milk
(hypothetical data)

Price per litre Rs.	*Purchases per week by*			*Aggregate (all three)*
	Family A	*Family B*	*Family C*	
3-00	3	1	4	8
2-50	4	2	6	12
2-00	6	3	8	17
1-50	8	4	10	22

The demand schedules of the three families and total demand might be as given in Table 1.4. The market demand schedule for milk as seen by the cross roads milk marketing society, is the sum of the individual demands of all the customers. Market demand schedule can be derived and be plotted on graph as in Figure 1.7. In order to derive the market demand curve for milk, we must add all the individual quantities demanded by each family at a given price. In our given example there are only three families buying milk in the market. At a price of Rs. 2.50 per litre, family A will purchase 4 litres ; family B, 2 litres and C, 6 litres. The sum of these quantities (4+2+6=12) is the total quantity of milk demanded in the market at a price of Rs. 2.50, per litre.

Nature of Demand Curve

We need to repeat again the point that price and quantity demanded of a given product are inversely related. When price falls demand increases and when price rises demand falls. Such an inverse *relationship* of price and demand underlines an important property of the demand curve. Barring few exceptions, demand curve slopes downward to the right. The negative slope of the demand curve implies itself the law of demand that more goods will be demanded at lower prices than at a higher price.

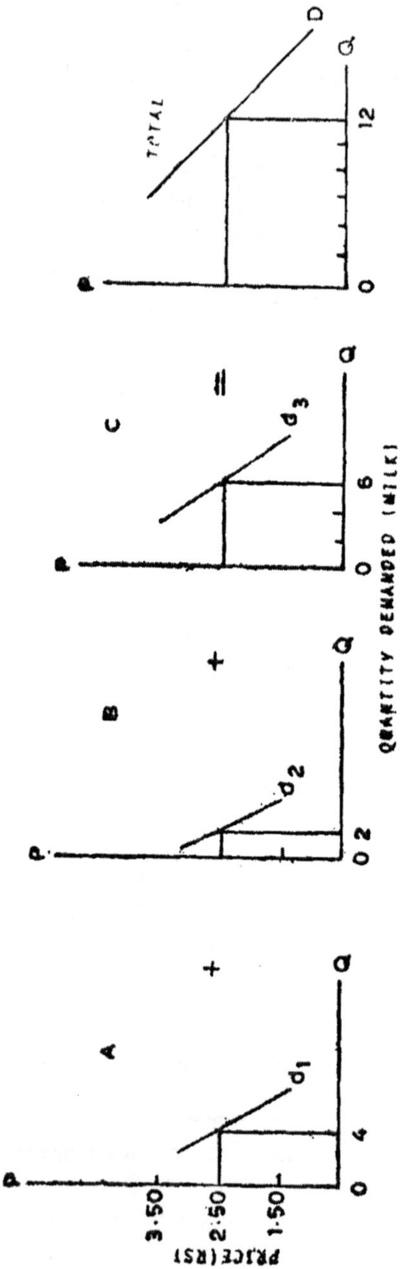

Figure 1.7 Deriving the Market Demand Curve for Milk.

Why, then, we demand more of a good when its price falls? The reasons are not hard to identify. These are in accordance with the common observance. The basic notion underlies in the law of demand is the. law of diminishing marginal utility. As we consume more of a good, the marginal utility derived from the consumption of that commodity tends to fall. That is, consumption of successive units of a goods would yield lesser and lesser satisfaction. As we take more doses of a goods, our psychological ability to appreciate more of that goods will rationally decline. This is the fundamental tendency of human mind. And any more dose of a goods will be purchased only when there is considerable fall in price.

Again, a fall in price of a goods may necessarily be equivalent to an increase in the income of the consumer. The consumer has to spend only lesser amount of money for purchasing the same quantity of goods as before. This is called the *income effect*. The amount of money gained by a fall in price of a goods enables the consumer to purchase some more units of that commodity.

Thirdly, a fall in price of a given commodity means that it is comparatively cheaper than the commodities whose prices remain unchanged. The consumer would, therefore, prefer cheaper commodities to the dearer ones. He would purchase more of a goods whose price has fallen and less of a goods whose price has remained unchanged. That is, he would substitute the cheaper commodities for the dearer ones. This is called the *substitution effect*.

Determinants of Individual Demand

Demand, as we have defined, refers to the quantities of a commodity that the buyers are able and willing to buy at various prices suring some given period of time. It shows the entire schedule of price-quantity combinations. What actually determines the demand for a product? The various factors that influence demand are called the determinants of demand. Any change in those influencing factors may cause changes in demand. The factors that influence individual demand are, mainly, income of the buyer, availability of substitutes and complementary goods, expectations of future changes in price and buyers' tastes and preferences.

Income

We may know that at every possible price a poor man with

small income demands lesser amounts of any one commodity than a rich person. As income rises, so does demand for many goods. Additional earnings enable us to purchase more of the commodities we usually consume and to purchase many more commodities as well.

An increase in income provides a greater ability to pay the price for a commodity which in turn raise the demand for the product. As income increases, demand for many goods will increase, and as income falls, demand for many goods will fall. Goods whose demand varies directly with personal income are called 'normal goods'. Products such as vegetables, tea, meat and sugar are included in this category. But there are certain goods whose demand actually falls as income increase and *vice versa*. Such goods are called 'inferior goods'. Millet, maize and bajra are the possible examples of inferior goods. A poorman who purchases a given amount of millet will purchase smaller amount of it when his income increases, instead, he will switch on to more wheat or rice. Inferior goods are, thus, defined as those goods whose consumption falls when real income increases.

The case of inferior goods resembles the famous Giffen Paradox, named after Robert Giffen, the British Army Officer who first observed it in Ireland. Giffen noted that when the price of potatoes declined, the quantity of potatoes consumed usually declined—exactly contrary to what one would expect. This happened because potatoes were inferior goods in Ireland at that time.

Substitutes and Complementary Goods

An individual's demand for a particular commodity will also be influenced by the changes in price of a related goods. Those goods which can be used for the same purpose and are competed with each other are substitutes. If the price of a given goods rises, the demand for its substitutes will increase. For example, when price of tea rises, people will decide to switch to a substitute, say, coffee, which is now relatively less expensive.

Another influencing factor of demand for a specific goods is the price of its complements—the commodities that will be jointly used. For example, the demand for motor bikes will be directly affected by the price of petrol. When the price of commodity rises, the demand for its complement will fall.

Future Expectations

One's own willingness and ability to pay for a product is

also influenced by the future expectations of changing prices. Expectations of changing prices in future tend to increase present demand. If the consumers expect a further considerable rise in prices of, say, electric fans, they will decide to purchase them even before the rise. The pre-budget bargain of many of the electrical goods and luxury items is the result of the expectations of future rise in prices due to budgetary proposals.

Tastes and Preferences of the Buyer

Personal preferences are the last but not least important determinant of individual demand. When individual preferences favour a particular commodity—say, bell-bottom pants—demand for that product will rise. When tastes shift, demand for that product declines.

Changes in Demand

We may note that our "demand" for a particular commodity, say, oranges, is our entire set of intentions about buying oranges. These depend, mainly, on how much income we have, our taste for oranges compared with other fruits and the prices of other fruits available in the market. Now, suppose that our hypothetical consumer get tired of oranges and develop a taste of mangoes. He will now buy fewer oranges than before at each of the prices shown. This change in attitude changes demand.

A change in demand can, easily, be illustrated with the help of demand curves. We have seen that demand changes as a result of price changes, if other things are held constant. If changes in quantity demanded occurres in response to a change in price alone, other factors held constant, that change can be graphically shown as a movement along the demand curve. If quantity demanded changes for the reasons other than price changes, the graphic representation would take a different turn necessitating shifts in the demand curve.

Consider, for example, a local milk marketing store in a village. There are few buyers of milk in that village. The hypothetical demand schedule for milk in that market might be as :

Now, consider Figure 1.8 for a while. The demand curve d1 is drawn on the assumptions that consumers' income, prices of related goods and their expectations about the future changes in price are all held constant. Given these assumptions, as price falls from, say, Rs. 3.00 to Rs. 1.50, the quantity of milk increases from 5 litres to 20 litres. This change in demand as a result of a change in

TABLE 1.5

Demand Schedule for Milk
(Hypothetical data)

Price per litre (Rs.)	*Milk demand per week*
3.00	5 litres
2.00	10 "
2.50	15 "
1.50	20 "

price is represented by a movement along the demand curve d1 from Point A to Point B.

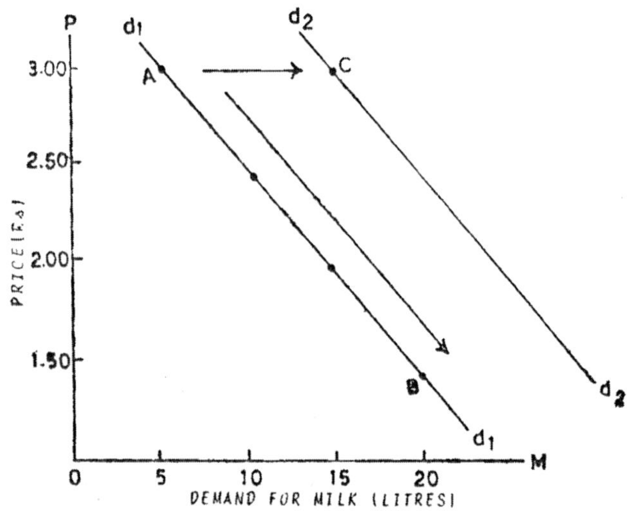

Demand for Milk (litres)
Figure 1.8 : Changes in Demand.

Return to the Point A again. Assume that price does not change, but something else changes, say, consumers' income rises. A sufficiently large increase in consumers' income would cause to raise demand for milk even if the price doesnot fall. This change (increase in demand) is represented by a movement from Point A to Point C in the diagram, a movement of the demand curve d1. With a higher level of income or expectations, changes in demand would cause movements along the new demand curve d2 which lies above and right to the initial demand curve d1. The new demand curve indicates that whatever be the price of milk, at a higher level of income or expectations quantity demanded would be larger than that at the same or old level of prices.

If the prices of related goods change, we could have the same story. We may establish a general point thus : When quantity demanded of a goods changes due to the reasons other than changes in price of the given good, the change occurs on a different demand curve represented by a shift in the demand curve to a new position.

Supply

We now turn to supply and examine the relationship between price and quantity supplied. We defined demand as a schedule of the quantities of a goods that would be purchased by the consumers at all possible prices. Supply is also defined as a schedule : Schedule of the quantities of any goods offered for sale at all possible prices during some specified period of time.

Like demand, supply can also be drawn on graph. But it differs from demand when it is plotted, supply curve ordinarily slopes upward, whereas the demand curve ordinarily slopes downward. The uphill slope of the supply curve implies that more quantities are usually offered for sale at a higher price than at lower ones. Thus quantity supplied, like the quantity demanded, is a function of price. Like the market demand for an commodity is derived by adding up the quantities demanded by all the consumers at each price, the market supply of a product is derived by adding up the quantities offered for sale at each price.

Law of Supply

We may repeat that supply is a function of price. Other things remaining constant, as price of any commodity during a given period of time rises, its supply extends and as price falls, its supply counteracts. The supply varies directly with the price. That is, price of a given commodity and its quantity offered for sale are positively related. We may now recognise the fact that the inducement of higher price will normally call forth increased output. This relation can, best, be illustrated by a farmer who, for instances, can use his land to produce a given product, say, wheat. The higher the price offered for wheat, the more of his land the farmer will allocate to produce wheat.

Supply Schedule

The behaviour of the suppliers can, conveniently, be summarised, in a supply schedule which focuses on the relationship between price and quantity supplied. The quantity of wheat offered for sale by a single farmer at each of a series of prices of wheat might be as indicated in Table 1.6.

TABLE 1.6

Individual Demand Schedule for Wheat (hypothetical data)

If the price is (Rs. per kg.)	*The farmer will supply (kg.)*
2	100
4	200
6	300
8	400
10	500

The supply schedule entertains the relation between price and quantity offered for sale. It shows that at any price there is a definite amount of wheat that the farmer is willing and able to offer. The supply schedule is, thus, defined as the tabular statement of the quantity of any commodity offered for sale at a variety of prices. It is seen from Table 1.6 that at a higher price, say, Rs. 10 per kg. the farmer would like to cultivate more wheat and as such they would like to offer larger quantity, say, 500 kgs. On the contrary, at a lower price of Rs. 2 per kg. the farmer would like to reduce wheat production, and in place he would like to cultivate other produce. say, maize. As per the schedule, at Rs. 2 per kg. he would only supply a lesser amount of wheat-100 kg.

Supply Curve

The relation between price and quantity offered for sale is graphically represented in Figure 1.9 in which the numerical data from the supply schedule are plotted. If we plot price on the vertical axis and the amount of wheat supplied on the horizontal axis and connect the points, we can read off the resulting curve how many kgs. of wheat the farmer will offer for sale during a given period of time at any price shown. Thus, at Rs. 2 the farmer will produce and sell 100 kgs. of wheat, at Rs. 4, 200 kgs. and so on-up the curve. By connecting the dots we get a curve labelled as 'ss' which we call individual supply curve.

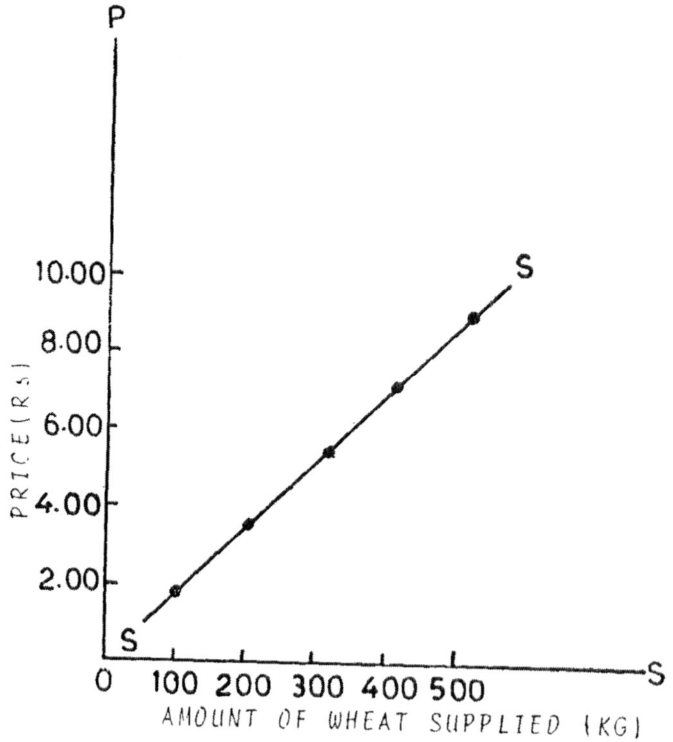

Figure 1.9 : Individual Supply Curve for Wheat.

Market Supply

We aggregate the individual supplies to obtain the market supply schedule. Suppose there are three farmers producing wheat in a particular area. At various prices, each will produce and offer different amounts for sale, as shows in Table 1.7. This is the market supply schedule which is the sum of all individual supply schedules for wheat-in that area.

The numerical data given in the above schedule can be plotted on a graph. Again, plotting price on the vertical axis and quantity of wheat offered for sale on the horizontal axis, we get the market supply curve as shown in Figure 1.10

Exceptions : The Law of Supply

There are few exceptions to the law of supply which are worth

TABLE 1.7

Market Supply Schedule for Wheat (hypothetical data)

Price	*Amounts of wheat*			*Supplied by*
	Farmer A.	*Farmer B.*	*Farmer C.*	*All (aggregate)*
(Rs. per kg.)	*(kg.)*	*(kg.)*	*(kg.)*	*(kg.)*
2	100	80	40	220
4	200	100	60	360
6	300	140	70	610
8	400	200	100	700
10	500	300	150	1050

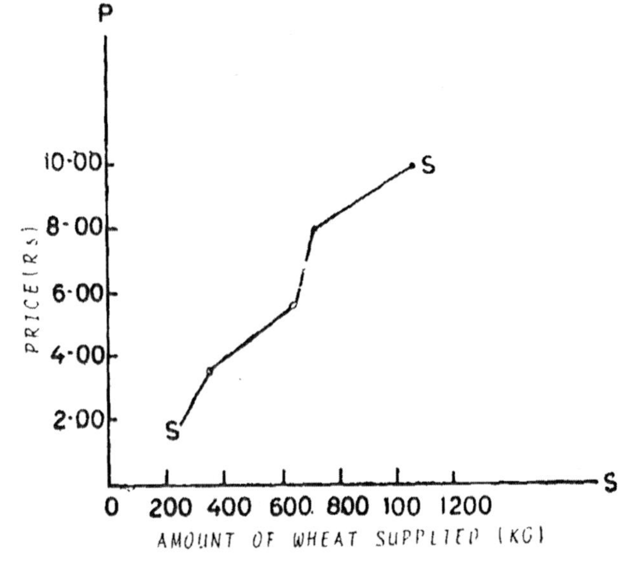

Figure 1.10 Market Supply Curve for Wheat.

noting. There may be the cases where the supply of certain goods cannot be increased at any cost. Original paintings of Raja Ravi Verma are the possible examples. In such a case the supply curve will be a vertical straight line as shown in Figure 1.11a.

There are certain other cases of markets where producers can be persuaded to increase the supply without any increase in price. The local market for icecream can be cited as an example. With in a reasonable range of price, any amounts of icecream can be supplied

(A) Paintings of Ravi Verma. (B) ocal Supply of Icecream.
(C) Supply of Automobies

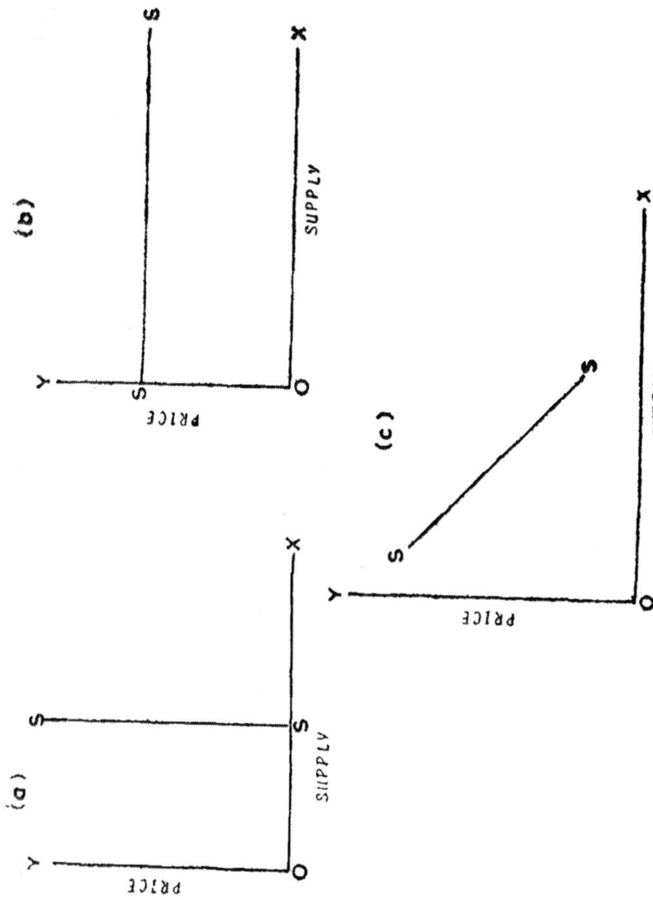

Figure 1.11 : Supply Curves : Exceptional Cases.

without much difficulty. The shape of the supply curve in an ice-cream market is depicted in Figure 1.11b.

There are some products, the cost of production of which can be reduced as quantity of output rises. Automobiles belong to these category. Because of the economies of large scale production, their supply can be increased with a possible reduction is cost of production. The shape of the supply curve in such a case is as shown in Figure 1.11c.

Determinants of Supply

Like that of demand, there are several factors affecting supply. The most important of them is cost of production. Cost of inputs, availability of resources and the state of technology are the main determinants of cost of production. If there is any change in any of these factors, the entire supply schedule will change. When cost increases, the suppliers are able to supply only a very limited amount at each and every price. If costs of production fall, the producers will be able to produce more and able to supply more at every possible price.

Profitability

Producers are producing and supplying products for getting profits. Changes in the price of any product may cause changes in the revenue receipt from the sale of that commodity and hence changes in profits. When the price of a goods increases and the production of that goods becomes more profitable its supply will increase, for suppliers of competitive commodities will change their productive activities in favour of the products that earn maximum possible profits. For example, suppose that demand for pepper rises and the price of pepper also goes up. Since the profit obtainable from growing pepper are greater than those from other produces, many more farmers will plant less cashew or cocoa and more pepper.

Expectations

Decisions regarding the production and supply of a good also depends upon expected future price of that product. An anticipation of higher prices for groundnut producers may tend them to cutshort the current supply in order to boost up the future profit by supplying more.

Changes in Supply

Supply changes for many reasons. A change in price necessitates change in quantity supplied. Supply also changes due to the reasons other than price changes.

When supply changes solely because of a change in price, the effect can be seen as a movement along the supply curve. A change in supply in response to a change in price is graphically presented in Figure 1.12. It shows that when price rises from Rs. 4 to Rs. 6, the supply of wheat increases from 200 kg. to 300 kg. This change in supply is seen by a movement along the supply curve S1 from Points A to Point B.

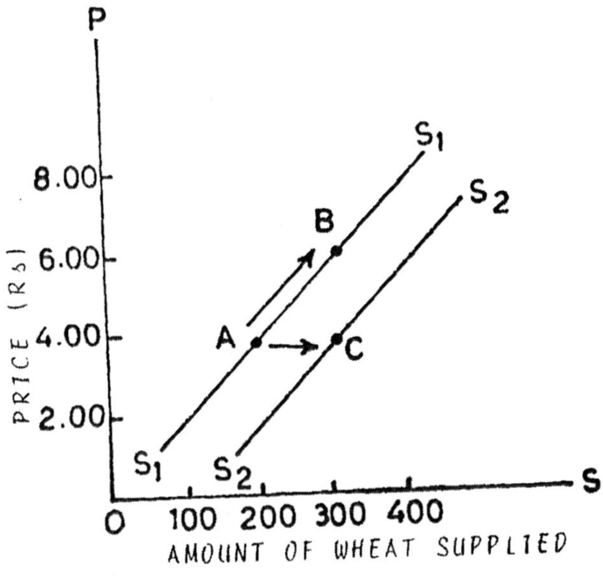

Figure 1.12 : Changes in Supply. (in Kg)

Suppose, further, that a good wheather condition has taken place and cheap fertilisers are made available to the farmers, an increase in supply of wheat is possible. This would cause a shift in the supply curve from S1 to S2 which implies that the farmers would be able to supply more, say, 300 kg. of wheat without an increase in price-level.

Market Equilibrium : Demand, Supply and Price

Let us combine our analysis of supply and demand to examine

the market mechanism which necessarily explains determination of price by the forces of demand and supply. A market is said to be in equilibrium when quantity demanded and quantity supplied are identical at some price. And the price at which quantity demanded equal quantity supplied is called equilibrium price.

If we have demand and supply schedules for a given commodity in a market, equilibrium condition can easily be explained. Let us consider an example of a cotton market. In Table 1.8 columns 1 to 3 give the supply and demand schedules. It is clear from the given schedules that at a higher price, say, Rs. 5 per bale, 30,000 bales are offered for sale, but millowners are willing to purchase only a smaller amount, say, 10,000 bales. There exists surplus amounts of cotton to the extent of 20,000 bales. To sell out this unsold amounts, farmers would compete among themselves which would bid down the price to a lower level to, say, Rs. 2. At that low price farmers would be willing to offer only a small amount, say, 15,000 bales. But the millowners demand a high amount of cotton, say, 25,000 bales which would cause a shortage of 10,000 bales. The unsatisfied millowners would, then, offer a still higher price which would bid up the price to a higher level. Only at Rs. 3, both the farmers and the millowners would be satisfied. At that price, market would be in equilibrium where quantity offered and quantity demanded are equal.

TABLE 1.8

Supply and Demand Schedules for Cotton (hypothetical data)

Price (per bale) Rs.	*Quantity supplied (1000 bales)*	*Quantity demanded (1000 bales)*	*Shortages*	*Surpluses*	*Direction of pressure on price*
5	30	10	..	20 ↓	Downward
4	25	15	..	10 ↓	Downward
3	20	20	..	..	Equilibrium
2	15	25	10	.. ↑	Upward
1	10	30	20	.. ↑	Upward

The market equilibrium condition is graphically shown in Figure 1.13 where both demand curve and supply curve for cotton are drawn. The horizontal distance between demand and supply curves indicate the surplus or shortage at any price. At the price of Rs. 3 per bale the supply and demand curves intersect. The intersection point of supply and demand curves indicates price and quantity at which both purchasers and sellers contend. At that price, which is

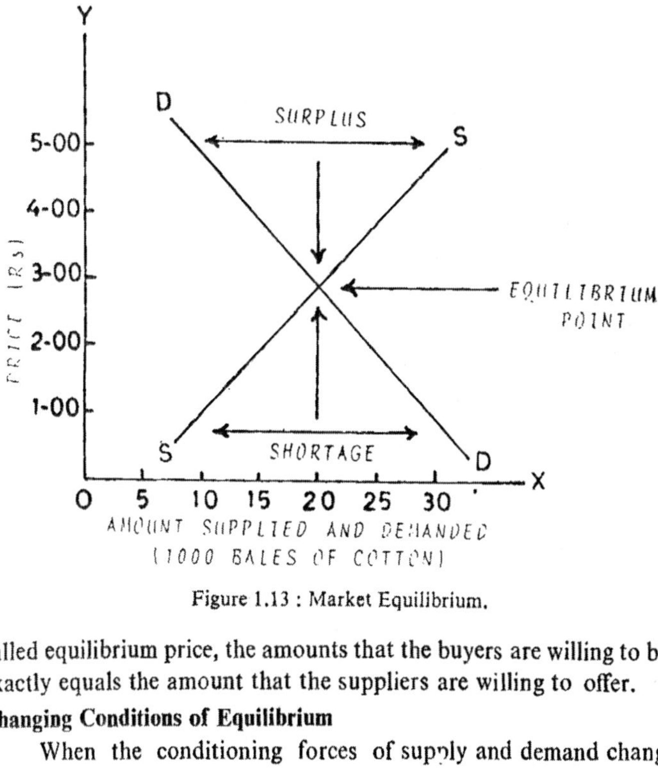

Figure 1.13 : Market Equilibrium.

called equilibrium price, the amounts that the buyers are willing to buy exactly equals the amount that the suppliers are willing to offer.

Changing Conditions of Equilibrium

When the conditioning forces of supply and demand change, the equilibrium position would also change. The changing equilibrium positions would necessitate the supply and demand curve to shift to new positions. Let us examine briefly such changing equilibrium situation.

Consider our given example, once more. Suppose that bad weather affects adversely the cotton cultivation in the State. This would reduce the production of cotton considerably and the farmers would unable to supply the required amount of cotton in the market. This situation is shown in Figure 1.14. The original supply curve intersects the demand curve dd at Point A. The production of cotton has reduced due to bad weather and as a result of fall in output, the supply curve shifts to a new position and has become S1 to S1. The new supply curve S1 to S1 intersect the demand curve at Point A1. This implies a rise in price as a result of fall in quantity supplied.

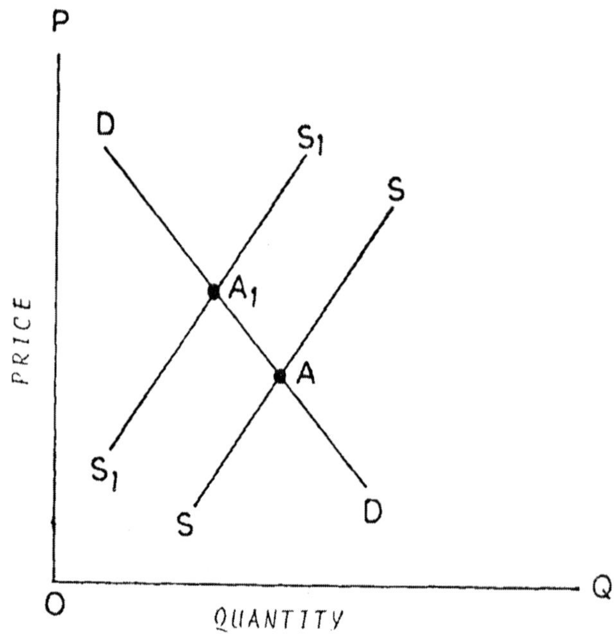

Figure 1.14 Changing Equilibrium : Supply Changes

Similarly, the effect of change in demand can also be explained. Assume that the income of the people is increased which would tend to raise the demand for cotton cloths. This would raise the demand for cotton by millowners. This would necessitate a shift in the demand curve from dd to d1d1 as shown in Figure 1.15 The equilibrium position at which demand and supply curves intersect, then, changes from Point B to B1. This implies a rise in price.

From the given analysis, it is seen that when supply or demand changes, equilibrium price also changes, necessitating shift in supply curve or demand curve.

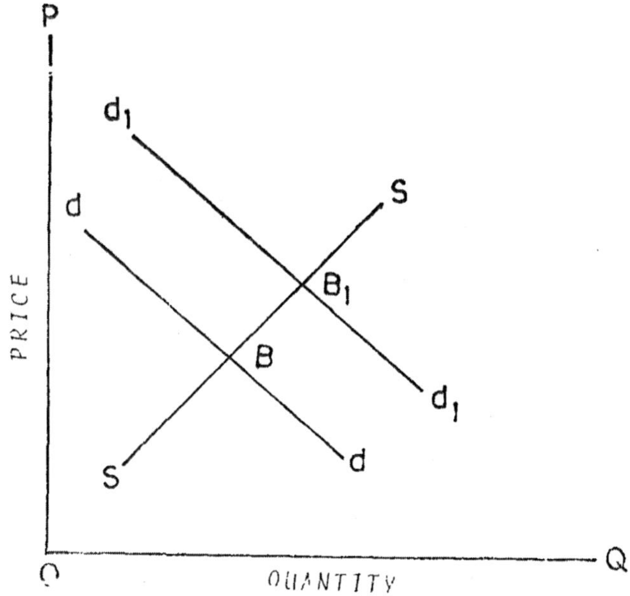

Figure. 1.15 : Changing Equilibrium : Demand Changes.

THE CONCEPT OF ELASTICITY

Behaviour of Demand

The law of demand holds that quantity demanded increases as price falls. It only states the direction of change in quantity demanded in response to a change in price. For one or other, we may want to know how much or to what extent the quantity increases with a given price fall. This information is provided by the concept of elasticity of demand.

It is price elasticity of demand which is commonly referred to as elasticity of demand. Elasticity is simply a measure of responsiveness of quantity demanded to a change in price. It may be defined as the degree of responsiveness of demand to changes in price. If a slight change in price leads to a big change in quantity demanded, then demand is said to be elastic. If, however, a fairly considerable change in price causes a little difference in the quantity demanded, then demand is said to be inelastic. Demand is perfectly inelastic if same quantity is purchased whatever the price, while demand is perfectly elastic when infinite-samlly small change in price leads to an infinite change in demand.

Elasticity determines the shape of the demand curve. If demand is perfectly elastic the demand curve will be a horizontal straight line. Perfectly elastic demand curve is drawn in Figure 1. 16. If demand perfectly inelastic the demand curve will be

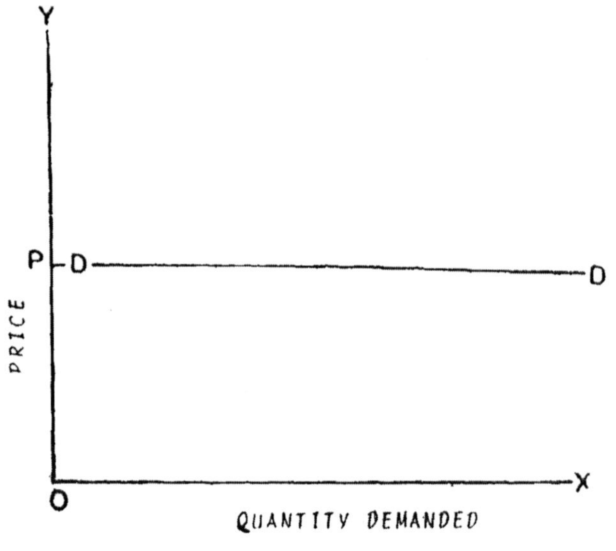

Figure 1.16 : Perfectly Elastic Demand.

vertical straight line parallel to Y-axis as shown in Figure 1.17. Between these two extremes there exists an infinite number of possibilities. A fairly elastic demand is represented by a gradually sloping demand curve as shown in Figure 1.18. While a fairly elastic demand is represented by a gradually sloping demand curve as shown in Figure 1.18, a fairly inelastic demand is represented by a steeply sloping demand curve as shown in Figure 1.19.

We may note the fundamental point that there is no product for which the elasticity of demand is the same at all prices and most demand curves show varying elasticities over various parts of their lengths. Varying elasticities of demand for a product is graphically

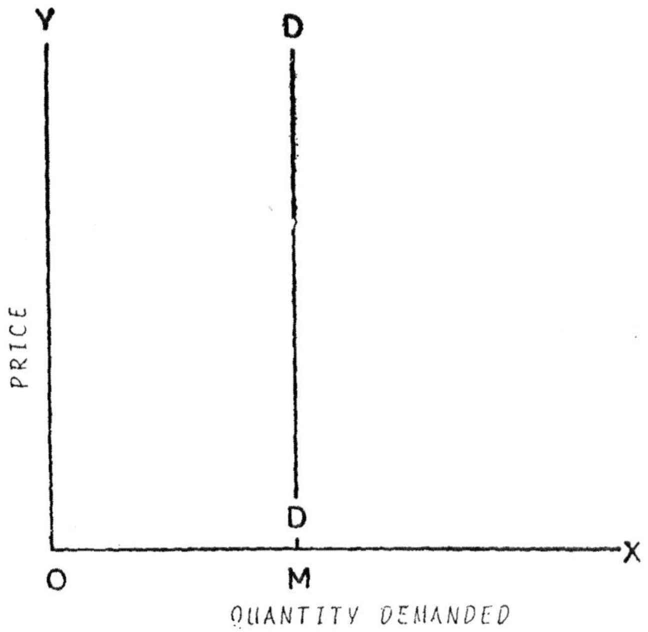

Figure 1.17 Perfectly Inelastic Demand.

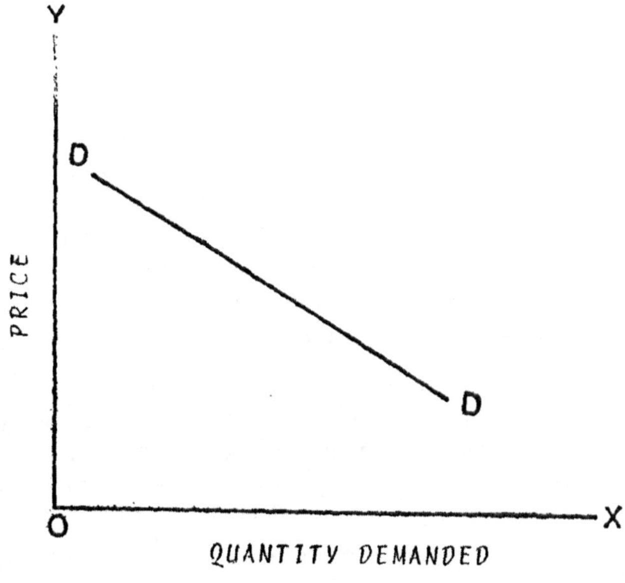

Figure 1.18 Fairly Elastic Demand.

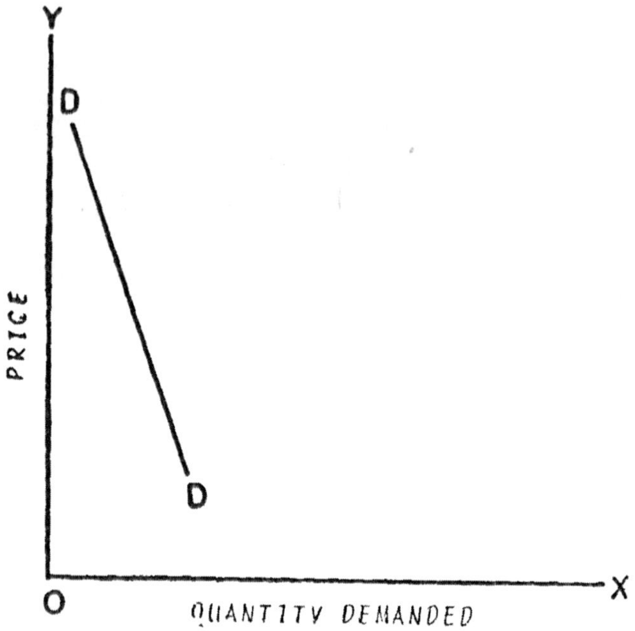

Figure 1.19 Fairly Inelastic Demand.

shown in Figure 1.20. The demand curve DD shows that at low prices up to OPI demand is inelastic but between prices OPI and OP2 demand is elastic, becoming inelastic again at higher prices over OP2. It is seen from the diagram that when the curve is steep, as between prices OP2 and OP3, there is little change (OM2 to OM3) in the quantity demanded, and so demand is inelastic. On the other-hand, then the curve has a more gradual slope, as between prices OPI and DP2, there is a considerable change (OMI to OM2) in quantity demanded and so demand is elastic.

We may also note the relation between elasticity of demand and change of supply. If demand is elastic and increase in supply will cause a large increase in the quantity demanded, but a small change in price. This is graphically shown in Figure 1.21. If, on the other hand, demand is inelastic an increase in supply will cause a small increase in quantity demanded, but a big fall in price as shown in Figure 1.22.

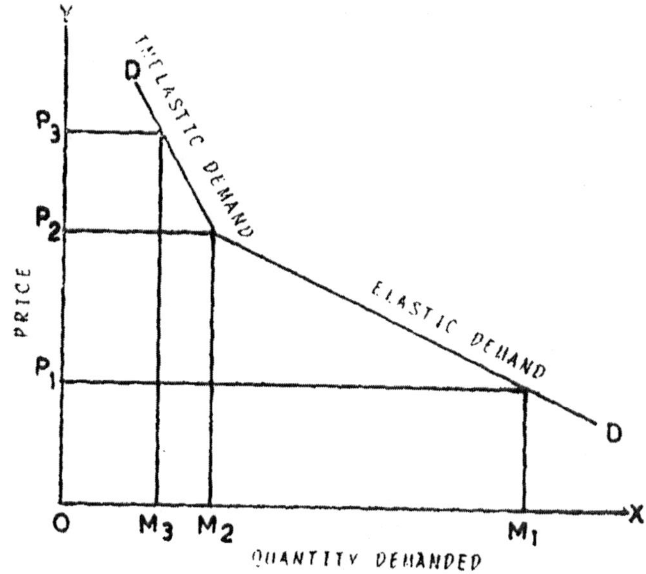

Figure 1.20 : Varying Elasticities of Demand.

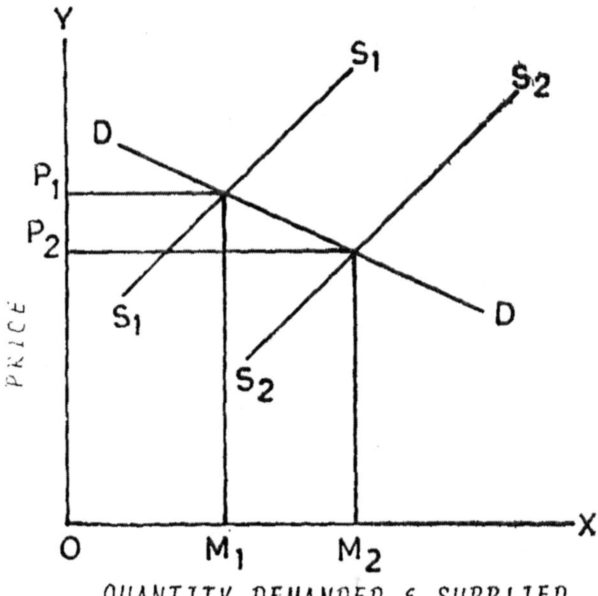

Figure 1.21 : Elastic Demand and Change in supply.

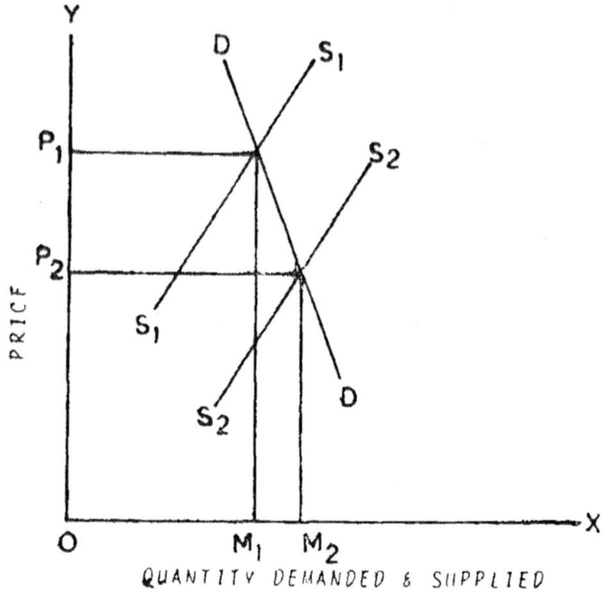

Figure 1.22 : Inelastic Demand and Change in Supply.

Measurement of Elasticity of Demand

If a change in price of a commodity results in a proportionate change in quantity demanded, then the elasticity of demand is equivalent to unity. In such cases there will be no change in total expenditure on the commodity.

If a change in price leads to more than proportionate change in quantity demanded, elasticity of demand is greater than unity. The total expenditure on commodity will be less than before.

If there is a less than proportionate change in quantity demanded as a result of a change, in price, elasticity of demand is less than unity and the total outlay on commodity will be greater than before.

When there is perfect elasticity, elasticity of demand will be equal to infinity whereas if there is perfect inelasticity, elasticity will be equal to zero.

Cross Elasticity

It is a measure of responsiveness of quantity demanded of a given commodity to a change in price of the related commodity.

Factors Determining Elasticity of Demand

The main factors influencing the responsiveness of demand to changes in price are :

1. *The Possibility of Substitutions* : The most important influencing factor of the elasticity of demand is the availability of substitutes for the commodity. If there are closer substitutes for the product, the demand for the commodity will be more elastic. But the substitutes must be within the same price range. The demand for cocacola is elastic because fairly close substitutes for it exist at approximately the same price. If there are no close substitutes within the same price range demand for a commodity is likely to be inelastic. Ex. salt.

2. *The Degree of Necessity* : Another factor influencing elasticity of demand is whether the good is luxury or necessary. Higher the degree of necessity, the less elastic is likely to be the demand for the commodity. Rice is a possible example.

3. *Consumer's Income* : Generally the higher the income of the consumer, the more elastic will be his demand for commodities. The demand of a rich man for all commodities may be quite unaffected by any changes of price.

4. *Habit* : It is a fact that once certain habits have been formed, they may be sufficiently strong for a time to effect the effect of changes in price. Hence, the demand for such commodities becomes inelastic. This has been particularly in the case of cigarettes. Though the price has been considerably increased by taxation, the demand for it has remained unchanged.

Behaviour of Supply : Elasticity

Elasticity of supply relates to the responsiveness of supply to a change in price. If a change in price leads to a more than proportionate change in quantity supplied, the supply is said to be elastic. The supply is said to be inelastic when a change in price causes a less than proportionate change in quantity supplied.

As we have seen in the case of demand, here too, elasticity determines the shape of the supply curve. If supply is perfectly inelastic, i.e., if the supply is fixed whatever the price, the supply curve will be a vertical straight line as shown in Figure 1.23.

If supply is perfectly elastic, i.e., if a small change in price leads to an infinite change in quantity supplied, the supply curve will be a horizontal straightline as presented in Figure 1.24. These are two

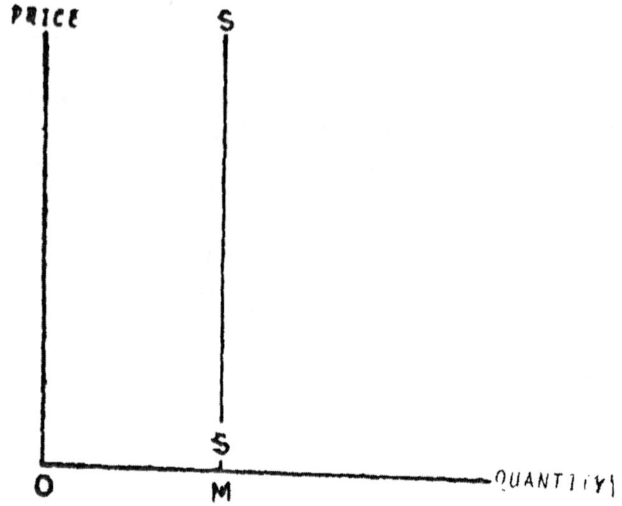

Figure 1.23 : Perfectly Inelastic Supply.

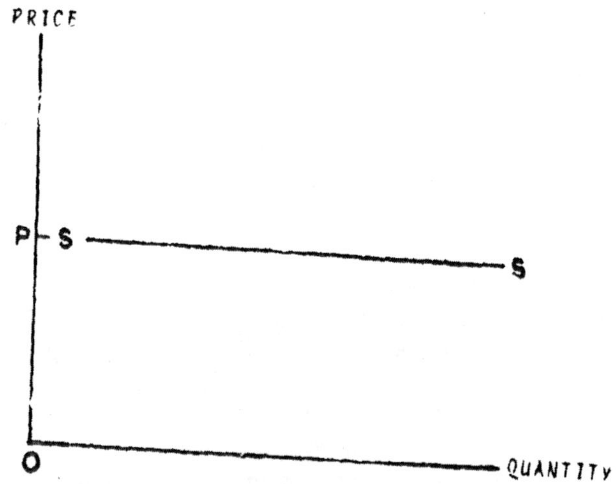

Figure 1.24 Perfectly Elastic Supply.

extremes. We may also note that the greater the degree of inelasticity, the steeper will be the slope of the supply curve (Figure 1.25) while, the greater the degree of elasticity, the supply curve will be of gradual slope. (Figure 1.26).

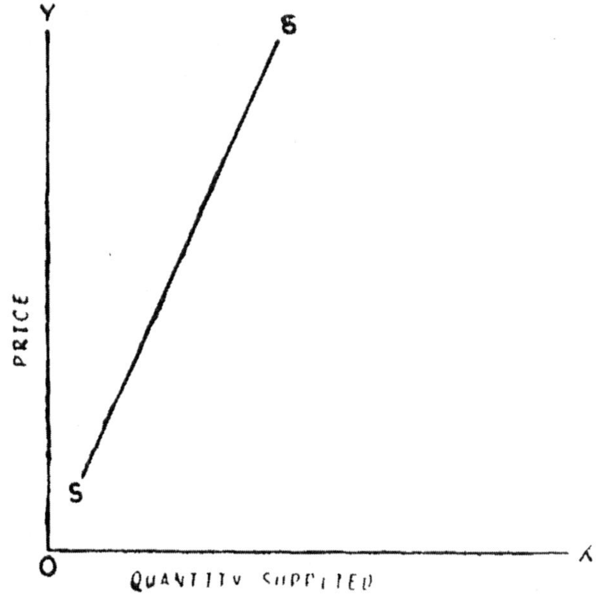

Figure 1.25 Fairly Inelastic Supply.

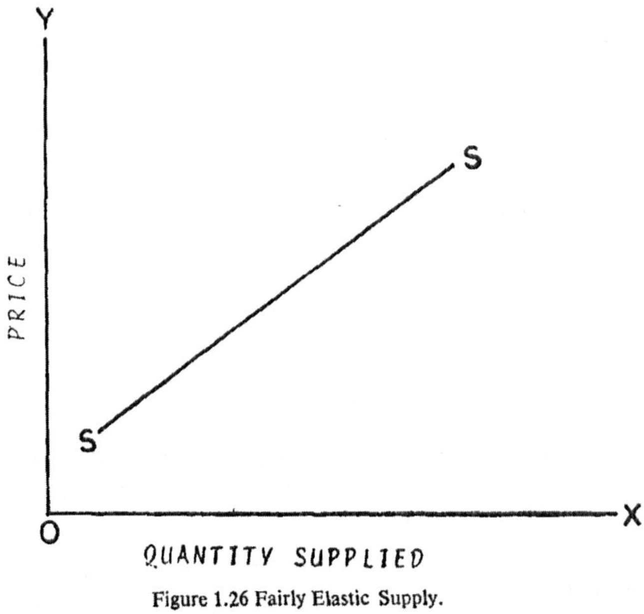

Figure 1.26 Fairly Elastic Supply.

Change of demand on price can be effected by elasticity of supply. If supply is fairly elastic an increase in quantity demanded will cause a large increase in the quantity supplied, but only a small rise in price. This case is represented in Figure 1.27.

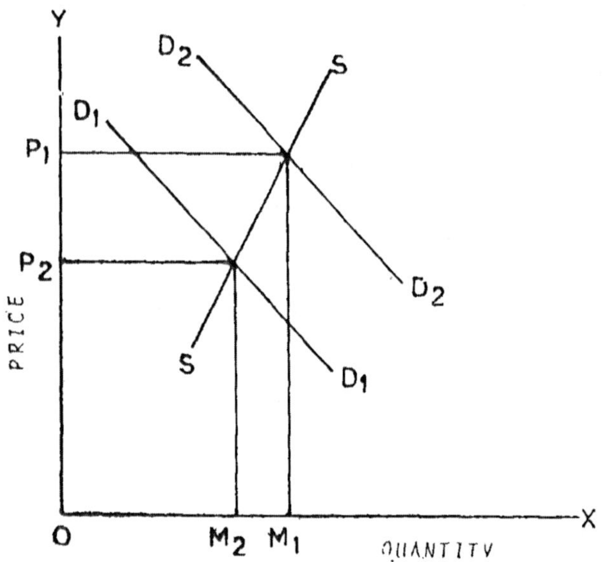

Figure 1.27 Elastic Supply and Change in Demand.

If supply is fairly inelastic a rise in demand will result in a small increase in the quantity supplied but will cause a big increase in price. This is shown in Figure 1.28.

Thus, we note that the more elastic the supply the less variable will be the price.

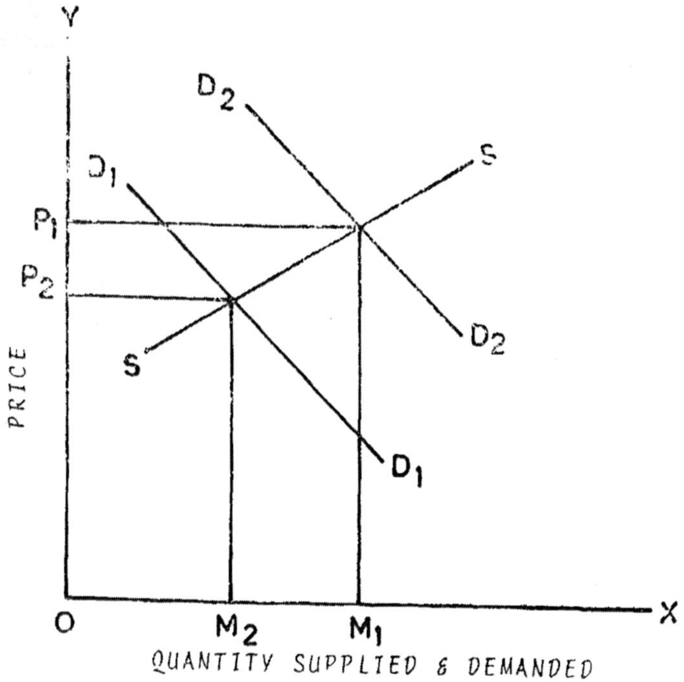

Figure 1.28 Inelastic Supply and Change in Demand.

NOTES AND REFERENCE

1. J.N. Keyues : Scope and Method of Political Economy, p. 3.
2. Alfred Marshall : Principles of Economics, Eight Edition, p. 1.
3. *Ibid.*, p. 41.
4. *Ibid.*, p. 12.
5. E. Cannan : Elementary Political Economy, p. 1.
6. W. Beveridge : Economics, Vol. 1.
7. A.C. Pigon : The Economics of Welfare, p. II.
8. L. Robbins : Nature and Significance of Economic Science, p. 15.
9. E. Roll : Elements of Economics, p. 13.
10. William Loucks: Comparative Economic systems, p. 5.
11. Paul A. Samuelson : Economics, Eleventh Edition, MeGrawttill-Kogakusha, p. 38.
12. Adam Smith : The Wealth of Nations, Pelican Classics, Penguinbooks 1977, p. 110.
13. George L. Bach : Economics—An Introduction to Analysis and Policy, Prentice Hall of India, New Delhi, (1977) page 26.
14. K.E. Boulding : A Reconstruction of Economics, p. 3.
15. K.E. Boulding : Economic Analysis, p. 25.
16. The term derived from the Greek "mikros" which means small.
17. A.P. Lerner : Micro economic theory, Reprinted in Perspectives in Econo mics, editied by Brown, Neuberger and Palmatir, p. 29.
18. G. Ackley : Macro Economic Theory, p. 4.
19. D.S. Watson : Price Theory and its Uses, p. 5.
20. G. Ackley, *op. cit.*, p. 4.

2

THE THEORY OF CONSUMER BEHAVIOUR

THE UTILITY ANALYSIS

We have already explained how market prices are determined in a competitive market. In a market system, as already noted, price is determined by the schedules of demand and supply. Now, let us explain the principles that lie behind the demand schedule and supply schedule. The present chapter investigates briefly the economic principles of utility that lie behind the market demand schedule. The subsequent chapters will survey the principles of cost that underlie the market supply schedule.

To explain the theory of consumer behaviour we begin with the usual assumption that the consumers with a given income are making rational choices in allocating many of their economic resources. The ultimate goal of any individual consumer is to maximise his satisfaction. In economic jargon he is to maximise utility by spending his rupees on goods and services that he thinks well give him most satisfaction. If an alternative pattern of expenditure is possible to increase his satisfaction, he will definitely adopt the same.

Utility of a good is its capacity to satisfy a human want. In other words, it is "the want satisfying power" of any goods or service. Anything has utility if it possesses the ability to satisfy a particular want. A goods may be either a physical thing such as an orange, a fountain pen, a cup of tea; or a service such as economics teaching, a dance or a musical concert. The want satisfying ability of a goods or service is neither visible nor uniform. Utility does not arise altogether from the properties of the goods because utility is purely a subjective concept and it is necessarily dependent upon consumer's taste and the objective qualities of the goods as well. Thus, utility derived from a package of cigarettes is zero to a non-smoker, but the same may give much utility to a fellowman.

Since utility is a subjective concept it can hardly be uniquely measured. Though immeasurable in quantitative terms, it may not prevent us from using the concepts of "total utility" and "marginal utility". The concept of total utility measures the sum of all utilities derived from the consumption of a goods or service. For example, the total utility of a set of pelican classics that you purchase is the utility you derive from the first book plus utility from the second book and so on, right down to the utility of the Classics you are currently purchasing from the nearby bookstall. Marginal utility, on the other hand, measures the additional satisfaction derived from the consumption of an additional unit of a goods.

This distinction between total utility and marginal utility is helpful to explain the "diamond water paradox" which was first pointed out by Adam Smith. We know that water is more useful than diamond and diamond is more valuable than water. Water is an essential requisite for human existence and diamond is to show the proud and prestige of richness. Why we pay more for a piece of diamond and less or nil for a cup of water ? It is because of the reason that total utility of water is more than that of diamond and marginal utility of diamond is greater than that of water. For water is available in plenty and the marginal utility of it is less, whereas diamond is scarce in supply, the marginal utility of it is comparatively larger. Thus, the theory explains why diamond is more valuable than water, though water is so useful than diamond.

Consumer Demand

We may now repeat the point that it is market demand which consists of demand of many households, that determines market price of any commodity along with forces of its supply. The behaviour of the individual consumer, thus, forms the basis of the law of demand and this section briefly examines the same.

To investigate consumer's demand and the factors governing it, let us begin with the basic fact : Anyone's demand for a given commodity depends on the price of the product, his income, prices of related goods and his habit, tastes and preferences. It may be given a functional form as—

$$Dm = F (Pm, Y, P1, P2 \ldots\ldots, T)$$

where Dm represents demand for the given commodity M, Y is consumer's income, P1. P2. . . ., are prices of related goods and T represents consumer's tastes and preferences. To formulate a valid demand theorem, economists assume that income, tastes and preferences of the consumer and the prices of the related goods are all held constant. The theory of demand, thus, establishes a relation between quantity demanded and the price. Now, we may get the new functional form as—

$$D = f (P)$$

which means that demand is a function of price.

From time to time many theories have been formulated to explain consumer's demand. Utility analysis of demand developed by Alfred Marshall is the basic one which provides a simple explanation of consumer's demand.

Utility hypothesis is the basis of the demand theory. It assumes that people derives satisfaction from consuming any goods or service and the satisfaction is synonymous with 'utility'. Since it is difficult to know whether people derives satisfaction from consuming commodities, then this approach is apparently based on introspection. In other words, what economists knew about their own behaviour is assumed to be true about the behaviour of other. As one writer points out, "introspection is the ability of the observer to reconstruct events which go in the mind of another person with the help of self-observation."[1] The utility analysis is thus introspective.

Another basic tenet of the utility analysis is 'cardinalism'. It assumes that utility is a cardinal concept, atleast conceptually. That is, utility is a measurable and quantitable entity. A cardinal utility function gives numerically comparable estimates of the intensities of preferences. Individual preferences are assumed to be constant over the period of analysis.

The amount of utility the individual derives in a given period from the consumption of the X1 units of Goods X, Y1 units of Goods Y and Z1 units of Goods Z, can be written in a functional form as—

$$u1 = u\,(x1,\ y1,\ z1)$$

where the symbol u(. . . .) denotes the cardinal utility function.

Marshall used to measure utility in terms of money. Money relates to the general purchasing power and commands over utility obtainable from goods. Money is considered as a measuring unit of utility.

It is also assumed that marginal utility of money is constant. When comparisons are made, a monetary unit of purchasing power has the same utility for an individual consumer. A rational consumer would buy an additional unit of the commodity if he expected to obtain more utility from the consumption of that commodity than the utility he gave up in money to buy it.

Law of Diminishing Marginal Utility

Though human wants are many, each particular want is sateable. It is on this premise that one of the basic economic laws is built.

Our demand for a commodity is not based on its total utility but on marginal utility, for our choice is not whether to buy all of that commodity or none. Instead, we decide whether or not we want to acquire an additional unit. That is, in the market our purchases are conditioned in terms of marginal units or at the margin.

To verify the hypothesis, economists often think of 'law of diminishing marginal utility' developed by William Stanley Jevons of Britain. It is our common experience that as we go on consuming more and more of any commodity, the additional satisfaction derived from its consumption goes on diminishing. This is the simple law of diminishing marginal utility.

The law holds that as we consume more and more units of a goods, total utility derived from the consumption of that goods increases by smaller and smaller amounts. In other words, with the consumption of successive unit, marginal utility may diminish.

This notion of diminishing marginal utility is easily illustrated. Consider the state of your satisfaction after consuming one orange for a time. Now imagine by eating a second. So far it is good. But does a third one is so appealing as the second ? What about the fourth one ? With the consumption of the successive unit, the amount of satisfaction will, no doubt, increase, but only by smaller and smaller amounts. In the words of Alfred Marshall, "the additional benefit which a person derives from a given increase of his stock of a thing diminishes with every increase in the stock that he already has."

Assume for a moment that utility is measurable so as to illustrate the relation between total utility and marginal utility. A certain number of utilities are added with the consumption of each orange and note that each successive orange yields lesser utility. The utility schedule for oranges might be shown as in Table 2.1.

TABLE 2.1

Utility Schedule for Oranges (hypothetical data)

Number of Oranges	*Total Utility*	*Marginal Utility*
1	10	10
2	20	10
3	26	6
4	30	4
5	30	4
6	28	—2

In the above schedule, the consumers total utility continued to increase through the consumption of the fourth orange, although the marginal utility began to decline after the consumption of the second orange. Also note that the total utility starts decline after the fifth orange and with the consumption of the fifth one, no utility is added. The consumer will then buy no more oranges instead he will buy any other alternatives, say, a magazine or a world atlas, which yield him more satisfaction.

These hypothetical data depicting the utility schedule for oranges are shown graphically in Figure 2.1.

Marginal Utility and Expenditure

Let us now see how utility schedule affect the consumer's purchases. We may know the consumer's size of total expenditure, price of oranges in the market and his utility schedules for other goods so as to determine the number of oranges bought.

At the time he is purchasing oranges, our hypothetical consumer is assumed to be confronted with a wide range of other demands. He wants to buy, say, bread, vegetables, and fish. Each of them has utility and the behaviour of utility schedules for each good may be in the same manner. Marginal utility diminishes with the consumption of successive unit. The consumer will, then, try to apportion his total money expenditure in such a way as to maximise

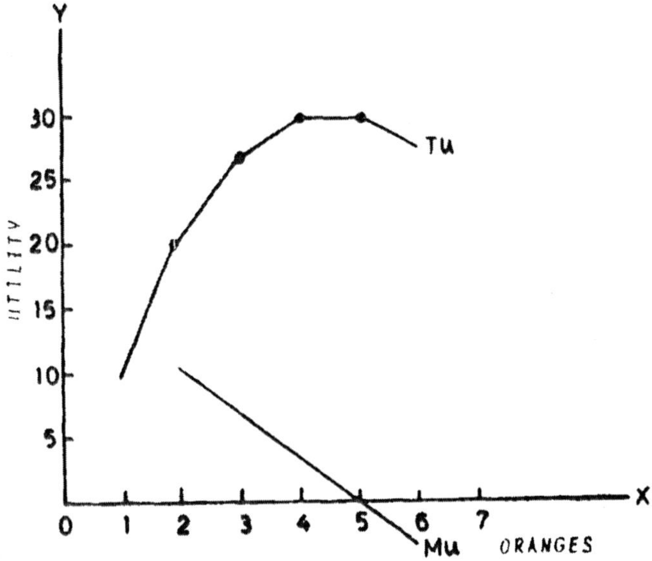

Fig. 2.1 : Total and Marginal Utility.

his total utility from all goods and he could achieve this position by spending additional units of his money expenditure on those goods which yield him the greatest marginal utilities.

Marginal Utility and Price

Marginal utility is the change in total utility resulting from a change in the consumption level of the commodity by one unit. When we are purchasing a commodity, we are consciously or unconsciously weighing in our mind the price we have to pay and the utility of each unit. We will continue purchasing the commodity till the marginal utility equals price. Here we draw a fundamental proposition of the theory of consumer demand. As Stonier and Hague point out, "A consumer will change money for units of any commodity A, up to the point where the last (marginal) unit of A which he buys has for him a marginal significance in terms of money just equals to its money price."[2]

A consumer gets maximum satisfaction when he purchases a commodity in such a way that marginal utility of the commodity equals its price. The equality of marginal utility and price is graphically shown in Figure 2.2. Mu is the marginal utility curve the slope of which implies that marginal utility diminishes as more units are purchased. When the price of the commodity is OP, which is equal to marginal utility, MS, the consumer would purchase OM units.

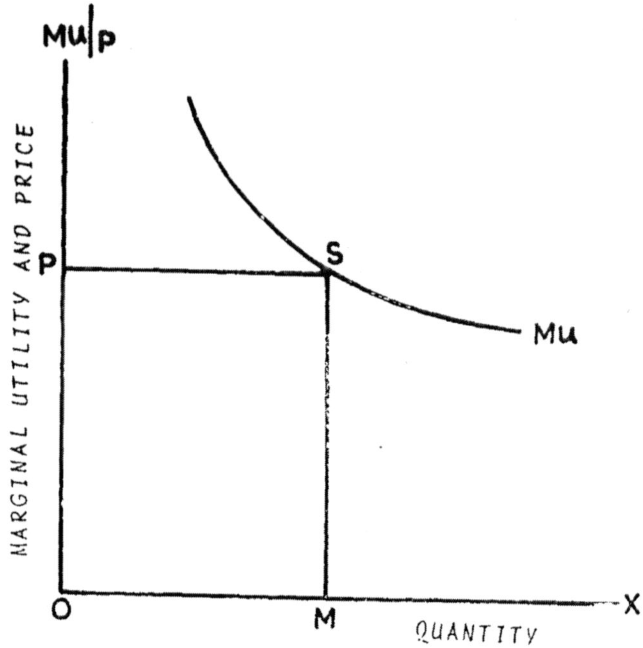

Figure 2.2 : Marginal Utility and Price.

Consumer's Equilibrium

Let us have a look at a general theory of consumer demand. As is well known we spend our money incomes to maximise our satisfactions. This follows an important proposition : Each consumer will change the volume of goods and services he buys whenever he gets more utility by spending an extra rupee on a given commodity than on alternatives. He will maximise his total utility when he allocates his money income so as to equalise the marginal utility he obtains from the last rupee spent on each item he buys. When he so allocates his income, we may say that the consumer is in "equilibrium", in the sense that he is maximising satisfaction he can receive by spending his money income.

If we get a larger marginal utility by spending a rupee on commodity A than on commodity B obviously we should spent it on commodity A. Whenever the marginal utility of the last rupee spent on different items is not same we can increase our total utility by switching from lower to higher marginal utility items. To simplify our analysis, we assume that the price of every item is the same. We may allocate our income as to obtain the same marginal utility from every item we buy. It can be written in an equational form as—

Mux=Muy=Muz and so on; x, y and z are the units of commodities when x, y and z are purchased.

If the prices of different goods are different, we may not expect that we could get the same marginal utility from each goods. It would be a sheer non-sense to think that the marginal utilities obtained from a movie and a fountain pen are the same. But if we divide the marginal utility from each by the price of each, it is possible to make them comparable. We may now repeat our central proposition : the consumer will be in equilibrium when the marginal utility of the last rupee spent on each commodity are equal.

Let us make it more clear. A consumer with a given income has to spend on various goods he wants. Now, the question is how he would allocate his money income among various goods. Consider that he is confronted with a wide range of commodities. He wants to buy a loaf of bread, a pen, a magazine and an apple. Each commodity has utility and each utility would behave in a similar manner. Marginal utility diminishes with the successive consumption of commodity. The consumer would, then, try to apportion his total money expenditure in such a way as to maximise his total utility from consuming all the commodities in question. He would reach this position by spending additional amount of his money on those goods that yield him greatest marginal utilities at the current level of consumption.

The consumer would maximise his satisfaction from spending his total income on all commodities when he reaches the point where marginal utility is equal in all the cases of expenditure. In other words, an individual consumer is said to be in equilibrium when he is purchasing that amount of commodity at which the money measure of the expected utility from purchasing an additional unit is equal to the market price. The monetary measure of the expected utility derived from consuming an additional unit is called the marginal demand price for that commodity. It is necessarily equal to the expected marginal utility of the commodity in question divided by the marginal utility of money.

In algebaric form

$$\text{Px} = \text{MDPx} = \frac{\text{Mux}}{\text{Mum}}$$

$$Py = MDPy = \frac{Muy}{Mum}$$

$$Pz = MDPz = \frac{Muz}{Mum} \text{ etc.}$$

where Px. Py, Pz are the market prices of commodities X, Y, and Z respectively, MDPx, MDPy and MDPz are marginal demand price of the goods X, Y and Z respectively and MUm is the marginal utility of money.

From the given equalities it is proved that an individual consumer is in equilibrium when the ratio of marginal utilities of any two goods purchased is equal to the ratio of their market price.

In symbols,

$$\frac{Mux}{Muy} = \frac{Px}{Py}$$

If it covers several commodities, the equality forms as—

$$MUm \frac{MUx}{Px} = \frac{MUy}{Py} = \ldots\ldots\ldots \frac{MUn}{Pn}$$

Consumer's equilibrium is graphically presented in Figure 2.3- Since marginal utility diminishes, the curves $\frac{MUx}{Px}$ and $\frac{MUy}{Py}$ are shown down ward-sloping. It is assumed that marginal utility of money is constant for a sufficient length of time and is shown as OM in Figure 2.3. $\frac{MUx}{Px}$ is equal to OM when ON1 amount of Goods X is consumed. $\frac{MUy}{Py}$ is equal to OM when ON 2 amount of Goods Y is consumed. Thus consumer is in equilibrium when he purchases ON 1 amount of Goods X and ON 2 amount of Goods Y at which

$$MUm = \frac{MUx}{Px} = \frac{MUy}{Py}$$

Utility Function and Law of Demand

We are now in a position to derive the demand curve from the cardinal utility function. The derivation of the demand curve from the principle of diminishing marginal utility is shown in

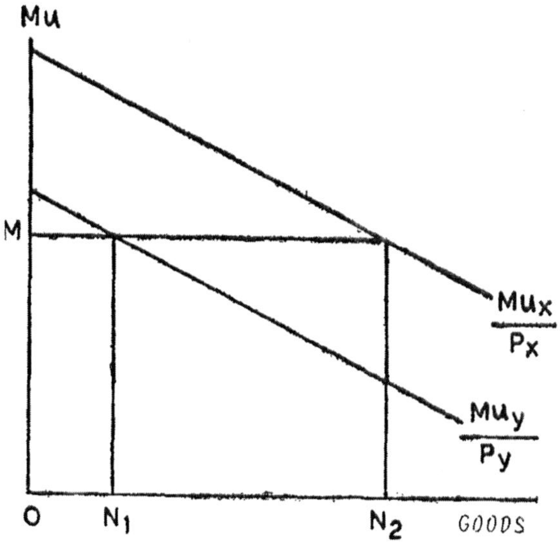

Figure 2.3. Consumer's Equilibrium.

Figure 2.4. The slope of the demand curve so derived is down-ward to the right since more is demanded at low prices. In otherwords, demand varies inversely with price, ceteris paribus. According to Marshall, "the greater the amount to be sold, the smaller must be the price at which it is offered in order that it may find purchasers, or in other words, the amount demanded increases with a fall in price, and diminishes with a rise in price."[3]

The theory holds good only on the assumption of constant tastes, constant money income, constant quantities of all related goods and constant prices of other commodities. It is also assumed that the utility derived from consuming a commodity independent of the quantities consumed of other commodities is independent of the quantities consumed of other commodities and inverse relationship between price and quantity demanded is the necessary consequence of these assumptions.

Critical Evaluation

Marshallian utility analysis has been criticised on various grounds. The following are the main shortcomings :

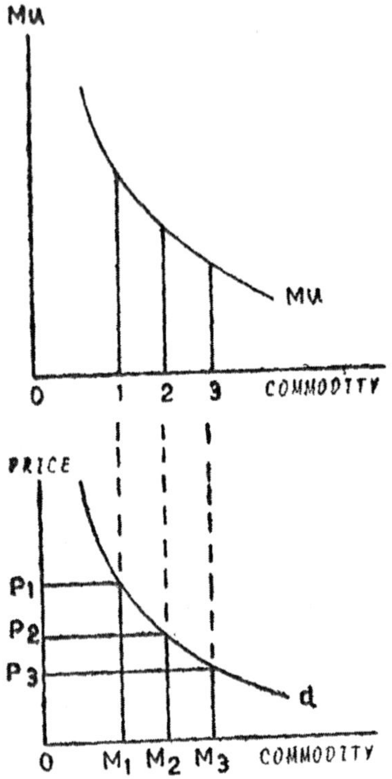

Figure 2.4 Derivation of Demand Curve.

1. Cardinal Measurement of Utility is Unrealistic :

The Marshallian utility analysis is based on the fundamental assumption that utility is measurable in quantitative terms. But in actual practice it is impossible to measure utility quantitatively. It cannot be measurable or quantifiable but comparable. We can compare the satisfactions derived from the consumption of various goods or combination of goods.

2. Utility is a Dependent Hypothesis :

The utility analysis, further, assumes that utility derived from the consumption of a goods is the function of that goods and that goods only. That is, utility derived from the consumption of one commodity is indepedent of the other. But utility of one commodity depends, usually, upon the availability of the other commodity. For instance, utility of pen depends on the availability of ink. Hence we my state that utility is a dependent, rather than independent hypothesis.

3. Marginal Utility of Money is not Constant

Another basic assumption of Marshallian utility analysis of demand is that marginal utility of money remains constant. But this is incorrect. As real income changes, marginal utility of money also changes. For instance, as we spend more from a giver money income on goods and services, the money income left wit us declines. With the decline in money income as a result of larger expenses, marginal utility of money rises. If, on the other hand, price level falls, real income may rise and as a result marginal utility of money will fall. By assuming marginal utility of money as constant, Marshall ignores the income effect of price changes. He could remain also unable to explain the Giffen paradox through his utility analysis.

THE DOCTRINE OF CONSUMER'S SURPLUS

In modern societies we are able to buy a multitude of commodities. For any one of the commodities, taken by itself, we may prepare to pay much more than we do infact have to pay. The difference between the amount a consumer would pay for the quantity of a commodity he buys and the amount he does pay is called "consumer's surplus".

The doctrine of consumer's surplus was first introduced by Alfred Marshall. Because of its simplicity, Marshall's doctrine remains sturdy even today. We are all experiencing some cosumer's surplus even in our daily purchases, since we may prepare to pay more than we actually pay in certain cases. The excess satisfaction that we derive from the purchase of commodities by paying a lesser amount than we actually are willing to pay is called consumer's surplus. According to Marshall, "The excess of the price which he (consumer) would be willing to pay rather than go without the thing over that which he actually does pay is the economic measure of this surplus satisfaction....It may be called consume-'s Surplus."

As an example, consider the consumer's surplus that a hypothetical consumer gets from his monthly purchases of vegitables, say, tomato.

Table 2.2 gives the hypothetical data :

TABLE 2.2

Calculation of Consumer's Surplus

Prices per K.g. Rs.	*Quantity bought Kg.*	*Total Expen-diture Rs.*	*Utility of Expen-diture**	*Total Utility**	*Consumer's Surplus**
(1)	(2)	(3)	(4)	(5)	(6)
2.50	1	2.50	2½	2½	
1.50	2	3.50	3	4	1
1.00	3	3.00	3	5	2
0.75	4	3.00	3	5½	4½

*By assumption, the utility of one rupee is one utltiy and remains constant.

The first-two columns are a demand schedule, the quantities being kilograms per month. The third column is total expenditure. For this consumer lets one rupee yields one utility. The fourth column gives the utility of the expenditure on tomato. The fifth column shows total utility. The first quantity, i.e., 1 kg. of tomato, has a utility of 2½ utility, but a second one—(2kgs) yields only 1½ utility, so that the first two kilograms afford a total of 4 utility. Consumer's surplus is obtained by subtracting the utility of expenditure from the total utility.

If the actual price is Rs. 0.75 per kg. the consumer buys 4 kilograms of tomato a month. His consumer's surplus is 2½ utility.

The Figure 2.5 given below displays the diagram for consumer's surplus. The diagram shows the number contained in the given Table 2.2. The stippled area is consumer's surplus.

If the price of a commodity or a service rises, the consumer is said be in less. Similary, if a price falls, the consumer benefits. What does the loss or benefit consist of? It is a loss or gain of consumer's surplus. This is illustrated in the Figure 2.6. Let the initial price be Po. At this price the consumer's surplus is the sum of the areas A and B. When price rises to P1 consumer's surplus shrinks to the area A., thus area B is the loss of consumer's surplus from the price rise. Similarly a fall in price from Po to P2 brings a gain of consumer's surplus equal to the area C.

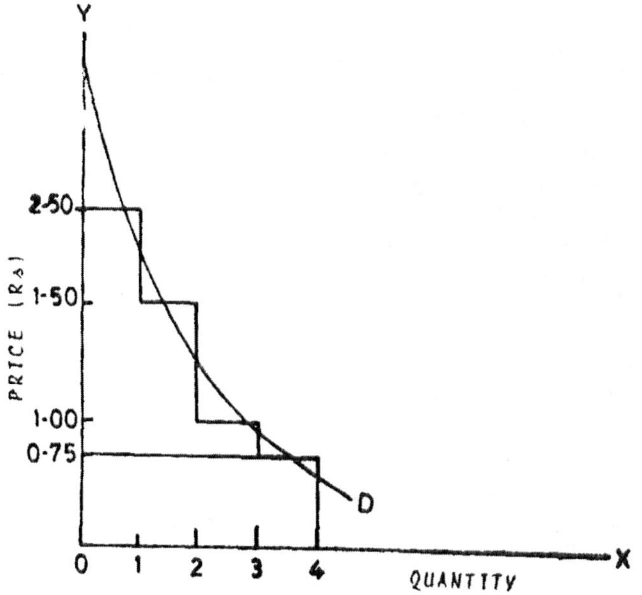

Figure 2.5. Consumer's Surplus.

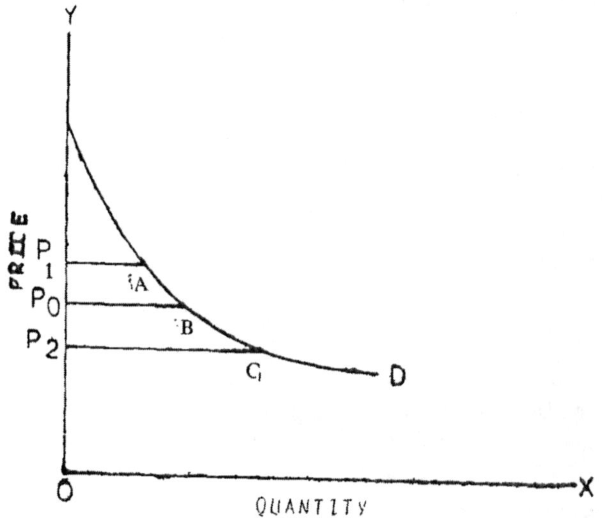

Figure 2.6 Consumer's Benefits and Losses

THE CONCEPT OF MARGIN

The concept of margin has an important place in economic analysis. By marginal unit we mean the last unit to be added to a supply or the first to be taken away from it. If a consumer already possesses 3 oranges and is deciding to a fourth one, this fourth orange might be considered to be his "marginal" unit. Whether he buys it or not will depend on whether he thinks that the additional benefit to be derived from this 4th orange is worth the price he will have to pay for it—that is he considers its marginal worth to him. If a farmer has two acres of land under wheat, a rise in the price of wheat may tempt him to devote another acre to wheat. This additional acre is the marginal unit. Alternatively, if he had decided to withdraw one acre from wheat cultivation the acre that ceased to grow wheat would be the marginal unit.

Marginal considerations concern the smallest possible rise or fall in the stock of anything. It is always marginal consideration that determines whether a person will add to his existing stock of a thing. The marginal significance of anything, therefore, depends on how much of its is already possessed. If a person already possesses a number of oranges the marginal significance to him of oranges is likely to be below ; if he has only one orange, the marginal significance of oranges may be high.

The margin is not fixed, for an increase in one's supply will push up the margin. Further, every fall in one's supply will bring down the margin nearer. A change in price will have a similar effect, a fall in price will push the margin further away and rise in price will bring down it nearer. We may thus speak of marginal unit of supply. The concept of margin can also be used in connection with cost, income, production etc., so as to speak of marginal cost, marginal income and marginal product.

THE INDIFFERENCE CURVE THEOREM

In place of cardinal utility approach to the theory of consumer behaviour, Vilfredo Pareto, a continental economist has evolved an alternative technique known as indifference curve analysis based on ordinal rankings of utility levels. Pareto's results were developed by Slutsky, a Russian economist and later by two noted English economists J.R. Hicks and R.G.D. Allen* The indifference curve theory in contrast to the marginal utility theory, results on the fact that while utility cannot be measured, it is possible to observe from experiences and experiment the preferences which people display when choosing between different commodities.[4]

The fundamental premise of the indifference curve theory is the ordinal utility function. A function that provides only alternatives is called ordinal utility function.[5] It assumes that utility is comparable and not measurable or quantifiable. Ordinal utility means that the consumer is assumed to order or rank the subjective utilities of goods.[6] The taste of the consumer is, therefore, described with the ideas of preferences or indifference. If a consumer is presented with different sets of commodities he, then, prefers one to the other or else he is indifferent. It is important to note that the consumer behaviour can be derived from the tastes of the consumers by ordinal rankings without numerical measurement.

The analytical tool in ordinal utility analysis is the indifference curve which can be derived from indifference set. Let us begin with the indifference set.

Indifference Set

Suppose that a certain consumer is offered a set of baskets containing two range of consumables, say, apples and oranges. If he obtains the same level of satisfaction from different set of combinations, we can say that he is indifferent among them or that he has no special preference to any of them. An indifference set can, therefore, be defined as a set of consumption alternatives yielding the s ame level of utility or satisfaction.

Exploring matters further, a typical indifference set is given in Table 2.3.

With the data in hand, a geometrical indifference curve can be drawn. Consider Figure 2.7. A set of ordinate axes are drawn first. Units of apples are measured on horizontal axis and units of oranges on vertical axis. Each basket of commodities can be shown as a point in the area between two axes. The point representing baskets A through D are shown in their proper spots in the diagram. The curve joining these points itself is an indifference curve. An

*The technique of indifference curve analysis was first introduced by Francis Edgeworth in 1881 in his famous monograph 'Mathematical psychics'. Later Fisher made use of this technique in his 'Mathematical investigations in the theory of value and prices, (1892).

TABLE 2.3
Indifference Set

Basket A	*Apples*	*Oranges*
A	8	3
B	6	4
C	5	5
D	4	7

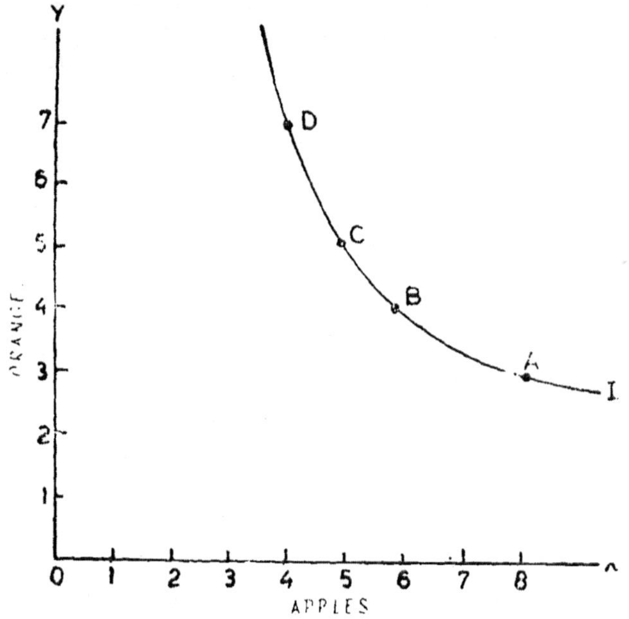

Figure 2.7 Indifference Curve.

indifference curve is thus a geographical representation of indifference set.

Each point in the diagram stands for a basket of apples and oranges. A,B,C, and D are baskets among which the consumer is indifferent. All give him the same utility. The curve I connecting these Points A,B, C and D constitutes an indifference curve.

Properties of Indifference Curve

Properties of indifference curve reflect certain basic regularities in behaviour pattern of consumer preferences. Five important properties of indifference curve are worth noting :

1. Indifference curves are downward sloping.

Consider the curve sketched in Figure 2.8. Consumption set shown by Point A contains more of both the goods than that shown by Point B. The higher combination would naturally give greater satisfaction and as such A must be preferred to B. The consumer is, therefore, not to be indifferent between them. The curve in Figure 2.8 represents an impossible upward sloping indifference curve.

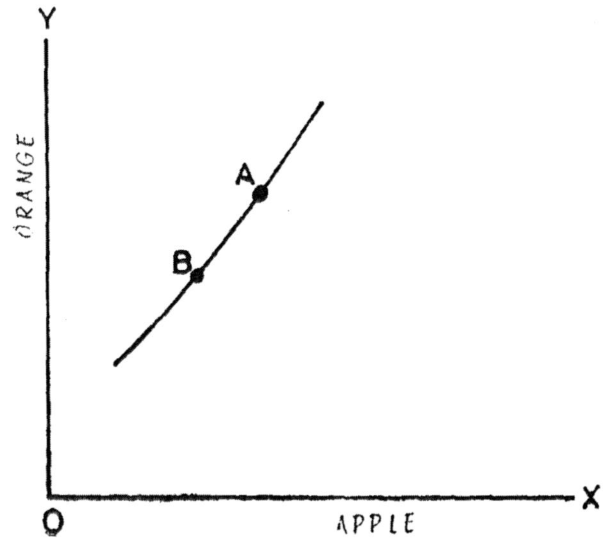

Figure 2.8 Impossible upward sloping Indifference Curve.

2. The slope of the indifference curve is the marginal rate of substitution.

As more and more units of one commodity are substituted for other the consumer will be willing to forgo fewer and fewer units of the other commodity for each additional units without gain or loss in satisfaction is called marginal rate of substitution. Marginal rate of substitution is the slope of the indifference curve.

Consider Figure 2.9. When the consumer moves from A to B on indifference I he gives up AC units of oranges (Y) and takes CB units of apples (X) and he enjoys the same level of satisfaction. It is seen that the consumer is prepared to exchange AC units of Y for CB units of X. That is marginal rate of substitution of X for Y is equal to AC units of Y (oranges) divided by CB units of X. That is marginal rate of substitution of X for Y is equal to AC units of Y (oranges) divided by CB units of X (apples).

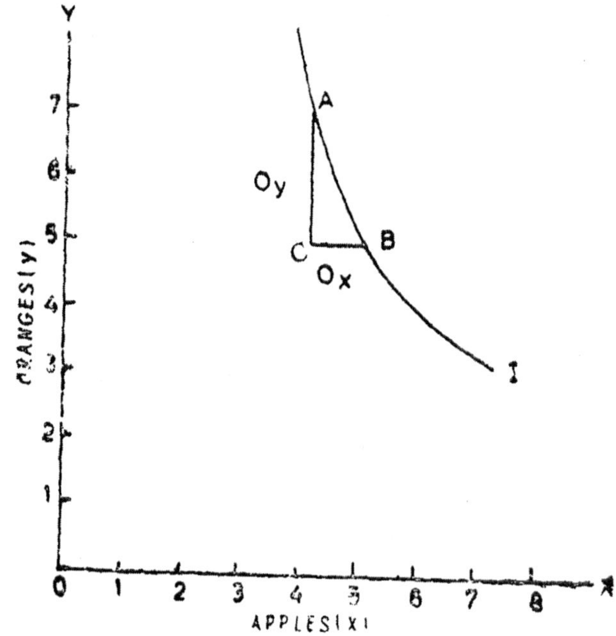

Figure 2.9 Marginal rate of Substitution.

In equation,

$$MRSxy = \frac{AC}{CB}$$

$$AC = \wedge Y$$

$$CB = \wedge X$$

$$\therefore MRSxy = \frac{\wedge Y}{\wedge X}$$

3. Indifference curves are convex to the origin.

It implies that their slope decreases as one moves down to the right. The convexity of indifference curve results from diminishing marginal utility. This is illustrated in the region between D and C in the diagram shown in Figure 2.10. The slope of the indifference curve is approximately-2 indicating that the ratio of marginal utility of apples to that of oranges is approximately 2:1. By comparison in the region between B and A, the slope is $-\frac{1}{2}$ indicating that marginal utility of apples to the marginal utility of oranges is 1 : 2.

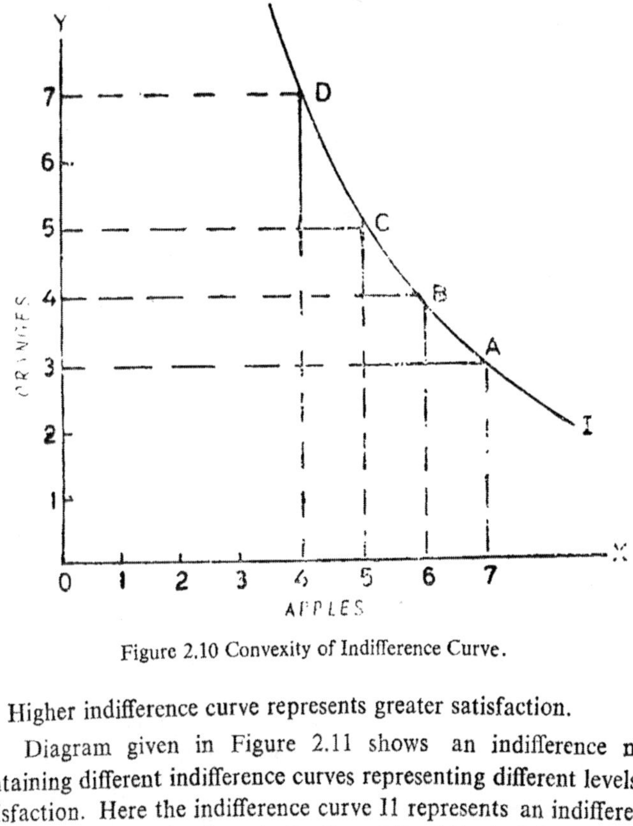

Figure 2.10 Convexity of Indifference Curve.

4. Higher indifference curve represents greater satisfaction.

Diagram given in Figure 2.11 shows an indifference map containing different indifference curves representing different levels of satisfaction. Here the indifference curve I1 represents an indifference set containing combinations A, B, C and D while indifference curve I2 represents another indifference set of combinations E, F, G and H. All combinations on I2 are better than the combinations on I1. The curve I2 is a higher indifference curve which ties to the right of the curve I1. The indifference curve I2 represents a higher level of satisfaction.

5. Indifference curves never cross or touch.

This is because of the transitivity assumption of the behavioural pattern of the consumer. The consumer preferences are transitive in the sense that if he prefers A to B and B to C he then prefers A to C.

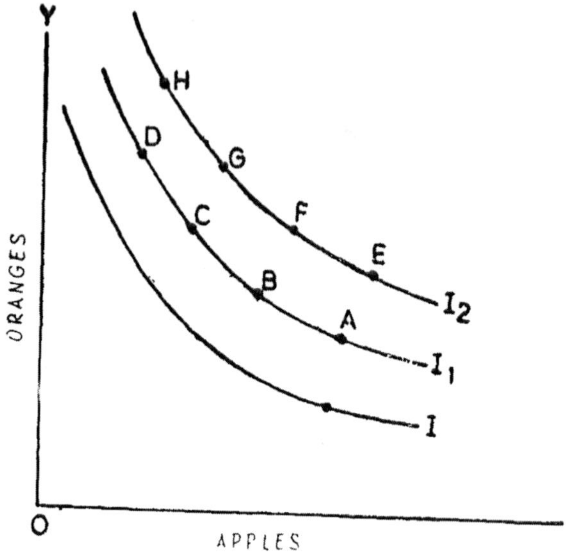

Figure 2.11 Indifference Map.

Figure 2.12 shows the crossed indifference curves which contradict—the assumption of transitivity. Look at the Points A, B and C. Since A and B lie on the same indifference Curve I1 the consumer is indifferent between these combinations. Again A and C lie on another indifference Curve I 2 between which also the consumer is indifferent. As per the transitivity assumption, if A is as goods as B and A is as goods as C, it is also concluded that C is as goods as B. But C lies above B which represents a combination of more of both goods. If more is preferred to less the consumer must prefer C to B. We, thus, see that crossed indifference curves imply a contradictory set of preferences.

Budget Constraint

Equipped with the consumer's indifference map, we may now set out to find what combination of goods will be purchased when his income and the prices of goods are given. He has, say, Rs. 50 to spend and he is confronted with fixed prices for each unit of commodities—Rs. 5 for Goods x and Rs. 10 for Goods Y. It is clear that he could spend his money on any one of a variety of alternative combinations of Goods X and Goods Y.

At one extreme he could buy 10 units of Goods X if he spends his whole income on that commodity, at the other, he could buy 5

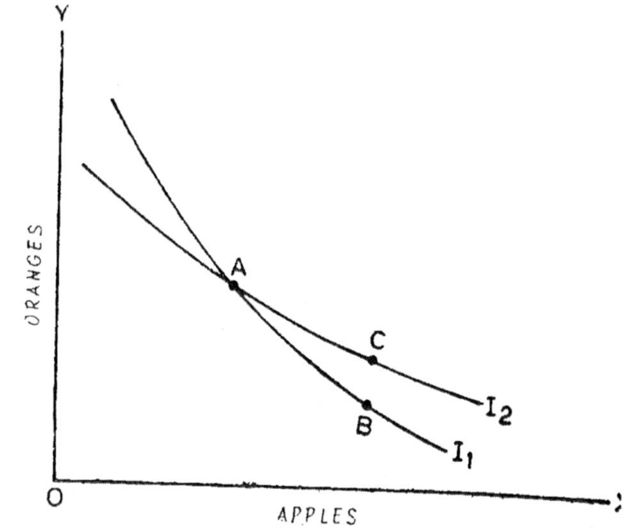

Figure 2.12 Crossed Indifference Curve.

units of commodity Y if he spent whole income on it. The Table 2.4 illustrates some of the positive ways in which his Rs. 50 could be allocated.

TABLE 2.4

Alternative Consumption Possibilities (hypothetical data)

	Goods X	*Goods Y*
B	10	0
	8	1
	6	2
	4	3
	2	4
A	0	5

Figure 2.13 shows these six possible positions on a diagram. Each position is marked by a small dot. Note that they all lie on a straightline, labelled as AB. The straight line sums up all the possible positions the consumer occupy in spending his total income Rs. 50. A budget line is thus a graphical representation of alternative consumption possibilities.

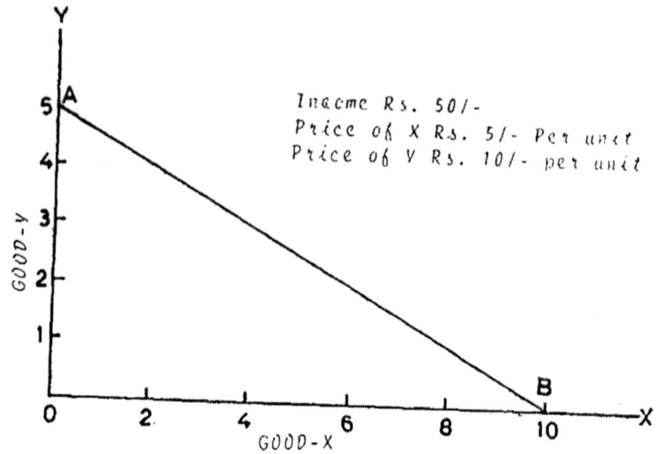

Figure 2.13 Budgetline.

The slope of AB is $\frac{1}{2}$ which is necessarily the ratio of the price of X to the price of Y.

Arithmatic slope of AB=
Price of X ÷ price of Y

$$\frac{\text{Rs. } 5}{\text{Rs. } 10} = \frac{\text{Price of X}}{\text{price of Y}} = \frac{PX}{PY}$$

Consumer's Equilibrium

It is now instructive to show graphically the position of consumer's equilibrium. This is explained with the help of the diagram, in Figure 2.14. AB is the budget line, slope of which expresses the price ratio of Goods X to Goods Y. Three indifference curves representing different levels satisfaction are drawn. Consumer would be in equilibrium when he obtains greatest satisfaction. The consumer would then move to the position of highest satisfaction, to the highest possible indifference curve. In this case this must be at Point L when he purchases OM amounts of X and OS amounts of Y. At Point L the budget line AB just touches the indifference Curve I1. The combination of Goods X and Goods Y at Point L is preferred to all other combinations available. If the consumer buys less X and more Y moving to Point P he will be on a lower indifference curve I 2. If he moves down to T he will also on the same lower indiffe-rence curve I 2. He would like to be on a higher indifference curve viz., I 3, but hecould hardly get them since his budget is too small.

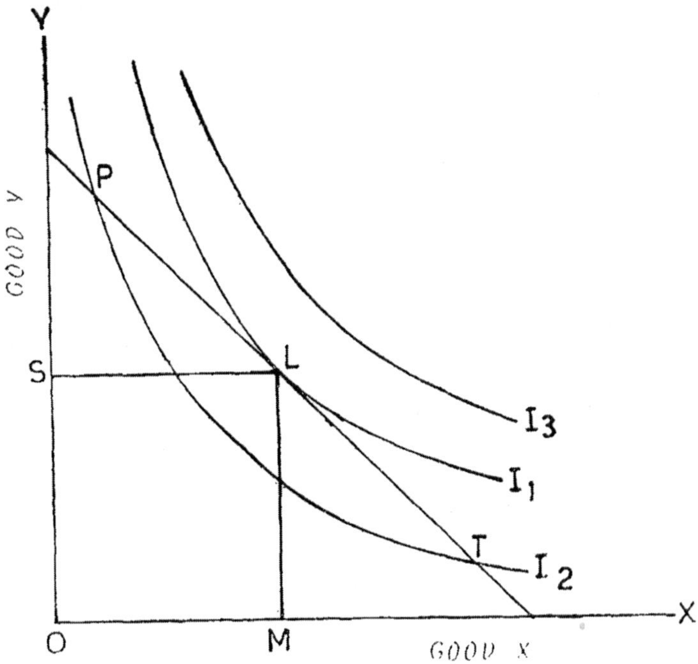

Figure 2.14 Consumer's equilibrium.

When the consumer is at equilibrium, the highest possible indifference curve is tangent to the budget line. Geometrically the slope of the budget line is exactly equal to the slope of the indifference curve. As stated, the slope of the indifference curve is $\frac{\Delta Y}{\Delta X}$ since utility of the loss is equal to the utility of gain,

$$\Delta Y \times Muy = \Delta X \times Mux$$

$$\therefore \quad \frac{\Delta Y}{\Delta X} = \frac{Mux}{Muy}$$

That is, slope of the indifference curve is equal to the ratio of marginal utilities.

To explain why marginal rate of substitution of X for Y $\left(\frac{\Delta Y}{\Delta X}\right)$ is equal to the ratio of marginal utility of X to the marginal utility of Y $\frac{(Mux)}{(Muy)}$ consider Figure 2.15. At point M the slope of the indifference curve is $\frac{\Delta Y}{\Delta X} = \frac{Iy}{2X.}$ Suppose that at Point M the consumer gives up I unit of Y he then moves down to the Point N on a lower indifference curve I2 to the loss of utility. The loss can be offset by gaining 2 units of X and the consumer moves to the Point O on indifference curve I1. That is utility lost by forgoing I unit of Y is made goods by obtaining 2 units of X.

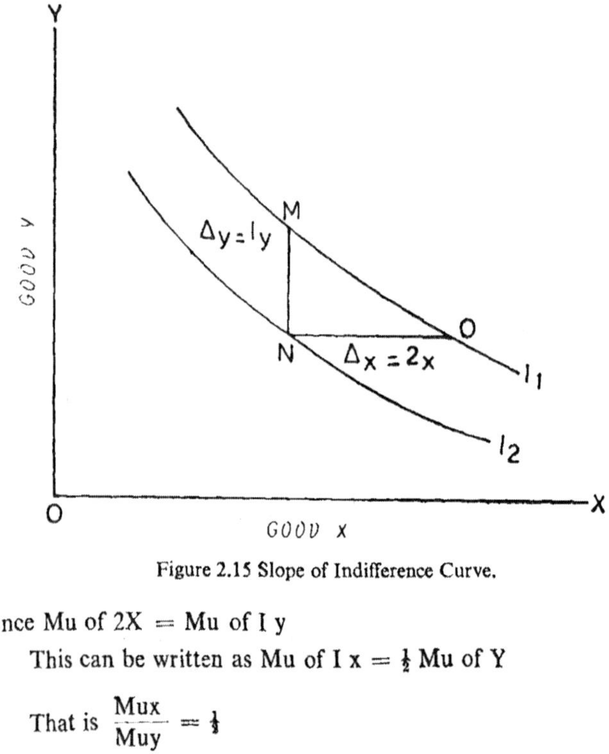

Figure 2.15 Slope of Indifference Curve.

Hence Mu of 2X = Mu of I y

This can be written as Mu of I x = ½ Mu of Y

That is $\frac{\text{Mux}}{\text{Muy}} = \frac{1}{2}$

The slope of the budget line is, as stated, $\frac{PX}{PY}$. At the point of equilibrium marginal rate of substitution of X for Y is equal to the ratio of marginal utility of X to the marginal utility of Y which is the price ratio of X to Y.

In equations,

$$\text{MRSxy} \ \frac{\Delta Y}{\Delta X}$$

$$\frac{Mux}{Muy} = \frac{Px}{Py}$$

At equilibrium $MRSxy = \frac{Mux}{Muy}$

That is $\frac{\Delta Y}{\Lambda X} = \frac{Px}{Py}$

Change in Income and Price

The study of the indifference analysis will be furthered by considering the effects of (i) a change in income and (ii) a change in price of one of the commodities.

The total effect of a change in price on quantity demanded is called price effect, which is composed of two important components income effect and substitution effect.

Income Effect

In the given analysis of consumer's equilibrium, we hold the assumption that the income of the consumer remains constant, given the prices of the commodities X and Y. It is interested to note that the consumer's behaviour in regard to his purchases when the income of the consumer changes, prices of commodities and attitude of the consumer are remaining constant. Income effect expresses the change in his money income, given the prices of commodities and attitude of the consumer.

The income effect is graphically illustrated in Figure 2.16. When the budget line is M1 N1, the equilibrium point is A where the budget line touches the indifference curve IC1. Suppose that the income of the consumer increases, the original budget line M1 N1 will shift to new position as M2N2 and the new equilibrium position is B—where the new budget line M2N2 touches the new indifference curve IC2. As income increases further the budget line will again shift forward and becomes M3N3 with C as its equilibrium point. It is possible to connect the various equilibrium points such as A. B and C with a curve commonly referred to as income-consumption curve (ICC). ICC is thus the locus of the various equilibrium points at the various levels of income.

Income effect may be positive or negative. If the volume of consumer's purchases increases as a result of increase in income, the income effect is said to be positive and in such cases the ICC will slope upward to the right as seen in Figure 2.16. Negative income effect may occur when the consummer purchases lesser

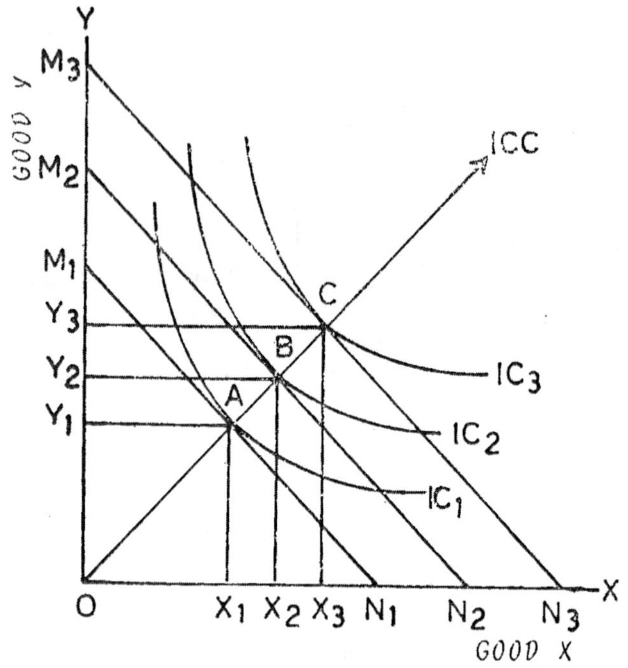

Figure 2.16 Income Effect.

volume of goods with a rise in his money income. In the case of inferior goods, the income effect will be negative since the income of the consumer rises, he may have to substitute more superior goods in place of inferior ones. In such cases, the ICC will slope upward to the left as seen in Figure 2.17a or downward to the right as seen in Figure 2.17b.

Substitution Effect.

Substitution effect shows the change in quantity demanded due to a change in the relative price. It means the difference in quantity demanded due to the difference in price when the purchasing power remaining constant. In other words, substitution effect means the change in the volume of purchases of a goods as a result of a change in relative prices, real income remains constant.

Prof. Hicks and Allen explained the substitution effect through compensating variation in income. When the price of a goods changes the real income or the purchasing power of the consumer also changes and to keep the real income constant so as to

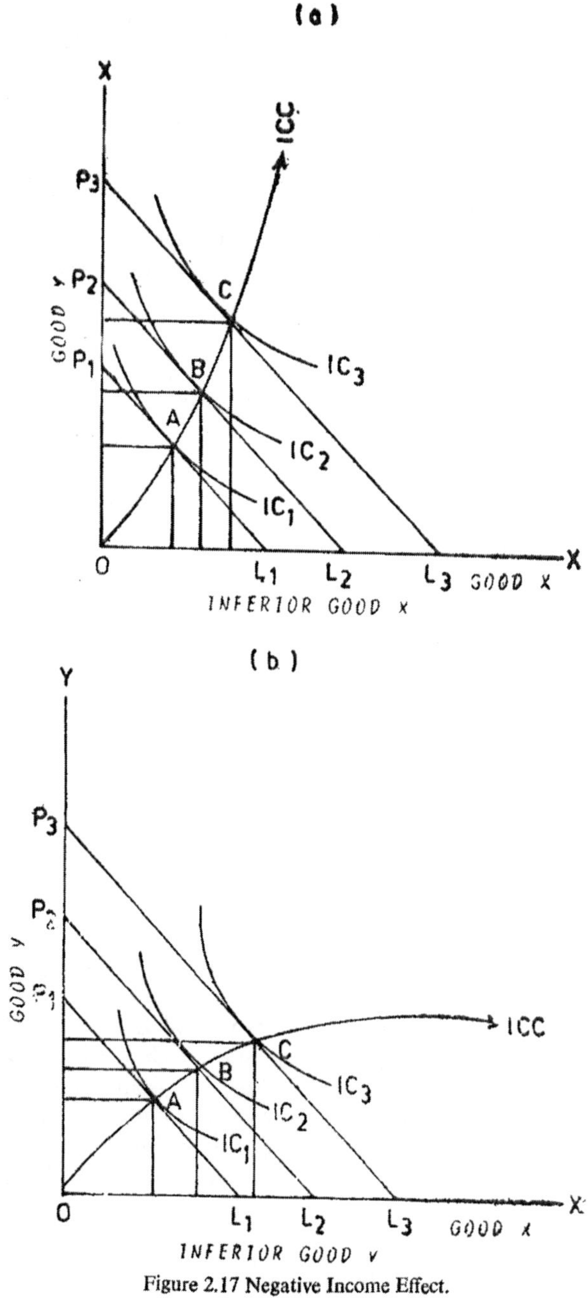

Figure 2.17 Negative Income Effect.

understand the change in the relative price alone, price change is compensated by so much change in income.

We may assume that when price of Goods X falls, the Goods Y becomes relatively dearer : The increases in the real income of the consumer as a consequence of the fall in the price of Good X is withdrawn so as to keep the consumer on the same position of satisfaction as before. He may be thus neither better off nor worse off than before. The substitution effect is clearly represented in Figure 2.18. The consumer is at equilibrium at Point A where the budget

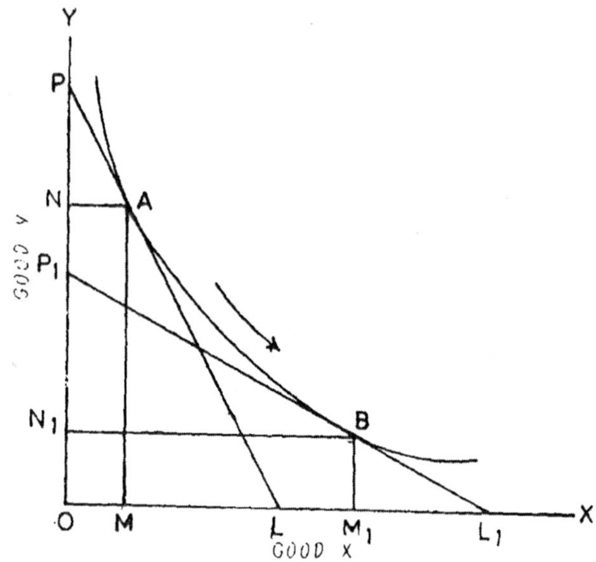

Figure 2.18 Substitution Effect.

line PL is tangent to the indifference curve ICI. Purchasing ON of Y and ON of X. Suppose that price of X falls. The new price line will be P1L1. If the consumer is to spend the whole of his income on the purchase of Goods X he can purchase OL1 of X instead of OP1. The commodity will become comparatively dearer and he will reduce the volume of purchases of commodity Y. The new price line P1L1 touches the IC1 at Point B, the new equilibrium position of the consumer. The consumer now purchases ON1 of Goods Y and OM1 of Goods X. The consumer reduces the purchases the consumption of commodity Y from ON to ON1 and increases the purchases of Goods X from OM to OM1. As a result he moves from the equilibrium Points A to B on the same indifference curve so as to make him neither better off nor worse off.

When the price of X falls the price of Y rises in the same proportion by PP1 so that the new budget line is P1L1 and the consumer remains on the same indifference curve. This is the compensating variation as a result of change in relative prices of X and Y.

Price Effect

The price effect shows the change in the volume of consumer's purchases of a goods, when its price changes giving his money income, tastes and preferences and the prices of related goods.

The price effect is graphically shown in Figure 2.19. Suppose the price of X falls. The price line PL will extend further as PL1 which shows that the consumer purchases more X than before since Goods X

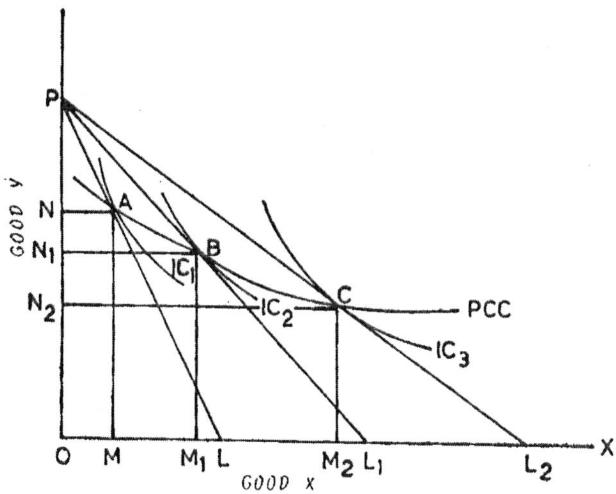

Figure 2.19 Price Effect.

has become cheaper. The price line PL2 shows a further fall in the price of X. Originally the consumer was in equilibrium at Point A where the indifference Curve IC1 is tangent to the price line PL1 purchasing ON of Goods Y and OM of Goods X. As a result of fall in price of Goods X, he purchases lesser amount of Y and more of Goods X, say, ON1 of Y and OM1 of Goods X. The price falls still further making the Good X more cheaper and the consumer purchases ON2 of Y and OM2 of X keeping on the equilibrium position

C where the indifference curve IC3 is tangent to the budgetline. The equilibrium positions at different level of prices, say, A, B and C can be joined with a curve as shown in Figure 2.19 the locus of these equilibrium points is called price—consumption curve.

The two effects—income and substitution effects—are illustrated in Figure 2.20 with the given price, and the consumer is in original equilibrium position at Point A, when indifference I1 is

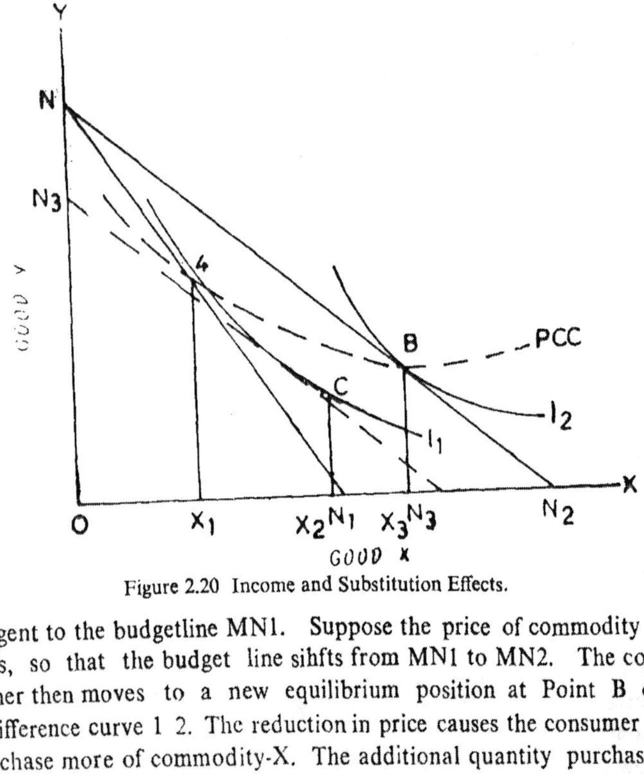

Figure 2.20 Income and Substitution Effects.

tangent to the budgetline MN1. Suppose the price of commodity X falls, so that the budget line sihfts from MN1 to MN2. The consumer then moves to a new equilibrium position at Point B on indifference curve 1 2. The reduction in price causes the consumer to purchase more of commodity-X. The additional quantity purchased X1 X3. The quantity X1 X3 is total effect of the change in price.

As stated, total effect is composed of substitution and income effects. The substitution effect is seen from the dotted budget line N3 N3 which expresses the new price ratio. The dotted budget line N3N3 is tangent to the indifference curve I1 at Point C. In terms of Goods X purchased the substitution effect is represented by an increases in demand from X1 to X2. Hence, substitution effect is formed as X1 X2.

The other part of price effect is income effect. The income effect is found by constructing a fictitious budget line N N2. The consumer would be at equilibrium at Point B on a higher indifference curve I 2. He now buys more of the commodity X to the extent of X2 X3. This change represents income effect.

Thus total effect of a change in price is the sum of substitution and income effects.

In quantity terms,

Total effect = X3 − X1

Substitution effect = X2 — X1

Income effect = X3 — X2

Therefore,

X3 − X1 = (X2 — X1) + (X3 − X2)

That is,

Total effect (Price effect) = Substitution Effect + Income Effect.

Derivation of Demand Curve

To derive an individual's demand curve different price situations are assumed. In Panel A of the budget line A B1 depicts a situation in which the individual's money income is equal to OA and the price of the commodity X is equal to $\frac{OA}{OB1}$. The budget line AB2 shows the same money income OA, but the price of commodity X is lower which is equal to $\frac{OA}{OB2}$. If the individual's budget line is AB1, he is in equilibrium at Point R1. At this points he purchases OMI units of Goods and spends AN1 amounts of his money. Suppose that price of X falls. A new equilibrium position now originates at R2 on the budget line AB2. He would then consume a larger quantity of X say, OM2 and spend lesser amount AN2 on commodity X. A curve is derived by joining the points R1 and R2 and labelled price—consumption curve (PCC). In Panel—B of the Figure 2.21 the demand curve is derived. Point K1 on demand curve corresponds to R1 on indifference curve I1 in Panel—A. It shows that quantity OM1 units of commodity X would be demanded when the price of X is equal to $\frac{OA}{OB1}$. It

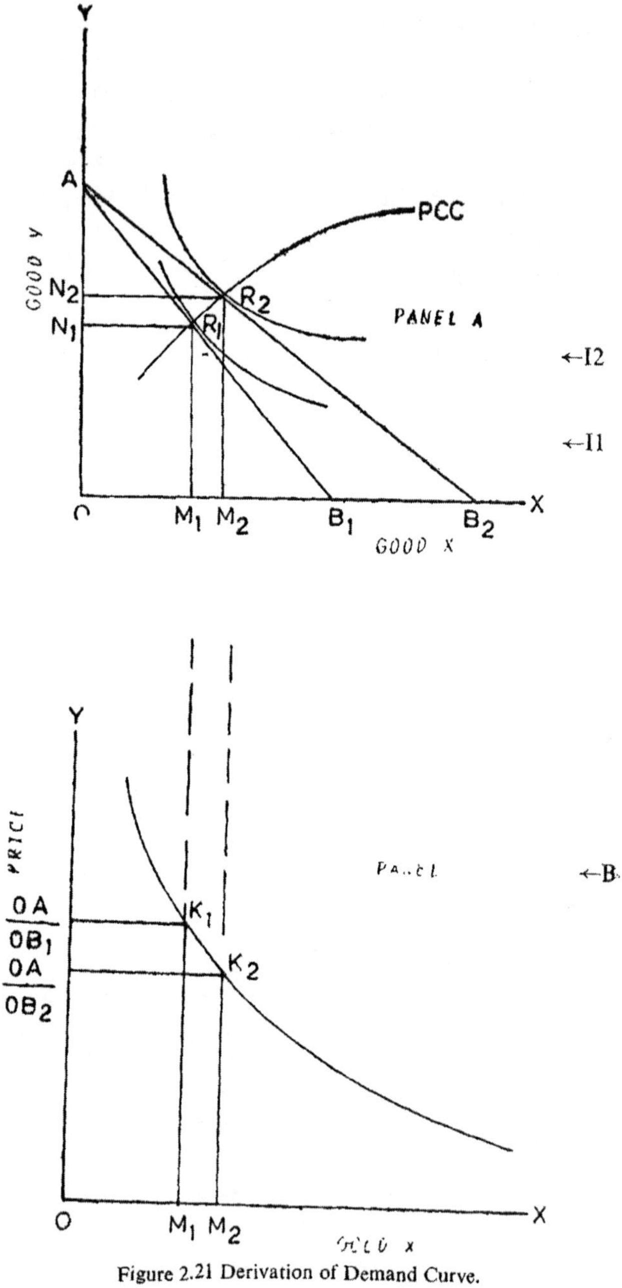

Figure 2.21 Derivation of Demand Curve.

explains that more is demanded at low price if consumer's attitude, income and prices of related goods remain unchanged.

Critical Evaluation

The indifference curve analysis, though superior to the marginal utility analysis of consumer behaviour, is not free from defects. Critics denounced it on various grounds. Prof. Robertson made a frontal attack on indifference curve technique and regarded it as "the old wine in the new bottle". The concept of preference has been substituted for utility. Introspective cardinalism has been replaced by introspective ordinalism in the indifference curve analysis. Marginal utility is substituted by marginal rate of substitution and it places the principle of diminishing marginal rate of substitution in the root of the law of diminishing marginal utility. Thus, Robertson has firmly believed that the indifference curve analysis has failed to bring a positive approach to the utility analysis and has given new names of the old concept.

Prof. F.H. Knight argues that the indifference curve technique fails to explain the observed behaviour of the consumer in the market objectively. Since the individual consumer thinks and acts subjectively it is hardly possible to make a positive demand theorem based on market observations.

Prof. Armstrong is of opinion that indifference curves are non-transitive. He argues that the consumer is indifferent in most cases because of his inability to perceive difference between alternative combinations of commodities. That is, the consumer is indifferent— between any combinations of goods which are having slightest difference from each other not because they give him equal satisfaction but because the differences between the combinations are so small that he is unable to perceive. Thus, the relation of indifference becomes non-transitive and with the non-transitivity of indifferences relation, the whole indifference curve analysis dilapidates.

Prof. Armstrong's argument can be illustrated in the Figure 2.22. On indifference curve IC1, points Q,R and S represent different combinations of Goods X and Y. The points are so drawn that the difference between each combination is imperceptible.

According to Hicks-Allen indifference curve analysis, the consumer is indifferent between Q and R and between R and S. Further, as per the transitivity assumption, he will be indifferent between Q and S. Prof. Armstrong argues that the consumer is indifferent between Q and R not because the total utility of combination Q is equal to the total utility of combination R, but because

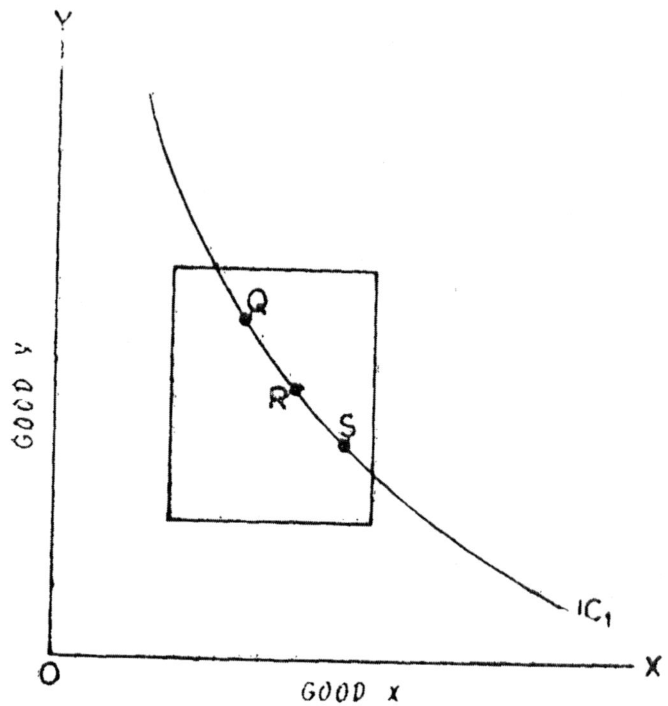

Figure 2.22 Imperceptible Combinations.

the difference between their total utilities becomes large enough to be perceptible. Thus, the consumer will not be indifferent between Q and S and will prefer Q to S or S to Q. This states that the points on indifference curve are not transitive.

THE REVEALED PREFERENCE THEORY

"Some economists, disenchanted with the subjective overtones of utility theory, have resorted to an alternative approach, that of revealed preference."[7] The essence of this theory is to look at observed behaviour, and from it deduce certain properties of consumer tastes. It was Paul Samuelson who propounded this theory as an alternative to the Hicks-Allen indifference curve technique. In sharp contrast to the psychological or introspective analysis, revealed preferences approach is a behaviouristic explanation of consumer's demand. This theory has been described by Prof. T. Majumdar as 'behaviourist ordinalist' since it applies behaviouristic method and also it uses the concept of ordinal utility.[8] It is distinct from the introspective ordinal utility theory as it requires no introspective information on the part of the consumer. The theory dispenses with the consumer's indifference for the combination of commodities and analyses his preferences for various combinations of goods on the basis of consumer's observed behaviour in the market. As Emil Kauder points out, "the behaviourist rejects introspection, his social insight is based entirely on experiment and controlled observation."[9]

Revealed preference theory is based on the fundamental premise that choice reveals preference. According to this hypothesis when a consumer is observed to choose a particular combination, say, carrot and tomato out of various alternative combinations, say, beans and potatoes, egg and fish, etc., open to him, then he reveals his preference for the combinations. Carrot and tomato over all other alternative combinations which he could have purchased. In other words, when a consumer chooses a particular combination, it means he considers all other alternative combinations which he could have purchased to be inferior to that.

Consider Figure 2.23 there are two commodities X and Y and there are various alternative combinations of these goods, say, A, B, C, D, and E. Given the prices of two commodities and income of the consumer PL is the price—income line. The triangle OPL is the area of choice for the consumer which shows the various combinations of X and Y on the given price—income situation PL.

Suppose the consumer chooses combination A, it is revealed that he also preferred to other combinations such as B,C,D, and E. Combinations B and C are lying below the price-income situation PL and hence he does not choose these combinations. Combination E is beyond the reach of the consumer since it lies above the given price-income situation. Therefore combination A is revealed to be preferred to all other alternative combinations.

Suppose we can observe a consumer at many equilibria-each with a different set of prices and quantities. At one time, as shown in Figure 2.24, he is at Q1 on price line P1. The individual consumer prefers this position to any other on or below this budget

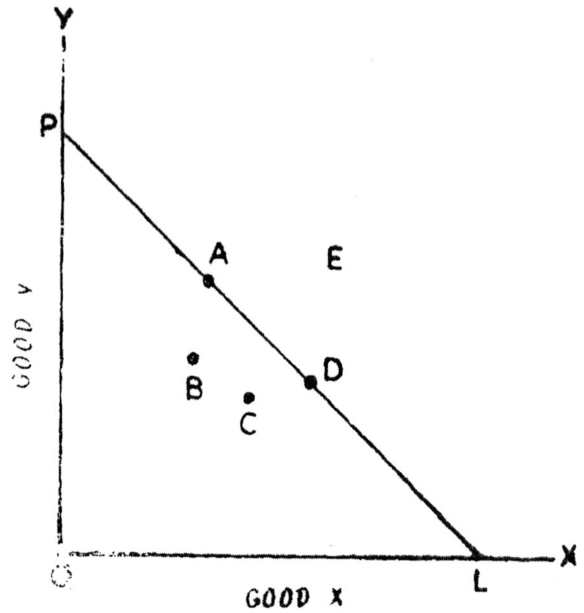

Figure 2.23 Alternative Combinations.

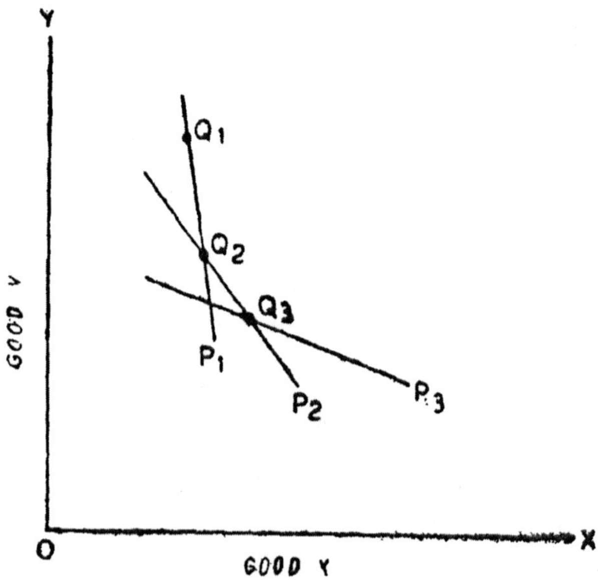

Figure 2.24 Alternative Budget Lines.

line or he would not have chosen it. Let us find the price line P2 which leads the consumer to choose combination Q2, a combination necessarily inferior to Q1. The choice of Q2 reveals it to be preferable to every other point on or below P2, so all these points are inferior to Q1. By similar argument Q3 is preferable to every point on or below the price line P3.

Another fundamental premise of Samuelson's revealed preference theory is the strong ordering, the consumer chooses only one item from a larger number of items making a definite choice of preferences. Here, the consumer definitely reveals his preference. In a 'weak ordering', on the otherhand, there may be many items which cannot be arranged in order of preference. So that the consumer is indifferent between alternative combinations. As J.R. Hicks points out, "the difference between the consequences of strong and weak ordering, so interpreted amounts to no more than this that under strong ordering the chosen position is shown to be preferred to all other positions in and on the triangle, while under weak ordering it is preferred to all positions within the triangle, but may be indifferent to other positions on the same boundary as itself."[10]

Assumptions

The revealed preference theory is based on the following assumptions.

1. The consumer's tastes and preferences remain unchanged.
2. The choice of the consumer for a combination reveals his preferences.
3. The consumer chooses only one combination at a given price-income situation.
4. The consumer prefers larger amount of goods to a lesser amount in any situation.
5. Consumer is always consistent regarding the preferences. Consistency of consumer behaviour states that If A is preferred to B in one situation, B cannot be preferred to A in other situations. This means that the consumer has a strong ordering in favour of combinat on A regarding the choice of combinations.

6. The theory is also based on the transitivity assumption which implies that if A is preferred to B, and B is preferred to C, then, the consumer prefers A to C.

Fundamental Theorem

Based on these fundamental assumptions, Samuelson states the 'Fundamental Theorem of Consumption Theory' as follows—"Any goods that is known always to increase in demand when money income alone rises must definitely shrink in demand when its price alone rises." It implies that when income elasticity of demand is positive, price elasticity of demand is negative.

Let us prove the Fundamental Theorem with the help of the following diagram (Figure 2.25).

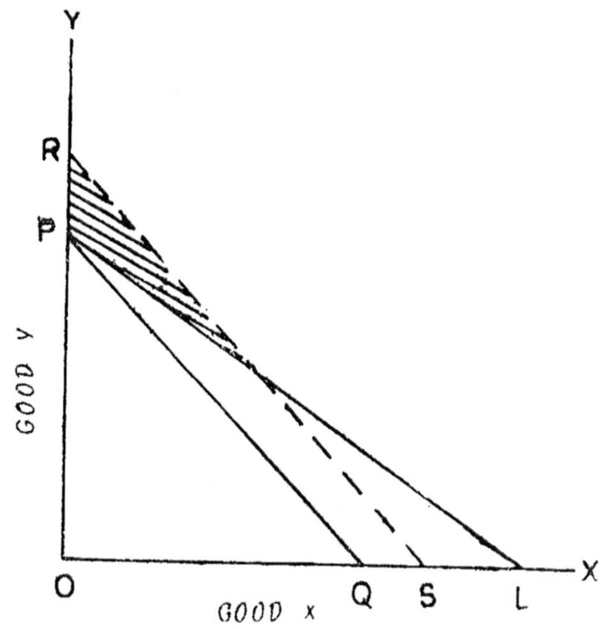

Figure 2.25 Fundamental Theorem of Consumption Theory.

Assume that the consumer spends his entire income on two Goods X and Y. PL is the original Price-income situation where the consumer is observed to have chosen the combination A. That means the combination A is revealed in prefernce to any other combinations available in the given situation. The triangle OPL is the choice area of the consumer for different combinations of X and Y.

Suppose, the price of X rises and the new price-income situation occurs which is represented by PQ as shown in Figure. When the price of a commodity rises, the real income of the consumer will naturally fall. We may now compensate the loss of the consumer in real income as a result of the rise in price of X, by giving him PR amount of money income in terms of Goods Y. In sequence, RS becomes the new price-income line which is drawn parallel to PQ and passes through the Point A. This is called the "Over compensation effect" which makes the choice traingle ORS. Since the combination A has been revealed preferred to any other combinations on the original price-income line PL, any choices below A on AL will be inconsistent with the consumer behaviour. Hence, the consumer may choose either the combination A itself or any other combinations lying above A in the shaded triangle ARP.

Suppose, we take back the extra money income provided to the consumer to compensate the loss due to the rise in price of goods what will be his choice ? He will definitely buy less of X if the income elasticity demand for X is positive. He will purchase any combination to the left of A on the budgetline PQ. As price of X rises, the demand for it shrinks and it is provided that when income elasticity of demand is positive, the price elasticity of demand is negative.

The Fundamental Theorem can also be explained with the assumption of a falling price. The inverseprice-demand relationship holds good in case of a fall in price also. This is demonstrated in Figure 2.26.

PQ is the original price-income line on which the consumer reveals his preference at Point A. Suppose the price of X falls and with the fall in price of X, the price-income line extends to the left as PL. The increase in the real income of the consumer as a result of the fall the price of X is taken away from the consumer in terms of PR amount of Y. As a result, RS becomes the new price-income line of the consumer which is parallel to PL and passes through the Point A. Now, ORS becomes the new choice triangle of the consumer. Since the consumer has revealed his preferences at Point A on the original price-income situation PQ, all points lying on AP will be revealed inferior to him. He cannot purchase lesser amount of X when its price falls. Thus he will either choose combination A or anyother combinations in the shaded triangle QAS. Any choice on AS implies that with the fall in price of X, the consumer buys more X and less of Y, since X becomes cheaper and Y dearer. If the money taken from the consumer is given to him, he will definitely buy more of X to the right of A on the budgetline PL. It is again established that positive income elasticity means negative price elasticity of demand.

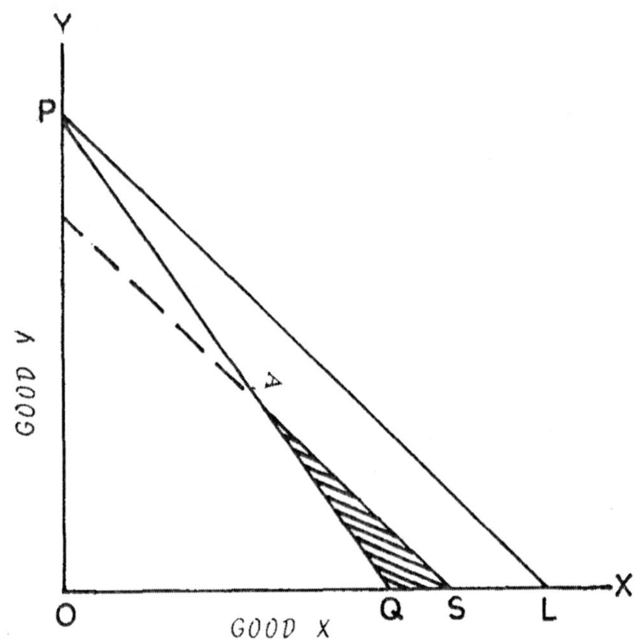

Figure 2.26 Invers Price Demand Relationship.

Superiority of Revealed Preference Theory

Paul Samuelson's revealed preference theory is superior to the Marshallian cardinal approach and Hicks—Allen ordinal approach to the theory of consumer behaviour. It hardly involves psychological or introspective information about the consumer behaviour. Rather, it is a behaviouristic analysis based on observed behaviour of the consumer in the market. This approach then divests the theory of demand of the last vestiges of the psychological analysis.

Thus, revealed preference technique is more realistic and scientific than earlier demand theories.

Again, it avoids the 'continuity' assumption of the earlier approaches. After Samuelson, Hicks in his 'Revision of Demand Theory' drops the continuity assumption and is replaced by strong and weak ordering hypothesis.

Critical Appraisal

Though Samuelson's revealed preference hypothesis is Superior to earlier hypothesis concerning consumer behaviour, it is not free from serious limitations.

First of all, Samuelson completely neglects the possibility of indifference in consumer behaviour. The neglect of indifference follows from his strong ordering hypothesis and his dictum preference to be revealed from a single act of choice. It is, of course, true that consumer reveals his preference over chosen combination. But

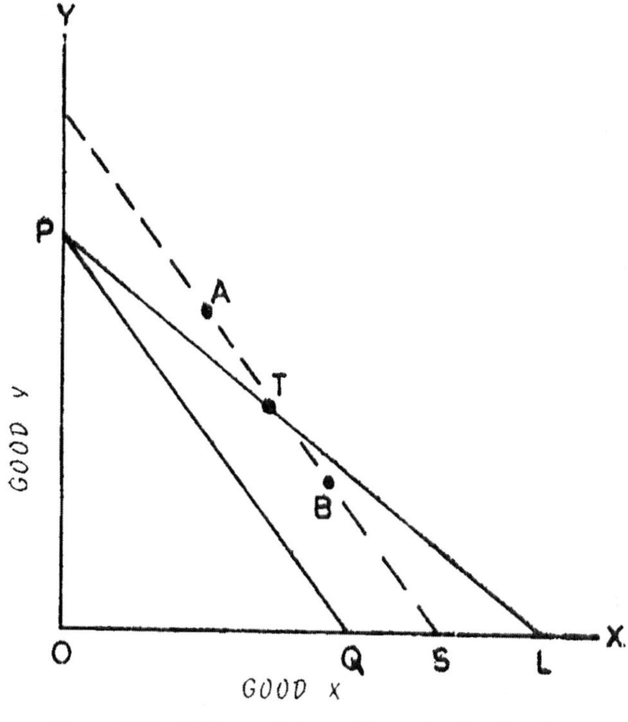

Figure 2.27 Indifference between Alternative Combinations.

we cannot avoid the possibility for being indifference between alternative combinations like A and B on every side of a given point T as shown in Figure 2.27.

Secondly, Hicks is of opinion that since the revealed preference theory is based on strong ordering hypothesis, it is impossible to assume that "all the geometrical points which lie within or on the triangle (OPL in Figure 2.27) represent effective alternatives. As such, two dimensional continuum cannot be strongly ordered. We have, therefore, not alternative but to assume that the commodities are only available in discrete units so that the diagram is to be thought of as being drawn on squared paper, and the only effective alternatives are the points at the corners of the squares."

Thirdly, Samuelson's Fundamental Theorem, though not universal, is conditional which is based on the assumption that positive income elasticities imply negative price elasticities of demand.

Fourthly, Samuelson's revealed preference theory doesnot explain the Giffen's paradox, since it considers only positive income elasticity of demand. The Giffen case, on the other hand, relates only to the negative income elasticity of demand.

Finally, the revealed preference hypothesis is applicable only to an individual consumer. It fails to analyse the market demand schedules. In this sense, Hicks-Allen indifference curve approach is bit superior to the revealed preference approach since it derives both the individual and market demand curves from the price-consumption curves.

Though it appears in no way an improvement over the Hicks-Allen indifference analysis, it presents a more realistic approach to the theory of consumer behaviour. Despite its weaknesses, Samuelson's behaviourist ordinalism appears to be a distinct alternative to Hicks-Allen introspective ordinalism.

NOTES AND REFERENCES

1. Emil Kauder : A History of Marginal Utility Theory, Princeton, New-Jersey, (1965) p. 120.
2. Stonier & Hague : A Text Book of Economic Theory, 1953, p. 40.
3. Alfred Marshall : Principles of Economics, p. 99.
4. Edward T. Nevin : A Text Book of Economic Analysis, Fourth Edition, Macmillan Education Ltd., (1976), p. 46.

5. A. Asimakopulos : An Introduction to Economic Theory, Microeconomics, Oxford University Press, Indian edition, (1979) p. 106.
6. Donald S. Watson : Price Theory and Its Uses, Scientific Book Agency, Calcutta, (1970) p. 78.
7. George J. Stigler : The Theory of Price, Third Edition, (Macmillan Publishing Co. Inc, 1966) p. 68.
8. See T. . Majumdar, Measurement of Utility.
9. Emil Kauder : A History of Marginal Utility Theory, (Princeton, New Jersey, 1965) p. 120.
10. J.R. Hicks: Revision of Demand Theory (1956) p. 43.

3

THE THEORY OF PRODUCTION

PRODUCTION AND ITS FACTORS

Every activity is productive when it creates goods and services. Production is defined as the creation of utilities or want satisfying goods. It is the creation or addition of utilities by transforming one set of commodities into another.

A goods may be physically changed from one form to another. A house is built by putting together bricks and mortar. A table is made by joining a large number of wooden pieces. This type of production or transformation is called creation of *form utilities.*

A goods may be transformed from one place to another, from where it is useful. A trader can taken commodities from places where they are available in plenty to the places where they are scarce. This is a process of creation of *place utilities.*

Certain commodities can be preserved overtime till they are taken for consumption. Keeping things and carrying them over from buys seasons to the periods of scarcity is an important form of creation of wealth. This type of production is called the creation of *time utilities.*

A part from this, exchange of commodities is also considered as an act of transformation.

Factors of Production

Production means transformation of inputs into outputs, change of one set of commodities into another. In order to produce any given commodity, certain resources are required.

Productive resources which are the pre-requisites for producing a commodity are called agents or factors of production. They are also known as "inputs'. The productive resources may be raw materials, or services of workers, capitalists or entrepreneurs.

Factors of production are classified by classical economists as land, labour, capital and organisation.

The term land refers to all kinds of natural resources. By 'labour' we mean human efforts employed in production. Capital consists of factory machines, equipments, raw-materials, semi-finished products and means of transport. Capital is accumulated by man's effort. Organisation is the special form of human labour. It is the activity of assembling the factors and co-ordinating and organising the work of production. The classical economists give importance to land and labour as being original factors of production, while capital is the produced means of production. Organisation includes office management, financial management, personnel management advertisment, Sales promotion activities and techniques, etc.

Land

Land consists of all resources provided by nature and whose supply is limited. Marshall defines land as "the materials and the forces which nature gives freely for man's aid in land and water, in air, light and heat."[1]

Land differs fundamentally from other factors of production in three ways.

1. Land is a gift of nature. Man is unable to make any effort to bring it into existence. The situation of land is the peculiar characteristic of land. Man is in no way responsible for the location of particular place. It has no cost of production and hence no supply price.
2. Supply of land is fixed. Man cannot increase the supply of land since it is nature's free gift. He cannot raise its supply by his own individual efforts. It is free in the sense that it is not the result of labour. The supply of land is inelastic.
3. Land is subject to the law of diminishing margina returns.

Labour

Labour is human effort exerted in production. Any work,

physical or mental, manul or nervous—which is undertaken for pecuniary benefit is called labour. According to Marshall, "any exertion of mind or body undergone partly or wholly with a view of some goods other than the pleasure derived directly from the work is called labour."[2]

Labour is indispensable in all forms of production. It differs from other factors of production such as land and capital in the sense that it is supplied by human beings. Labour is not only a factor of production but also the end for which all production is undertaken.

Labour as an agent of production possesses two important characteristics. (i) Labour is undergone not for its own sake but for the sake of getting any kind of reward. The bodily exertion of tennis player, however strenuous it may be, is not labour in the economic sense. But, if people have to pay to witness his play then it becomes labour. Labour involves strain and sacrifice entailed and the reward expected depend upon various considerations such as time of work, nature of surroundings of work, etc. This is the subjective aspect of labour. (ii) Labour must result in the creation of wealth. It possesses an exchange value. The reward offered for the labour will be in accordance with the results of labour which in otherwords known as efficiency of labour. This is the objective aspect of labour.

Condition of Labour Effiiciency

Efficiency of labour depends upon various factors such as health and strength, food and climate, intelligence and mental alertness. The health standard of labour, again, depends upon the level of income.

Satisfactory system of education is another determining factor of efficiency of labour. Education, in general, increases their general resourcefulness and capability of adaptation to surroundings and stimulate their ambitions.

The job surroundings of the labour also determine their efficiency. Better factory equipments, sanitary surroundings and full-ventilated factories are conducive for labour efficiency. Well balanced and nutritious diet, better housing facilities, hours of work also determine the efficiency of labour.

Racial qualities and climatic conditions also play an important role in determining labour efficiency.

Capital

Capital is defined as that part of wealth which is used in

producing further wealth. Capital, which yields income, generally refers to plant and equipments, tools and accessories, raw materials, etc. It is the means of production which is intended for further production. It is not a primary or original factor of production. All capital goods are the results of human labour. As the agents of production, land and capital are very well distinguished thus : capital is a man made instrument of production while land is a free gift of nature. Capital is produced by employing human labour with natural resources. According to Wiecksell. It is "a single coherent mass of saved-up labour and saved-up land which is accumulated in the course of Years."[3]

Capital has three important characteristics viz., revenue-yielding capacity, productivity and prospectiveness.

Forms of Capital

We may classify capital in following categories—

I. According to the nature of ownership, capital may be regarded from the stand point of society and of individual. Accordingly, capital is classified into *private capital* and *social capital.* Private capital is in the exclusive ownership of individuals. Social capital includes those things which are in public ownership.

(ii) According to the degree of durability, capital is classified as fixed capital and circulating capital. Circulating capital is that part of capital which can be used only ones and exhausts itself in one single use. It is required for everyday running of business. Fixed capital, on the other hand is that part of capital which can be utilised for various productive activities. It is more durable and it requires renwal at a fairly long interval.

(iii) According to the scope for alternative uses, capital is divided into sunk capital and floating capital.

Sunk capitals are those which are specialised in a particular use of productive activities and can hardly be adapted to an alternative use. Floating capital displays a greater degree of elasticity and adaptability of use and can be put into different uses.

Capital Formation

Capital plays an important role in the modern industrial societies. We cannot produce anything without capital. Capital is the mainspring of industrialisation and industrialisation forms the basis of economic progress.

Since capital would increase productivity, it occupies a central position in the proces of economic development. In fact, capital formation is the very core of economic development.

Capital formation refers to increasing the stock of capital. It involves creation of more producers' goods—the capital assets. Capital formation accelerates the process of economic development. Capital formation is conditioned by the level and rate of savings of the community. Saving is abstinence from present consumption. Abstention from consumption means refraining from spending on consumer goods. If consumers do not spend all their incomes, and save part of it, it will entail capital formation.

Organisation

Organisation refers to the task of directing an enterprise. Though it is only kind of labour due to its peculiarity, it is treated separately. In the modern industries the task of organisation to ensure maximum return is done by a specialised class of people commonly referred to as 'entrepreneurs'. They co-ordinate and correlate the factors with the other factors of production. They take risks of business uncertainties. The entrepreneur is infact an innovator. Innovation means something 'introducing new'. He may introduce a new product, a new method of production or a sbustitute. He may form a new organisation or can open a new vista to marketing the products.

Organisation of business may take the various forms, such as sole proprietorship, partnership, joint-stock companies or corporations, state enterprises and co-operative enterprises.

Sole proprietorship refers to a one-man concern. An individual entrepreneur himself becomes the organiser and the manager. When two or more people combine together, contribute capital and agree to share profits and bear losses, if any, in agreed proportions, it is called partnership. Joint-stock company is a form of large-scale business which enjoys the economics of largescale production. When enterprises are undertaken by central, state or local governments, they form state enterprises, Co-operative enterprises are the new forms of enterprises which are the results of co-operative endeavour of the members. Co-operative undertakings take the forms of producers' co-operative, consumers' co-operative etc.

PRODUCTION FUNCTION

The law of production plays a prominent role in the theory of pricing. It provides a base for the analysis of the relations between cost of production and quantum of output. It also serves as a base for the theory of demand of firms for factors of production.

We may know that the real economic world is certainly a complicated mechanism. This is also true in the case of production as well.

Production means creating of goods. It is a process of transformation of inputs into outputs. The production process not only consists to the physical changes in matter, but also includes those activities that make goods available at the time and place desired by the purchaser.

Production Function

Production, as a technical mechanism, requires different kinds of inputs such as labour, capital and raw materials. The firms which are actively engaged in manufacturing business combine different inputs to produce any final products.

For any business firm, the quantum of output depends directly upon quantities of inputs used. If more of a thing is to be produced, more units of various factors of production must be used. That is, quantities of inputs employed. This functional relationship between physical inputs and physical outputs of a firm is called production function. In other words, it is an input-output relationship. If a small industrial unit in a Mini Industrial Estate produces 10 steel chairs per week, then its production function consists of the minimum quantities of steel, screws, paints, labourtime, machines, building: electricity, etc., that are required to produce them. Or in other words, the production of that unit consists of the maximum number of steel chairs that can be produced with given quantities of steel, paints etc. Hence, a production function can be easily defined as "a flow of inputs resulting in a flow of outputs during some period of time."[4]

The form of the production of any firm is determined by the level of technology. Improvement in technology leads to new production function for firms. The new production function has a greater flow of outputs from the given inputs or lesser amounts of inputs for the same output.

Many more production functions have been examined by economists from time to time and Cobb—Douglas production function needs special mention. This production function generally applied to a sector of the economy, say manufacturing. Statistically, the production function takes the form as

$$Q=KLCa(1\text{-}a)$$

Where Q is output, L is quantity of labour, C is capital employed and K and a $(a<1)$ are positive constraints. In this function there are two inputs-labour and capital. Simply the Cobb-Douglas production function speaks that labour contributes nearly three-quarters of increases in production and capital contributes the remaining one quarters.

As an input-output relationship specifically in physical terms, the production function can be given in an equational form.

Let be the output and X1, X2.........Xn be inputs and T be the prevailing state of technology, then the nature of production process-transformation of resources into final goods—can be expressed by means of a simple equation—

$$q = f(X1, X2......Xn, T)$$

Production function may take two forms : Fixed proportion production function and variable proportion production function. When inputs, say, labour and capital, are used in a fixed proportion to produce a definite sum of output, the production function of which is said to be of fixed proportion. One unit of oxygen and two units of hydrogen combining together would produce water. Here, the two inputs hydrogen and oxygen are used in fixed proportion 2 : 1. This is a case of fixed proportion production function.

But in many cases of maufacturing industries, it is hardly possible, to employ inputs in fixed proportions. Outputs are generally produced under the conditions variable proportion production functions. When we are able to produce the same amounts of output by varying combinations of inputs we may say that the production function is of variable proportion.

Inputs or factors of production required for producing a given output may, conveniently, be classified as fixed factors of production and variable factors of production. Number of labourers employed by a firm can be easily changed according to the requirements. Such inputs whose quantities can be changed according to the requiements of a firm are called variable inputs. But unlike labour, the productive equipments like land or buildings cannot be easily changed. They are fixed factors of production. The quantities of plant or capital equipments tend to be fixed over short period of time. In our analysis labour represents variable factor of production and capital fixed factor of production.

The study of production analyses two kinds of input-output relations. One is the relation where the amounts of some inputs are fixed while amounts of other inputs vary. The other is the relation where all the inputs are variable. The study of the former refers to the law of variable proportions, while the study of the latter refers to the law of returns to scale.

Since many of the production processes are subjected to variable proportions, first of all our attention is directed to this type of production function.

To simplify our analysis, we may assume that there are two factors of production : labour and capital. Production, according to the law of variable proportion simply means that labour may be substituted for capital.

Consider a business firm actively engaged in manufacturing cigarettes. The business firm has its manufacturing plant. It is the capital inputs which is fixed in the short-run. The amounts of labour that can be varied according to the requirements. Let us see what will happen as more and more workers are employed with a fixed amount of capital.

The numerical production function of the cigarette manufacturing firm is given in Table 3.1.

Since capital is assumed to be fixed we may know that machinery doesnot run itself and output is zero when no workers are employed. When one worker is employed output becomes positive and tends to increase rather rapidly as the first few workers are employed. This is because when one worker is employed output increases even more. In our given example, this is true till the sixth worker is employed. Up to this point output increases more than proportionately. But after a certain point, further additions of workers expand output increases at a diminishing rate. Finally a point is reached beyond which further addition of employment would cause a decline in output.

The given numerical analysis of production is graphically presented in Figure 3.1. The curve TP represents total product which slopes steeply upward first, then flattens out and finally declines.

Let us now analyse the average and marginal concepts of the firm's output. Consider Table 3.2. Coloum 2 represents total output of the firm while Column 4 gives average output. Average output is the total output divided by the number of workers employed. Algebraically $AP = \frac{TP}{W}$, where TP is total porduct, AP is average product and W is the total number of workers employed. Column 3 illustrates the marginal output i.e., addition to total output attributable to the addition of one more unit of labour.

TABLE 3.1

Production Function of Cigarette.
(Hypothetical Data)

No. of Workers	*Total Product*
0	0
1	20
2	60
3	160
4	360
5	600
6	840
7	1000
8	1100
9	1180
10	1240
11	1260
12	1260
13	1240
14	1180
15	1060

TABLE 3.2

Total Product, Average and Marginal Product

No. of Workers	*Total Output*	*Marginal Output*	*Average Output*
0	0	—	—
1	20	20	20
2	60	40	30
3	160	100	53
4	360	200	90
5	600	260	120
6	840	240	140
7	1000	160	143
8	1100	100	131
9	1180	80	131
10	1240	60	124
11	1260	20	115
12	1260	0	105
13	1240	20	95
14	1180	60	84
15	1060	120	71

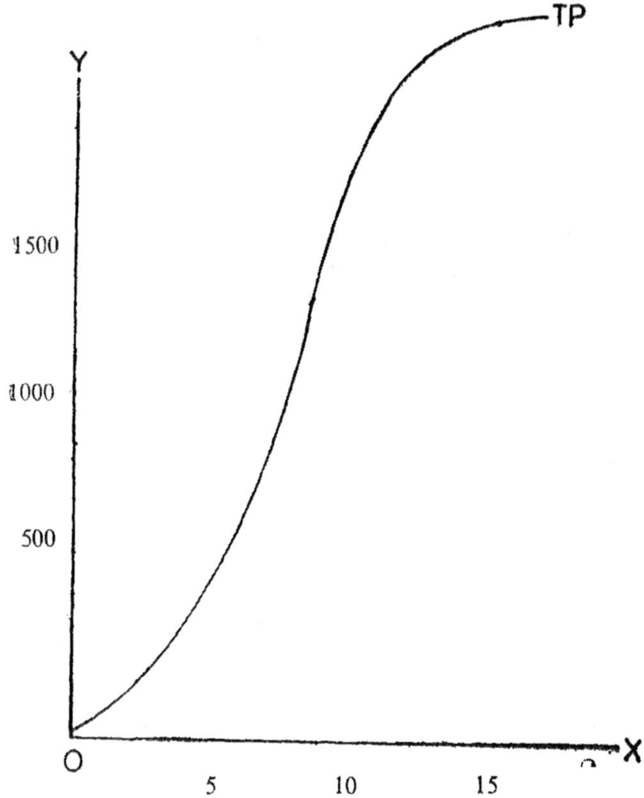

Figure 3.1 Total Production.

The nature of average and marginal output are shown graphically in Figure 3.2. We may note that the curve moves rapidly at first and then reaches a maximum and declines, thereafter. When total product began to decline, marginal product becomes negative.

Keeping this information in mind, we may now proceed to examine certain fundamental principles in economics.

Law of Diminishing Returns

The law of diminishing returns is a venerable economic principle. It tells the technical relation between output of the firm and inputs that are required to produce. The law states that as we employ more and more variable inputs, keeping the other factors fixed, the output increases at a diminishing rate. As George Stigler points out "as equal increments of one input are added, the inputs of other productive services being held constant, beyond a certain point the

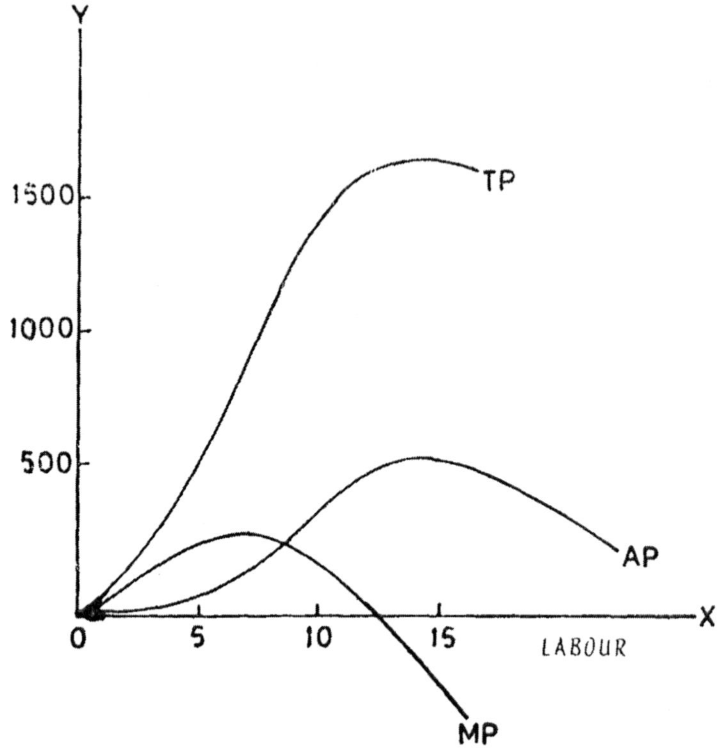

Figure 3.2

resulting increments of product will decrease—that is, the marginal products will diminish."[5] In simple terms that the law states that, in successive application of variable factors to a given amount of fixed factor, a point is reached beyond which marginal product declines indefinitely.

The tendency toward diminishing marginal product was first noticed by the French Economist Turgot and was further elaborated by the English Economists Malthus and Ricardo. It still holds good for almost all productive processes. The law is specially applicable in underdeveloped countries which are mostly agricultural oriented.

The population is normally concentrated in agricultural occupation in such economies. As the family members increase one is essentially adding more labour to a fixed amount of land. The marginal product of successive workers brings to decline, and if family grows large enough, the marginal product may drop to zero or even negative.

We may illustrate this fundamental principle with an example of controlled experiment. Given a fixed amount of land, say, 10 acres, for wheat cultivation. First of all, we add no labour to all, and with zero labour input there is no wheat production i.e., output is zero. When one labour is hired, output becomes positive and increases as more and more labourers are employed. This phenomenon is numerically stated in Table 3.3. One extra unit of labour is successively added to the same fixed amount of land, say, 10 acres. It is observed that when the number of workers employed increases from 1 to 2 units the total output increases from 20 to 30 quintals of wheat, but the marginal physical product diminishes from 20 to 10 quintals. Further addition of workers would cause the marginal physical product* to decline. It is this trend of diminishing marginal physical product that the law of diminishing returns explains.

TABLE 3.3

Law of Diminishing Returns

Land (Fixed input) Acres	*Labour (Variable input)*	*Total output (quintals)*	*Marginal output (extra output added by additional labour unit)*
10	0	0	—
10	1	20	20
10	2	30	10
10	3	35	5
10	4	38	3
10	5	40	2
10	6	40	0
10	7	38	2

The given numerical statement of the Law is graphically presented in Figure 3.3. In Panel-A of the Figure 3.3 the curve TP represents the total product and it is seen increasing at a diminishing rate as more and more workers are employed. The curve MP in Panel-B represents marginal physical product. It is down-ward sloping which implies that marginal physical product declines as more and more workers are employed.

* Marginal physical product is defined as the extra product added by an extra unit of a factor, while other factors are being held constant.

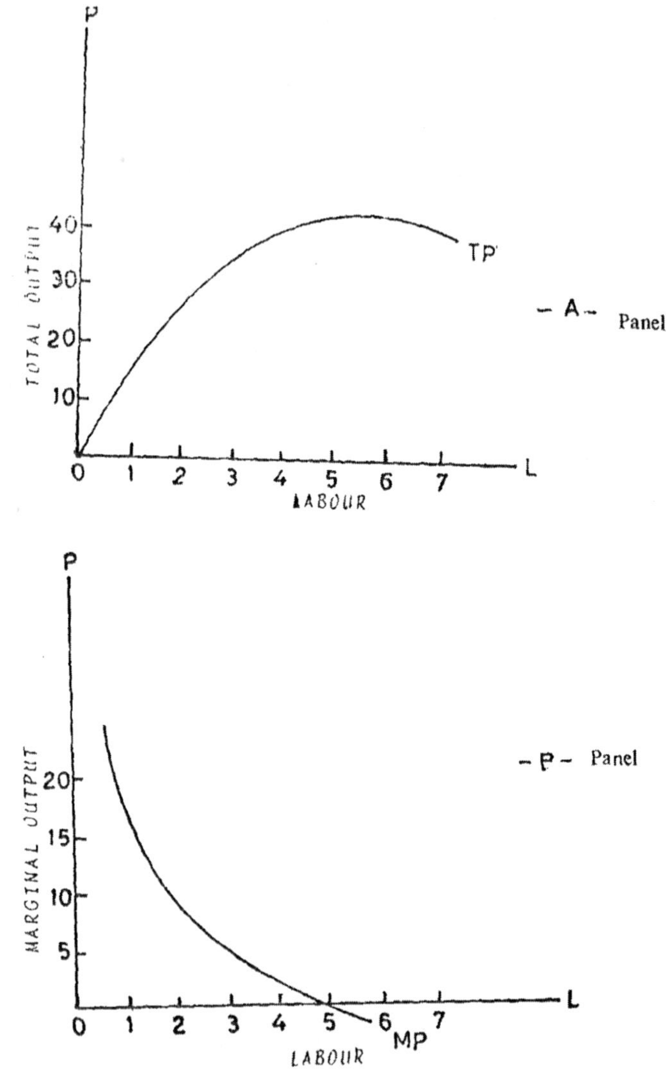

Fig. 3.3 Law of Diminishing Returns.

Law of Returns to Scale

Let us now examine the behaviour of output when all the factors vary. The law of returns to scale explains the changes in output in response to changes in all the factors of production. When we increase the quantities of inputs in the same proportion we call it as increase in scale. Increase in scale is numerically depicted in Table 3.4.

TABLE 3.4

Increase in Scale (hypothetical data)

Output (quintals)	*Inputs-I*		*Inputs-II*		*Inputs-III*	
	Labour	*Capital*	*Labour*	*Capital*	*Labour*	*Capital*
100	10	10	20	5	5	20
200	20	20	30	15	15	30
300	30	30	40	25	25	40
400	40	40	50	35	35	50
500	50	50	60	45	45	60

The two variables—labour and capital—are increased in different proportions. As per Table 3.4., 100 units of output can be produced in three ways : one by using 10 units of labour and 10 units of capital; second, with 20 units of labour and 5 units of capital, and third with 5 units of labour and 20 units of capital. To increase output, the units of labour and capital can be increased either in the same proportion or in varying proportions. The numerical statement of 'increase in scale' is graphically shown in Figure 3.4.

The law of returns to scale explains the relationship of outputs and inputs when all factors of production are varied. Accordingly we are driven to consider alternative possibilities : when all factors are increased in a given proportion, output may increase in greater or lesser or equal proportions.

If the increase in output is proportional to the increase in quantities of inputs, say, doubling of inputs causes a doubling of output, the returns to scale is said to be constant. If the increase in output is more than proportionate to the increase in quantities of inputs, returns to scale are increasing, whereas if increase in output is less than proportionately, it is a case of diminishing returns to scale.

Two Variable Inputs

So far we have discussed the production function of the firm using more of one input or more of all inputs. We may now turn

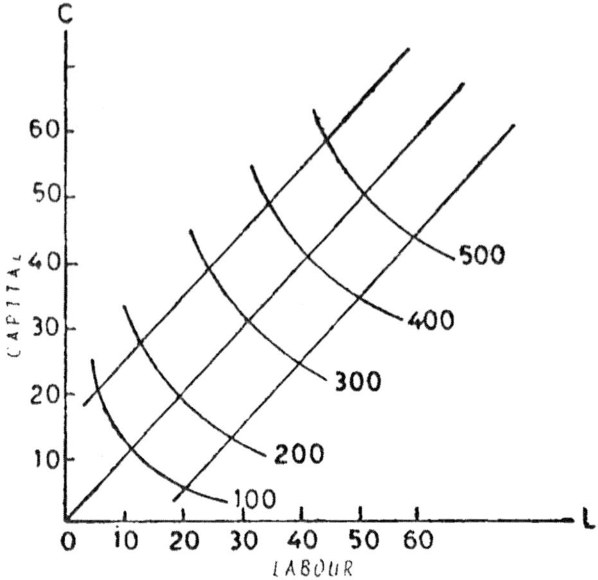

Fig. 3.4 Increase in Scale.

our attention to a firm's production function using more of two inputs that are substitutes for each other.

The production function that we conceive of is consisting of certain fixed inputs and of two variable inputs. The numerical illustration of substitution and combination of two variable inputs is presented in Table 3.5. It shows that 2 units of capital and 2 units of labour produce 10 units of output, 4 units of capital and 4 units of labour produce 20 units of output and so on. Thus, the numbers in the Table 3.5 exhibit constant returns to scale if both inputs are doubled then output is doubled.

TABLE 3.5

Substitution and Combination of Two Variable Inputs

Units of Capital	*Output*		
6	16	24	30
4	14	20	24
2	10	14	16
	2	4	6
	UNITS OF LABOUR		

Isoquants

Isoquants are equal product curves which represent all those input combinations producing the same level of output. A production function with two variable inputs can be represented by a family of isoquants which are simlar to the indifference curves.

Table 3.6 illustrates the concept of isoquant. Factor X and Factor Y are two variable inputs which are employed to produce a given output.

TABLE 3.6

Production Function with Two Variable Inputs

Factor Combinations	*Factor-X*	*Factor-Y*	*Output (Unit)*
A	1	10	50
B	2	8	50
C	3	6	50
D	4	3	50

Each of the factor combinations A, B, C and D produces the same level of output 50 units. Factor combination A consisting of 1 unit of factor X and 10 units of factor Y produces 50 units of output. Similarly, combination-B consisting of 2 units of X and 8 units of Y produces the same 50 units of output.

The given numerical illustrations in Table 3.6 are graphically shown in Figure 3.5 where we have plotted all those input combinations By joining them with a curve we get the equal product curve showing 50 units.

The Slope of the Isoquant

The slope of the isoquant is determined by the marginal rate of technical substitution. Marginal rate of technical substitution indicates the rate at which factors can be substituted at the margin without changing the level of output. More precisely, marginal rate of technical substitution of capital for labour may be defined as the unit of labour which can be replaced by one unit of capital.

The slope of the isoquant is thus the rate of trade-off one input for another at a point. It can be seen in Figure 3.6. Consider a small movement down on isoquant, where a small amount of capital is traded off for a small amount of labour. By the definition of an isoquant output is always constant, the gain in output from a little

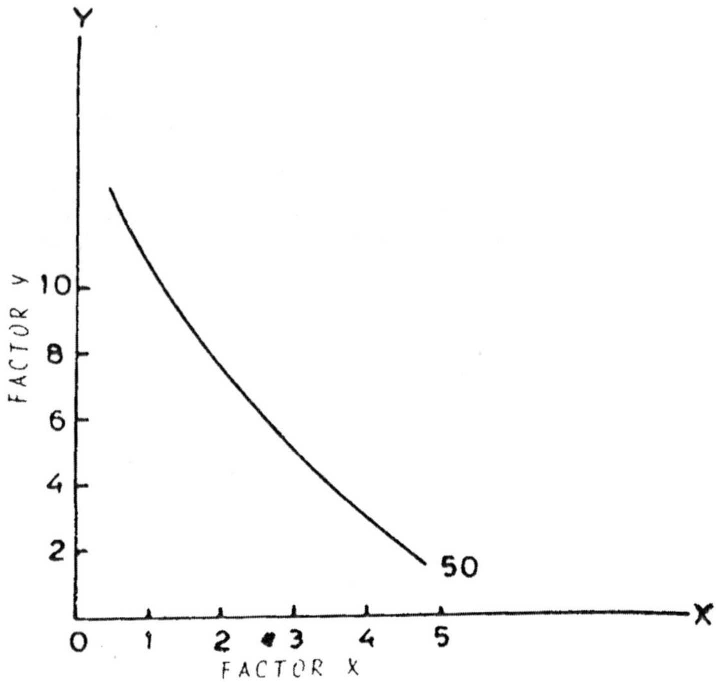

Fig. 3.5 Equal Product Curve.

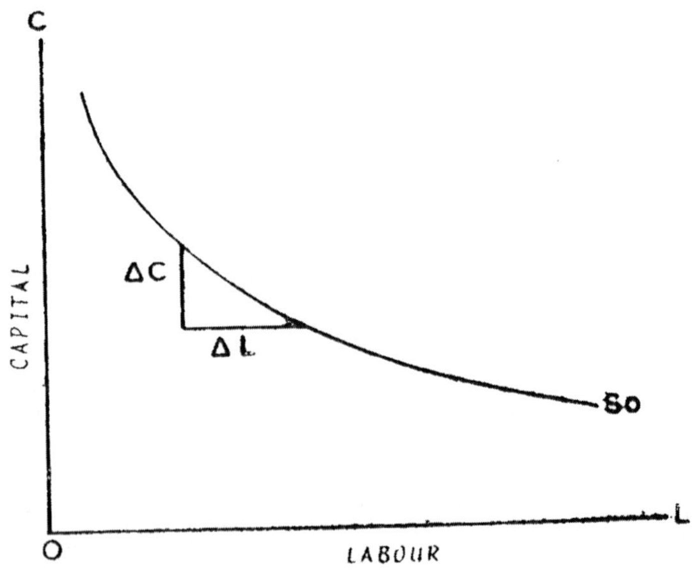

Fig. 3.6. Isoquant.

more labour being equal to the loss of output from a little less of capital. In other words, output loss by the withdrawal of capital made is good by additional labourers employed.

Geometrically, the slope of Isoquant is as—

$$=\text{MRTS}=\frac{\Delta C}{\Delta L}$$

Isocost Curves

Having discussed the nature of isoquants which represent the output possibilities of a firm from a given combination of inputs, we may pass on to the prices of inputs as represented by the isocost lines. Each isocost line represents the different combinations of two inputs that a firm can buy for a given sum of money at the given price.

Figure 3.7 shows these isocost lines, each represents a total outlay of Rs. 100, 200 and 300 respectively. The firm can hire OA of capital or OB of labour with Rs. 1000. Given the prices, if total outlay is raised the isocost line will shift to the right a CD and further raising outlay will again shift to the 150 cost line as EF.

The isocost lines are straight lines which implies that the firm has no control over the prices of the inputs and that the prices are the same no matter how many units the firm buys.

The slope of an isocost line is $\frac{PL}{PC}$ which is the ratio of price of labour to the price of capital.

For any isocost line

$$\text{Slope}=\frac{\text{Quantity of capital}}{\text{Quantity of labour}}$$

$$=\frac{\text{Expenditure}}{\text{Price of capital}} / \frac{\text{Expenditure}}{\text{Price of labour}}$$

$$=\frac{\text{Price of labour}}{\text{Price of Capital}}$$

$$=\frac{PL}{PC}$$

This property of an isocost line is identical with that of the budget line of the consumer. But there is an important contrast between the two lines. The consumer has only one budget and thus has only a single budget line. But the firm has a whole family of isocostline.

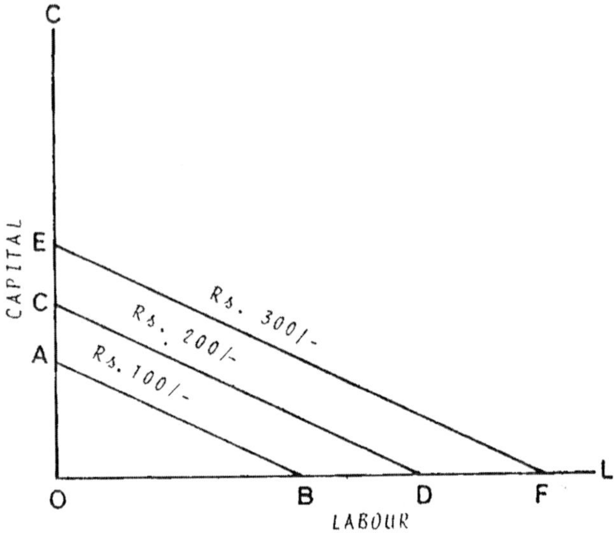

Figure 3.7 Isocost lines

The Optimum Factor Combinations

The firm, like the owner of any other factor of production, seeks to obtain the maximum possible monetary rewards from its economic activities. If the firm wants to produce a certain quantity of output and to sell at a certain price, the firm will seek the factor combination which results in production of goods at the lowest cost. The reward of the firm consists of the difference between what he has to pay for the factors of production as cost and what the product brings in as revenue; the lower the cost the greater his reward.

The least cost of any output is given by the point of tangency of isoquant curve OQ shows the combinations of capital and labour which will result in an output. If the relative price of one unit of capital and one unit of labour is represented by PA, the point of tangency X1 gives the combination of factors which will produce the output at minimum cost in this case OC1 units of capital and OL1 units of labour. At this point marginal rate of technical substitution is exactly equal to their relative price. At this point of tangency, slopes are equal. The slope of the isocost line is the ratio of the prices of inputs. The slope of isoquant is the ratio of marginal physical products of inputs.

Let C stand for Capital and L for labour.

We may note that—

$$\frac{PL}{PC} = \frac{MPPL}{MPPC}$$

$$\frac{MPPc}{Pc} = \frac{MPPL}{PL}$$

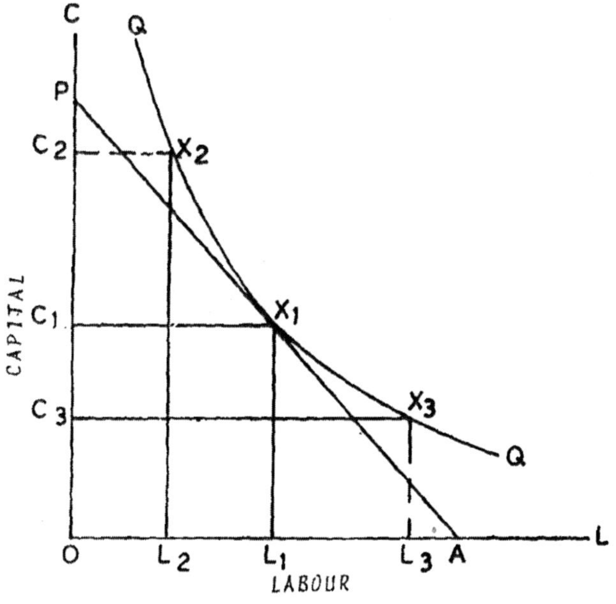

Fig. 3.8 Optimum Factor Combination.

Production-Possibility Curve*

Production-possibility curve is the locus of output combinations which are obtainable from a given amount of input. Consider a firm producing two different products, say, X and Y. Suppose that the firm has some given quantity of inputs—plant, equipment and labour. With this quantity of inputs the firm can produce X and Y in different proportions.

A hypothetical production possibility schedule is given in Table 3.7. A and D are possibilities in which the firm can produce either 200 units of Y or 150 units of X with the given quantities of

* A detailed account is given in Chapter 1.

inputs. There are many possibilities to produce two goods. Such possibilities are B and C. The firm can produce 100 units of X and 150 units of Y in possibility B, and 125 units of X and 100 units of Y in possibility C.

The hypothetical data given in Table 3.7 are diagrammed in Figure 3.9.

TABLE 3.7

Production-Possibility Schedule.

Possibility	*Output of X*	*Output of Y*
A	0	200
B	100	150
C	125	100
D	150	0

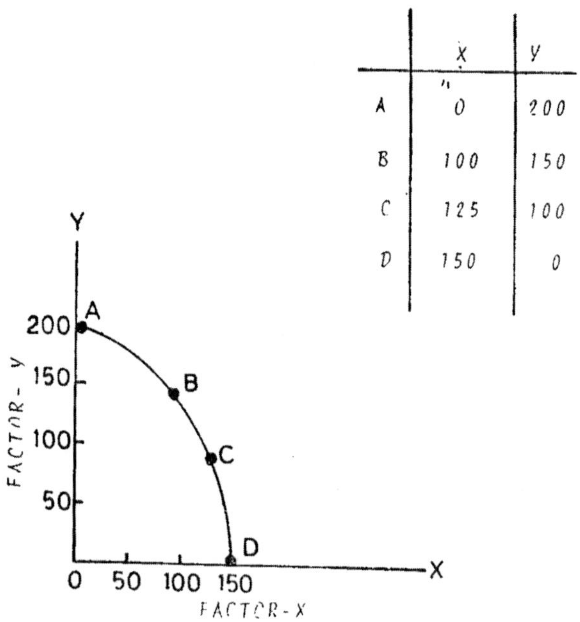

Fig. 3.9 Production Possibility Curve.

The curve AD is the firm's production possibility curve. Points B and C on the curve correspond with possibilities B and C in the Table 3.7. If the firm had a larger quantity of resources the curve would lie further. Thus, for each quantity of inputs, the firm has a different production-possibility curve.

ANALYSIS OF COSTS

Cost is sacrifice in any kind. When we say that something is costly, it means that something else of value must be sacrificed to get it. If we want to measure costs, we may add up these sacrifices in one way or the other. Let us examine how costs of producting output of a firm can be measured for analytical purposes.

Explicit and Implicit Costs

Cost of producting a good of a firm includes payments made for purchasing factor inputs such as labourers, raw materials, managerial personel and so many other things. All these factors are paid for their services rendered. The cost incurred by way of payment for services of such factors are called explicit costs. They are the total outlay for factor inputs and are paid out costs.

In addition to explicit costs, certain costs are incurred by way of supplying self-owned labour services or money even. They are called implicit costs which include physical exertions of the owner of the firm and the owner-supplied labour or money.

Implicit costs are, in a sense, opportunity costs of self-owned of the firm. When a firm uses its own machinery or occupies its own factory building it foregoes the opportunity of using that machinery or factory building. In some other ways, when an individual proprietor works for his own establishment, he foregoes his opportunity to work elsewhere.

Short-run and Long-run Perspective

We may now proceed to analyse the theory of cost which explains how costs change as output changes. For the better understanding of the theory, we may distinguish between short-run and long-run perspectives.

In order to produce output, many kinds of inputs are to be used. The firm can vary the quantum of output produced by varying the quantities of inputs that are put into operation. It is impossible to vary all inputs as easily as others. Quantities of certain factor inputs, such as raw materials, fuel, labourtime etc., can be very easily varied or adjusted according to the changing requirements. In contiast, factor inputs such as capital equipment, structure of the firm, salaried management cadres, etc. are not easily varied.

We may note, in this context, the distinction between short-run perspective and long-run perspective. Short-run may be defined as a time perspective so short enough that the amounts of atleast some factor inputs are kept fixed. Long-run, on tbe other hand, refers to a time perspective long enough that the amounts of all existing factor inputs can be varied. The factor inputs that can be changed or adjusted in the short-run are called variable factor inputs, while those inputs that cannot be varied in the short-run but are able to change or adjust in the long-run, are called fixed factor inputs.

The above given distinctions can be clearly illustrated with a simple example. Consider a wheat farmer who wants to increase his wheat production. In the short-run, it is known that, land is a fixed factor and assume that he has got only 1 acre of land. Even with this fixed input, 1 acre of land, he can raise his wheat production by increasing labour units or time; or by applying artificial manures or by adopting double or tripple cropping along with high yielding varieties of seeds. In the long-run, on the other hand, he can raise his output by purchasing more available land for cultivation. In short, in the long-run, it is learnt that all factor inputs are variable and none is fixed.

Diminishing Returns and Cost

To analyse the short-run theory of cost of production, a preliminary idea of the law of diminishing returns is essential. The law of diminishing returns explains that, as the output of a good increases by increasing the amounts of one variable input, other inputs remain fixed, after a point the quantum of output produced by each additional unit of variable input will decline.

Suppose, for example, that a wheat farmer who wants to raise his wheat production, applies more and more doses of labour on his given acre of land. As he employs more, and more units of labour would yield lesser amounts of output. Such a relationship between output and labour input is depicted in Figure 3.10. The shape of the total product curve TP in the digram shows that as more and more labourers are employed, output increases at a diminishing rate.

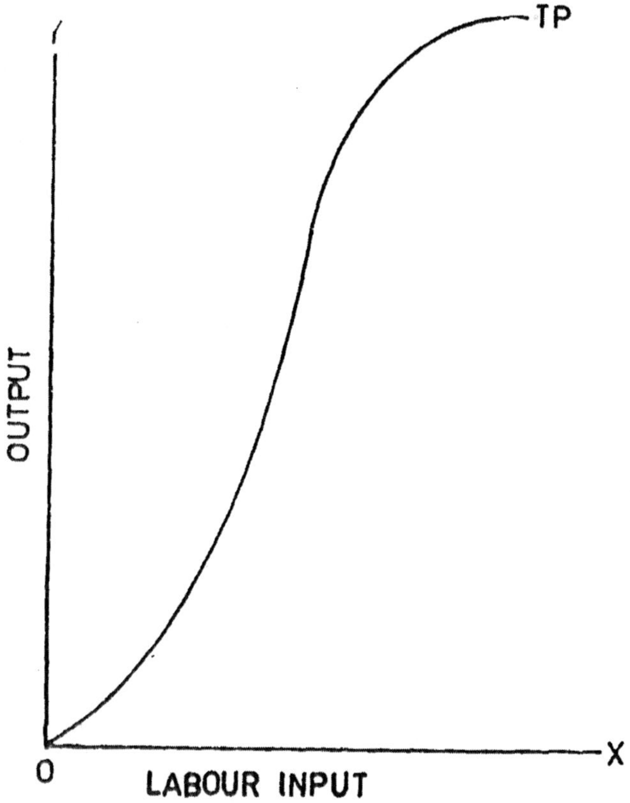

Figure 3.10 : Total Output

We may note from the given analysis that there is a close relationship between law of diminishing returns and cost of production. As the firm purchases more and more variable inputs at a constant price per unit and as successive units of inputs contribute lesser and lesser amount to total output than previous one, the cost of producing each additional output, in the short-run, rises. That is, in the short-run, total cost of production rises more than proportionately. The increasing total cost is represented by the curve TC in Figure 3.11.

A Variety of Short-run Costs

Let us examine the various short-run cost concepts of a typical firm. A variety of costs are numerically shown in Table 3.8 and each of which are graphically presented in Figure 3.12.

The key to the whole range of costs is total cost (TC) which can be broken into total fixed cost (TFC) and total variable cost (TVC). Hence, total cost (TC) is the sum of total fixed cost (TFC) and total variable cost (TVC) which is numerically shown in Table 3.8 at column 4. At any level of out put total fixed cost does not change. Total fixed cost is numerically shown in column 2 and is assumed to be Rs.2000 since total fixed cost curve is shown as horizontal straight-line in diagram (Fig. 3.11). Total variable costs change as output changes. As per our numerical example, total variable cost increases. Hence, total variable cost curve (TVC) is symetrical with the total cost curve, though lower by distance just equal to total fixed cost curve (see Figure 3.11).

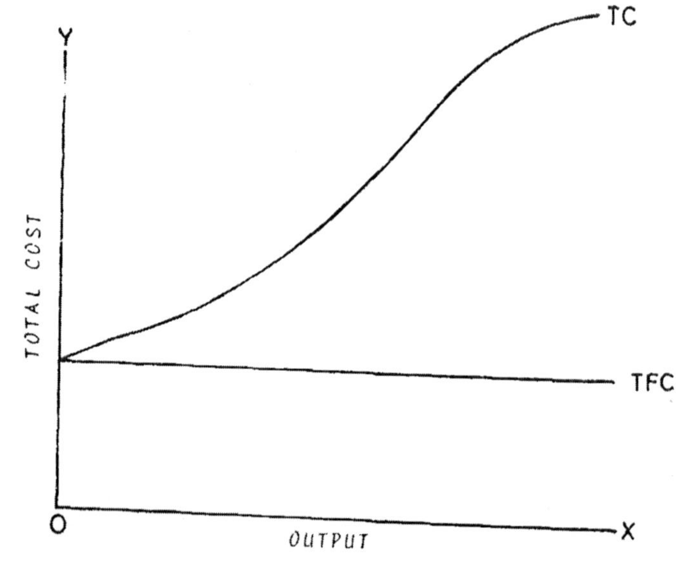

Figure 3.11 : Total Cost

Columns 6 through 8 give a variety of cost per unit measurements. Column 5 shows the numerical measurement of marginal cost (MC) which is the addition to total cost. It implies cost of producing one more unit.

As per the Table 3.8, the numerical measurement of marginal cost shows that it falls for the first 9 units and then begin to rise. This underlines the point that marginal cost curves are always U-shaped.

The other remaining costs are all averages. Average total cost is obtained by dividing the corresponding total cost by the units of

TABLE 3.8

Total Cost

Output (*q*)	*TFC* (*Rs.*)	*TVC* (*Rs.*)	*TC=TFC* +*TVC* (*Rs.*)	*MC* (*Rs.*)	*AC* $\frac{(TC)}{(q)}$	*AFC* $\frac{(FC)}{(q)}$	*AVC* $\frac{(VC)}{(q)}$
0	2000	0	2000	0	0	0	0
1	2000	380	2380	380	2380	2000	3800
2	2000	720	2720	340	1360	1000	360
3	2000	1025	3025	305	1009	667	342
4	2000	1300	3300	275	825	500	325
5	2000	1550	3550	250	710	400	310
6	2000	1780	3780	230	629	333	296
7	2000	1995	3995	215	517	286	285
8	2000	2200	4200	205	525	250	275
9	2000	2400	4400	200	488	222	266
10	2000	2605	4605	205	460	200	256

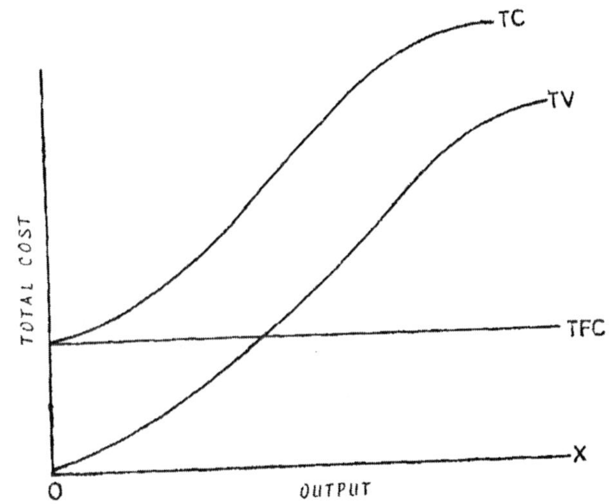

Figure 3.12 : Variable and Fixed Costs.

output produced. It is the cost per unit. In symbols,

$$ATC = \frac{TC}{q}$$

where ATC is average total cost, TC is total cost and q the total quantities of output produced. Similarly, average fixed cost is obtainable by dividing corresponding fixed cost by the quantities of output.

Algebraically—

$$AFC = \frac{TFC}{q}$$

where, AFC is average fixed cost, TFC is the corresponding total fixed cost and q is the number of units produced.

Like that of the above averages, average variable cost can be measured by dividing corresponding total variable cost by the number of output. That is, $AVC = \frac{TVC}{q}$ where, AVC is the average variable cost, TVC is the total variable cost and q is the number of output produced. As shown in Figure 3.13, both average total cost curve and average variable cost curve are u-shaped; while average fixed cost curve is a rectangular hyperbola.

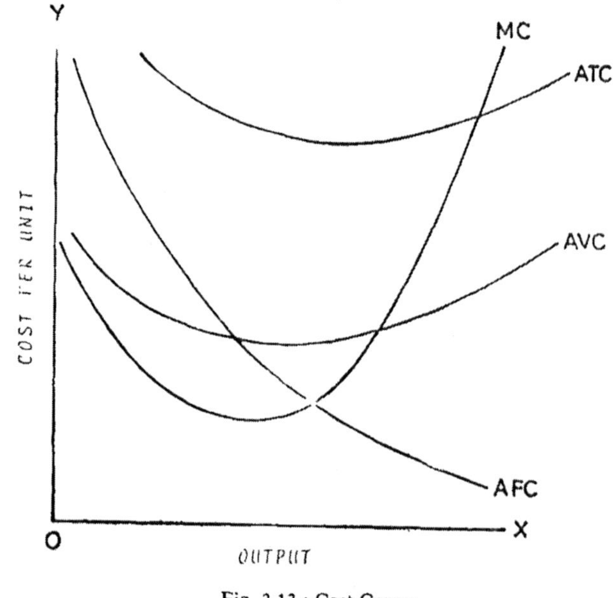

Fig. 3.13 : Cost Curves.

The Relation Between MC and AC

As we have seen, marginal cost of production refers to addition to total cost of production. It is the extra cost of producing one more unit. Benham points out that the marginal cost of a firm is "the addition to its total cost that must be made in order to increase its output per period of time by one unit."[6] According to Stonier and Hague, marginal cost is "the cost of increasing the output of the firm's product by a marginal unit.[7]"

In symbols,

$$MC = \frac{\wedge TC}{\wedge q}$$

Suppose that the total cost of producing 101 units is Rs. 203.

Then marginal cost is $MC = \frac{TC}{q} = 3/1 = \text{Rs. } 3.$

The relation between marginal cost and average cost of production can be clearly understood by the following table.

TABLE 3.9

Total, Average and Marginal Costs

Units of output	*Total cost (TC) Rs.*	*Average cost (AC) Rs.*	*Marginal cost (MC) Rs.*
0	30	—	—
1	40	40	10
2	48	24	8
3	54	18	6
4	62	15.5	8
5	80	16	18
6	102	17	22

The cost function, in which the relationship between marginal cost and average cost is shown, is represented in Figure 3.14. The nature of average and marginal cost curves are seen u-shaped. The average cost curve slopes downward at first as long as marginal cost curve, lies below average cost curve, it continues to fall and its rate of fall is greater than that of average cost curve. But average cost curve starts rising from the point T where the marginal cost curve touches the average cost curve. As seen in figure marginal cost curve passes through the minimum point of average cost curve.

There is a close relationship between AC and MC of a firm. Average and marginal costs are directly related. Consider Figure 3.15 when average cost falls marginal cost also falls but is below it. On the otherhand, when average cost is rising marginal cost is also rising but is above it. When average cost is minimum, marginal cost equals it.

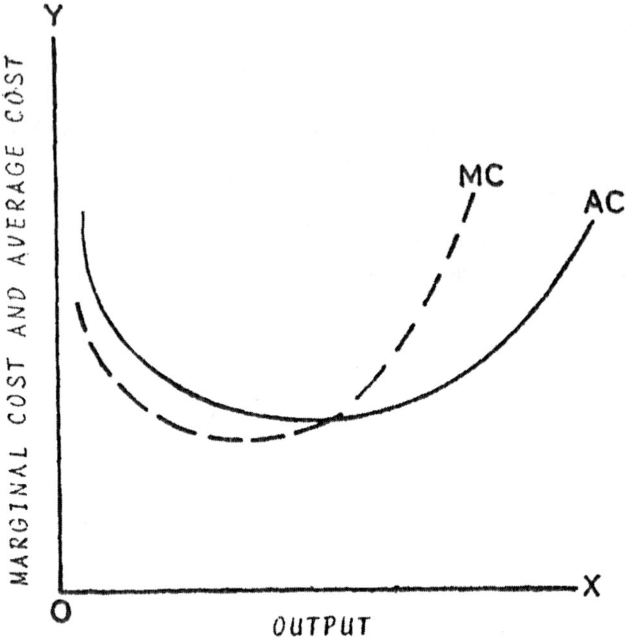

Fig. 3.14 : Marginal and Average Costs.

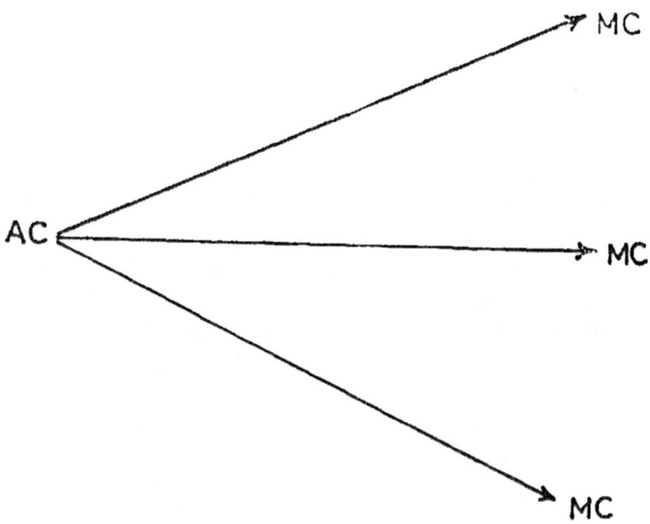

Fig. 3.15 : Relation between AC and MC.

Long-run Cost Curves

In the long-run, as we have seen earlier, all factors of production are variable. The production function of a firm has no fixed factors and hence has no fixed costs. The firm expands output by changing all the factors including the existing plants and equipments. So that input output relations in the production function of a firm are of returns to scale.

Consider Figure 3.16. There are three short-run cost curves—SAC1, SAC2 and SAC3. The three cost curves are for three sizes of Plants I, II and III in an industry. Plant I is the smallest with costs SAC1, Plant II is larger with costs of SAC2 and Plant III is still larger with a cost curve of SAC3. If the firm decides to produce the volume of output to the extent of OA, it will naturally operate the Plant I. If instead, larger quantities of output to be produced, say, to the extent of OB or OC, it would have to operate the Plant II or Plant III.

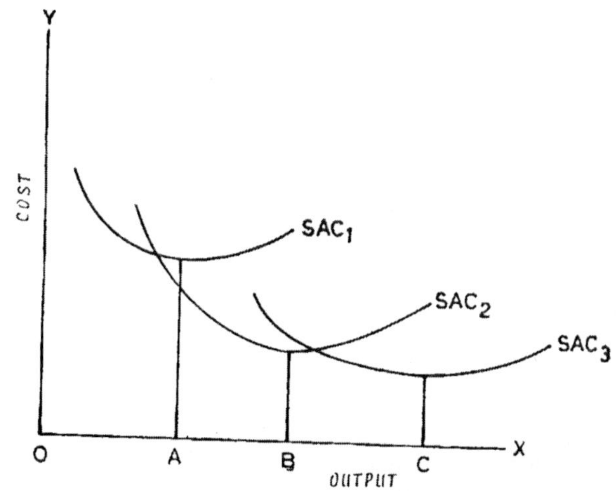

Fig. 3.16 :. Short-run Average Cost.

Suppose that the firm can build many plants, each one just a bit larger. The very many curves in Figure 3.12 are the short-run cost curves for successively opзarted plants. The curve LAC (long-run average cost curve) is tangent to the minimum points of the SAC curves. Graphically. long-run averag: co3t curve (LAC) is the "envelope" of the short-run averge cost curves.

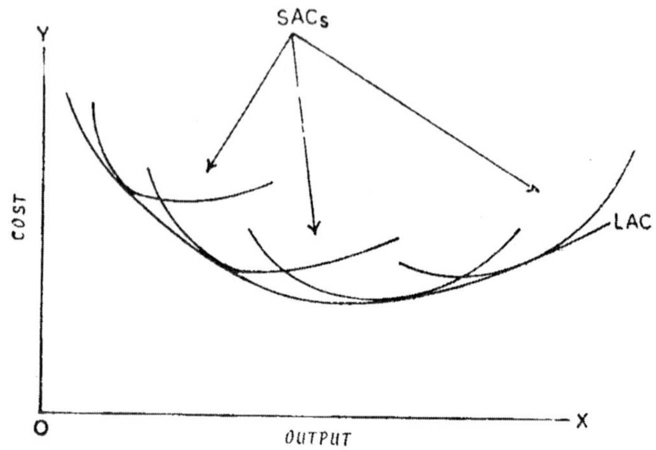

Figure 3.17 Long-run Ac Curves.

THE CONCEPT OF REVENUE

The revenue of a firm has an important role in determining its profits. The revenue with its costs of production determines profits of a firm. It is known that profit is the difference between revenue and cost. We may now turn our attention to the concept of revenue.

Revenue means the receipts derived by a firm from the sale of commodities at various prices. The concept of revenue relates to total revenue, average revenue and marginal revenue.

Total Revenue

Total revenue (TR) is the total sale proceeds of a firm by selling a commodity at a given price. If a firm sells 2 units of a commodity at Rs. 10. total revenue is 2x10=20. Thus total revenue is price per unit multiplied by the number of units sold.

Algebraically,

$$R = PQ$$

where R is total revenue, P the price per unit and Q quantities sold.

Average Revenue (AR)

Average revenue means the average receipts from the sale of

comodities of a firm. We may findout the average revenue by dividing the total revenue by the number of units sold. In our given example, average revenue is $\frac{20}{2}=10$. The average revenue of a firm is, thus, the price of the commodity at each level of output.

We have seen that R=PQ

Therefore, $AR=\frac{R}{Q}=\frac{PQ}{Q}=P$

Where AR is average revenue, R is total revenue, Q is Quantity sold and P price per unit.

Marginal Revenue (MR)

Mariginal revenue is the addition to total revenue by selling an additional unit. Algebrically, is same as price and marginal revenue (MR) is identical with average revenue.

Study the data given in Table 3.10–

TABLE 3.10

Revenue under Pure Competition

Q	*P* *Rs.*	*TR* *Rs.*	*AR* *Rs.*	*MR* *Rs.*
1	10	10	10	10
2	10	20	10	10
3	10	30	10	10
4	10	40	10	10
5	10	50	10	10

Since uniform price level prevails in a purely competitive. Market, the average revenue and marginal revenue are as same as price. The data given in Table 3.10 is graphically represented in Figure 3.18. As there is uniform price in the market the average revenue curve is a horizontal straightline parallel to X-ax is and MR curve coincides with it. The price is shown as OP. Each firm can sell as much as it can at the ruling market price, OP (Rs. 10). Thus demand for the product becomes infinitely elastic. The firm's demand curve is coincided with its average revenue.

AR And MR under Monopoly

Monopoly and Monopolistic Competitions are market situations where there are so many market imperfections. Under such a market situation there are no homogeneous products and hence no uniform prices. Under pure competition, as already pointed out, the

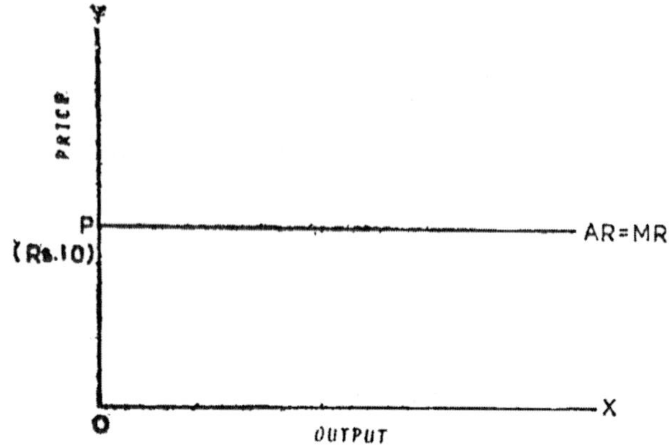

Figure 3.18 AR and MR under Pure Competition.

firm can sell any number of commodities at the ruling price. But unlike pure competition, under monopoly or monopolistic competition, the firm has to reduce prices to increase their sales. This is numerically illustrated in Table 3.11.

TABLE 3.11.

Revenue under Monopoly

Q	*P* *Rs.*	*TR* *Rs.*	*AR* *Rs.*	*MR* *Rs.*
1	10	10	10	10
2	9	18	9	8
3	8	24	8	6
4	7	28	7	4
5	6	30	6	2

It is seen from the given table that if the seller in an imperfectly Competitive market wants to sell more the prices will have to be reduced and that average revenue is falling along with marginal revenue but average revenue is always greater than marginal revenue.

The given numerical analysis can conveniently be transformed into a graph. This is done in Figure 3.19. The average revenue curve is seen downward sloping as shown in figure and marginal revenue curve is also downward sloping but is below the average revenue curve. This is because MR is lower than AR. Given the demand for the product, the monopolist can increase his sales by reducing price, MR is also falling but the rate of fall in MR is greater than that in AR.

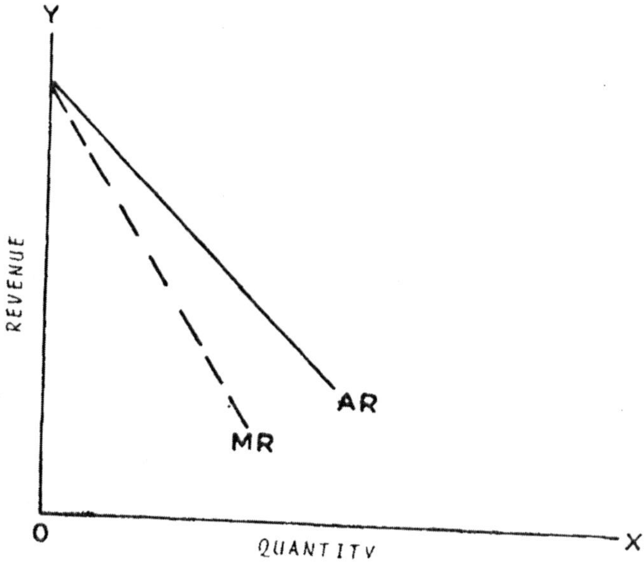

Figure 3.19. AR and MR Curves under Monopoly.

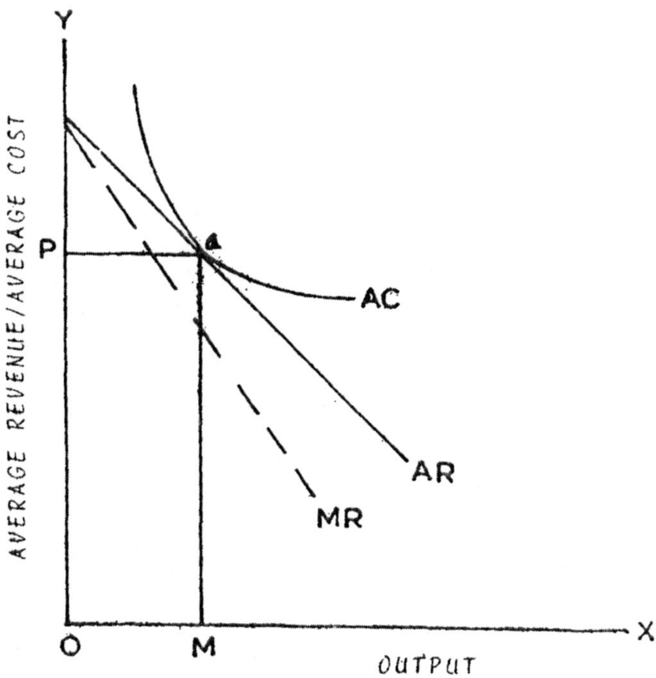

Figure 3.20 Normal Profit.

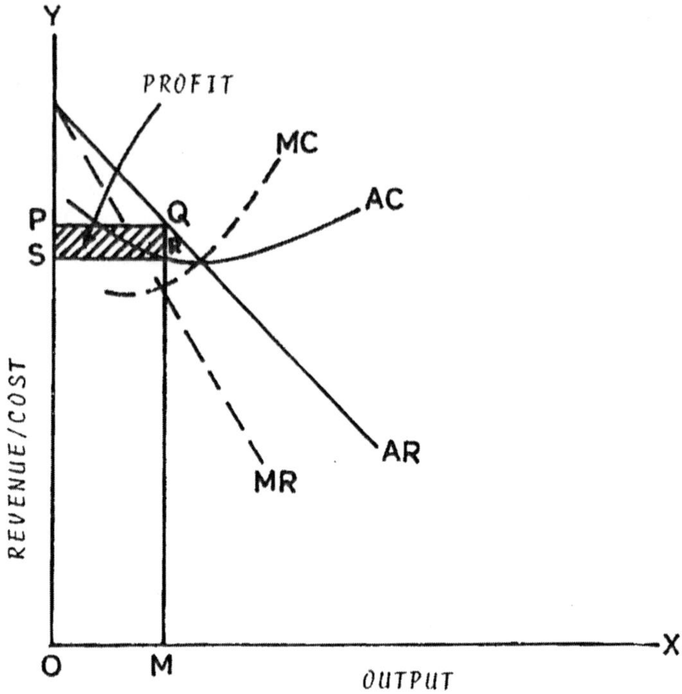

Figure 3.21. Abnormal Profits.

Practical Importance

The AR and MR curves are important tools of economic analysis. The AR curve is price curve for all the producers in different market situations. We may find out whether the firm is earning normal or abnormal profits or incurring losses by relating AR to the average cost (AC) of the firm. If the AR curve is tangent to the AC curve of the firm at the point of equilbrium (as in Figure3.20) We may know that the firm earning normal profits. If the AC curve is below the AR Curve, the firm makes supernormal profits Figure 3.21).

The firm incur losses if AC curve lies above the AR curve' as shown in figure 3.22.

ELEMENTS OF LINEAR PROGRAMMING

Linear programming is a mathematical device to solve certain kinds of production problems. Also called "mathematical programming" or "activity analysis" this technique was first formulated by the Russian mathematican L.V. Kantrovich. Later, the U.S.

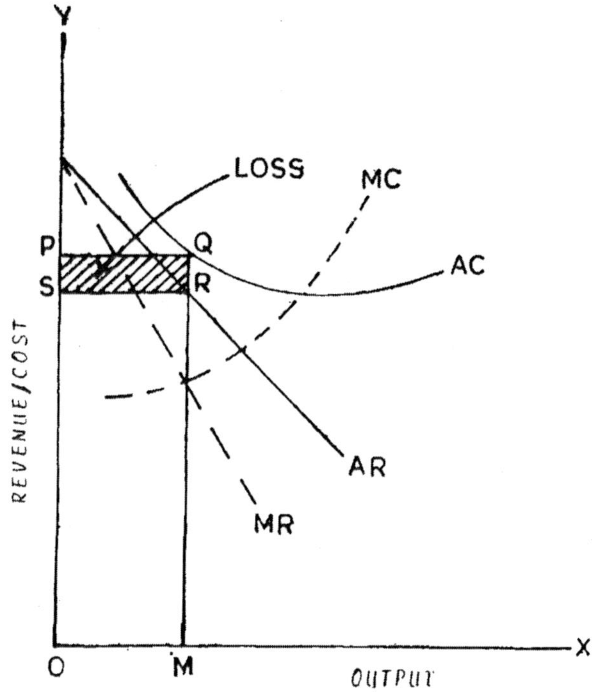

Figure 3.22 Loss.

Mathematician George B. Dantzig developed the technique of linear programming by inventing a superior technique of computation for the purpose of scheduling the complicated procurement activities of U.S. Air force. It has been further developed in its application to the economic theory of the firm, managerial economics and recently to development planning.

Linear programming is, simply, the maximisation or minimisation of linear function of variables subject to a constraint of line in equalities.[8] It gives actual numerical solutions to problems of making optimum choices when the problems have to be solved within the definit bounds or constraints.

The application of linear programming is based on certain conditions and generalisations. First, there is a *definite objective* to be achieved. It is called objective function which states the determinants of the quantity to be maximised or to be minimised. Profits or income are the objective function when they are to be maximised, while costs from the objective function when they are to be minimised. Cost minimisation is the 'dual' of profit maximisation and *vice versa.*

Second, there should be *alternative production processes* to achieve the definite objective. A process is a way of doing things. It is a combination of particular inputs to produce a particular output. A firm has serveral processes, each of which can be carried on at several levels to produce the firm's product. One process can be substituted for another.

Third, there must be certain *constraints or restraints* which are called linearar inequalities. They are certain linitations pertaining to any conditions of the problems as to what can't be done and what has to be done. The budget of a consumer is a constraint. If a firm is maximising revenue, then it is limited or constrained by the facts that it has, say, 5 machines.

Fourth, there are *choice variables.* We may choose the numbers in order to maximise or minimise the objective function within the linitations.

Last, there are *feasible and optimal solutions.* Feasible solutions for the consumer, given his income and prices of commodities are all of the possible combinations of commodities that he can possibly buy. Optimal solution, on the otherhand, is the best of feasible soultions.

Assumptions of Linear Programming

The linear programming technique is based up on the following assumptions.

Firstly, the decision-making authority or the firm is confronted with certain constraints or limitations in the form of credit, raw materials or space constraints on its activities.

Secondly, there are alternative production processes which are assumed to be limited in number.

Thirdly, it assumes linear relations among different variables. It implies that there exist a constant proportionality between inputs and output within a process.

Finally, certain period is assumed for the programming technique. For convencince and more accurate results the period is generally short.

Technique and Application : Maximising Profit

Let us analyse a "product mix" problem to understand linear programming technique and its application. The objective function is of maximsing profits in the production of two products where production is suject to three constraints. The two products X and Y can be produced indifferent proportions or mixes the problem is to find the profit maximising mix.

In the marginal analysis of the conventional theory of production, the firm with two products has a production possibility curve.

Consider Figure 3.23.

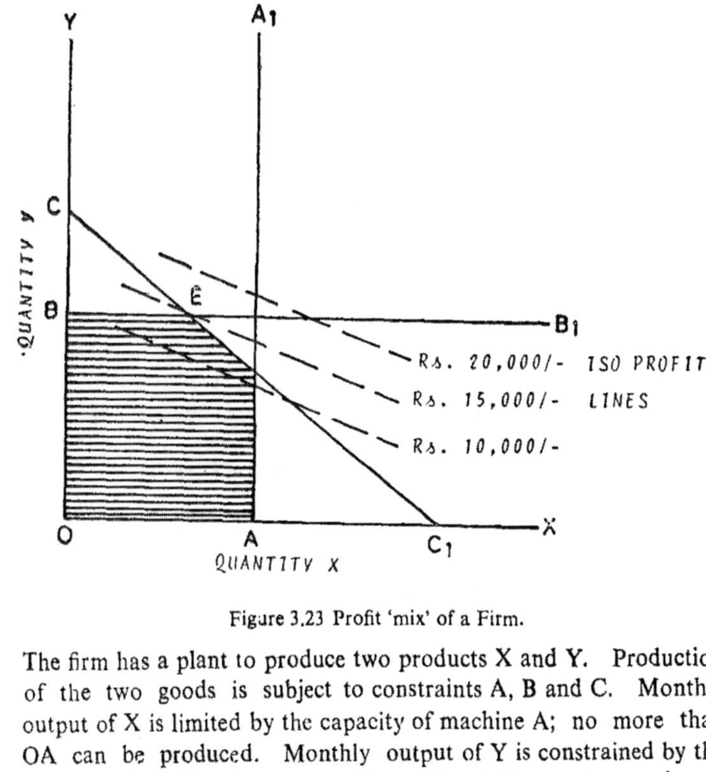

Figure 3.23 Profit 'mix' of a Firm.

The firm has a plant to produce two products X and Y. Production of the two goods is subject to constraints A, B and C. Monthly output of X is limited by the capacity of machine A; no more than OA can be produced. Monthly output of Y is constrained by the capacity of machine B; no more than OB of Y can be produced. The ractangle formed by the two axes and by lines 'A1' and 'B1' shows the combined effects of these two constraints. There is one more constraint C, which is, say, the packing unit. Both the products have to be packed by polythelene covers. The line CC1 defines the monthly capacity of the packing unit. The shape of the line. 'CC' indicates that if more of Y are to be packed, then fewer units X can be.

The shadedarea in Figure 3.23 is, thus, the zone of feasible production. The three straight lines BF, FF and FA together form the linear programming version of the production possibility curve. Any combination of X and Y on one of the straight lines is feasible, so also is any combination inside the zone. But it is impossible to produce X and Y in a combination shown by the point lying outside the zone.

Now, consider the profit side. The two products sell at certain prices. To find the profitable "mix", we may consider iso-profit lines which are constructed in the same way as isocost lines. Three iso-profit lines are shown in Figure 3.23. The optimum solution is at Point E where the iso-profit line labelled Rs. 15,000 is tangent to the production possibility curve BEFA. Here profits are maximum at Rs. 15,000 a month. Any other of the feasible combinations of the two products would yield a lower profit.

Take another firm whose objective function is to maximise output. Suppose that the firm decides to produce a commodity, say, coal, using capital and labour inputs. Its objective is to maximise output. It has two alternative production processes, capital intensive and labour intensive. The constraint is a given cost outlay MP as shown in Figure 3.24. Units of capital per period are measured along the vertical axis and labour units per period are shown as the horizontal axis. If the capital intensive process requires 2 units of capital to every unit of labour, it will produce 50 tons of coal. If the inputs of capital and labour are doubled to 4 units of capital and 2 units of labour output is also doubled to 100 tons of coal. These combinations of capital and labour are represented by the capital intensive process line OC. On the other hand, the same units (50 tons of coal) can be produced by labour intensive process by combining 3 units of labour with one unit of capital. 100 tons of coal can be produced by doubling the inputs of labour and capital to 6 units of labour and 2 units of capital. These output scales are established along the labour intensive process line OL as represented by the input combinations C and D. If the points a and C at the 50 tons of output level on the linear line OC and OL are joined they form an isoquant labelled Iaes. At the 100 tons output level the corresponding isoquant is I1 bdS1. The cost outlay constraint is represented by the isocost line MP and it places a limit on the production capacity of the firm. The firm can produce with either of the two variable techniques C and L with area represented by the triangle Obr. It is impossible for it to produce outside this area of the feasible solutions. The optimal solution which maximises

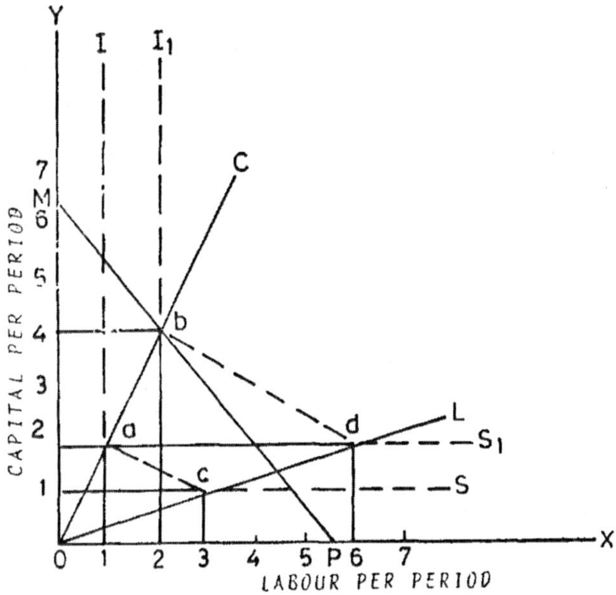

Labour per period.
Figure 3.24. Linear Programming.

the output of the firm will occur at the point where the isocost line touches the isoquant with the highest output. In the given figure the isocost line MP touches the isoquant I1bds1 at Point B on the production process line OC. It shows that the firm will use the capital intensive technique C by using 4 units of capital and 2 units of labour and produce 100 tons of coal.

APPENDIX

SCALE OF PRODUCTION

Scale of production refers to the amount of factors used, the quantum of products produced and the technique of production adopted by a producer. Production may be undertaken on small. scale or on large scale by the firms. When a firm operates by using less amounts of factors of production the scale of production is said to be small. When the firm employs large amounts of factors of production the scale of production is said to be large.

Scale of production, in otherwords, relates to the size of the unit of production or firm. There may be large scale production and small scale production. Production is said to be on a large scale when the size of the firm is large and it is on small scale, when the unit of production is comparatively small. There is a controversy whether an economy should have large scale or small scale productions. Most of the economists are of opinion that both are necessary but the sphere of each of which should be so determined that socio-economic interests of the country are not to be hindered. It is, therefore, desirable to examine the advantages and disadvantages of both the types of production.

To give brevity, let us make the point clear. Large scale production does not mean large volume of production. If, for example, all adults in India are engaged in making candles, we will have large amounts of candles in the country. This is not the case of large scale production but a case of large volume of production. Large scale production means production in bulk in a large sized unit of a firm.

It is the common experience of every manufacturer that large the scale of production, lower the average cost of production. i.e., cost per unit of the product. That is why the manufacturers are tempted to enlarge the scale of production. So that they may benefit from the resulting economies of scale. Economics of scale are broadly classified as internal economies and external economies. Before we pass on to a detailed discussion on both these economies, we may summarise the advantages and disadvantages of large scale production.

Advantages of Large Scale Production

When production is organised on large scale, a unit of production or firm derives certain economies which necessarily reduce the cost of production per unit of the product. These are called internal economies. They refer to the advantages derived by a firm from an increase in the scale of production. Internal economies are therefore, defined as the resultant advantages from an increase in the scale of production of a firm. The internal economies arise within a firm as a result of its own expansion independent of the size and expansion of the industry as a whole. The following are the internal economies accruing to a firm when its scale is increased.

1. Technical Economies : Technical advantages that a firm derives in five possible ways are detailed below :

(a) *Economy of specialised Machinery* : When the firm

increases the scale of production, it can afford to use large machinery to increase production. Use of large-machinery results in lower costs of production. The firm can instal sophisticated and modern machinery. If the firm employs specialised machinery, the production becomes more economical.

(b) *Economy of Division of Labour* : Large scale production gives rise to economy of specialisation. In a large firm, there is wide scope for division of labour. Each group of labour can be employed in specialised areas of production of the firm, specialised labour produces larger and quality products. When a firm increases its size and increases production, they are able to employ specialised labourers. This is impossible in the case of small scale production.

(c) *Economy of Linked Process* : Large scale production enables a firm to produce its own raw material and semi-finished products. For example, a large sugar mill can produce its own sugar canes in its firm and can supply it to its own self-owned sugar mill. It may depend upon the open market for its own materials. Since the firm links the different production processes and materials in the firm itself. It is called economy of linked processes.

(d) *Economy of Bi-products* : A big business firm will be able to utilise its bi-products and minimise wastes most effectively and productively and derive some sort of economies. A small sugar factory, for example, throws away its molasses. Whereas a big sugar factory can use it for the production of alcohol.

(e) *Economy of Research and Experiment* : A big business concern can maintain its own research wing and can afford to spend adequate funds for undertaking research experiments and discovery of new production techniques and related matters. Such an activity can hardly be afforded by a small firm.

2. *Managerial Economies* : A big business firm can easily employ an efficient manager which a small firm is unable to do so. In a small firm, the manager will have to do all kinds of jobs; but in a big business firm, the manager may look into the policy matters while the other related works are to be assigned to concerned

departments. Further, it can derive economies arising from the creation of specialised developments.

3. *Commercial Economies* : A big business concern can secure specially favourable terms of purchasing raw materials and other accessories. Similary, it can sell the products in bulk and can dictate its terms. Secondly, a big firm can secure concession from railways and other transport operating agencies for transporting its commodities. Thirdly, it can increase its volume of sales through advertisement and salesmanship.

4. *Financial Economies* : A big business firm can secure better credit facilities by providing adequate securities at cheaper rates of interest. Cheaper credits help to reduce cost of production. Further, it can secure more share capital by its own reputation.

5. *Risk-bearing Economies* : Large firms can show better resistence during the time of adversity. They have larger resistence to withstand unfavourable circumstances. Losses can be easily borne. They can also diversify their output by production technique.

6. *Economies of Overhead Costs* : In a large business firm the expenses of administration and distribution per unit of output are much less as output increases. Interest, wages and other overhead charges are the same whether production is large or small. Thus, the same amount of expenditure being distributed over a larger output the result of which is less cost per unit.

Disadvantages of Large Scale Production

Large scale production is not free from disadvantages. The following are some of the disadvantages of large scale production.

1. *Lack of Adequate Supervision* : As the scale of production increases, it becomes unwieldy and therefore too difficult to supervise the work more effectively. Costs often rise on account of the dishonesty of employees or wastes of material by them. Owing to laxity of control cost of production rises.

2. *Individual Tastes Ignored* : Large sized firm produces standardised products. Products are of uniform quality and size. Though the mass production helps to reduce cost of production per unit, uniformity of the product does not satisfy the tastes of different consumers.

3. *Absence of Personal Touch* : Large sized business firms are generally manged by paid employees who are not the owners of the firms. The owners have no direct control over the management of

the firm. The sympathy and personal touch, which ought to exist between the owners and the workers are lacking. The separation of ownership and management often leads to misunderstandings. Frequent misunderstandings lead to strikes and lockouts. This is harmful to the business firms.

4. Lack of Adaptability. A large scale producing unit finds it very difficult to change its pattern of production from one form to another according to the nature of fluctuating market conditions. It has specialised form of machinery and specialised labour, each engaged in producing particular type of products. If there is any change in the tastes of consumers or a fall in demand for products, it could not switch on from one line of production to another.

Inspite of these disadvantages, large scale production offers several economies. Manufacturing and transport industries tend to increase the scale of production. The advantages out weigh the disadvantages. The scale of production enlarges till the firm reaches the optimum size. At this scale of production, the total profit is maximised and cost per unit is minimised. Lower the cost more efficient will be the firm.

External Economies

External economies refer to those economies which accrue, to each firm as a result of the expansion of the industry as a whole. There are no peculiar advantages to any particular firm. They are the advantages enjoyed by all member firms of an industry. The benefits of localisation of industry are the examples of external economies. When certain industries are localised at a particular place, some common benefits spring up in the area which can be enjoyed by all firms.

External economies benefit all units of firms within the industry as the size of the industry expands. When the industry is localised in a particular place, makes inventions and evolves specialisation of production processes, external economies accrue to firms.

The following are the various types of external economies :

(*i*) *Economies of concentration* : Advantages of a localised industry can be reaped by all the member firms in the area. Advantages arising from the availability of workers, provision of better transport, communications and credit facilities, benefits from subsidiary industries etc., are common economies of concentration. Each firm in the industry shares in the common stock of knowledge and experience.

(*ii*) *Economies of Information* : Economies of information refer to the advantages enjoyed by all firms in an industry from the publication of trade journals, technical informations and research institutions. Research and experiments are centralised in a localised industry. The fruits of the research in research institutions in the form of new inventions are passed on to the firm through scientific journals. All these help in raising the productive efficiency of the firms and reducing their costs of production.

(*iii*) *Economies of Disintegration* : When an industry expands, it becomes possible to split up some of the processes for making specialisation. For example, concentration of cotton mills in a particular locality can separate the process of cotton ginning, spinning and weaving of cloths. This enables the firms to reduce cost of production.

It may be noted that increase in the size of an industry may ultimately lead to external dis-economies. Localisation of industry may lead to high cost of transportation due to congestion. Similarly, as industry expands there arises scarcity of raw materials and skilled labourers, the resultant of which is increasing cost of production. It is also a common experience that when industry expands there arises scarcity of raw materials and skilled labourers, the resultant of which is increasing cost of production. It is also a common experience that when industry expands, there exists keen competition among the firms for factors of production and raw materials. As a result, the prices of raw materials and cost of production go up. All firms have to pay higher wages, rent and interest apart from higher prices for raw materials. With the result of these, cost of production rises instead of falling.

As the firm expands its production beyond certain limits, it is possible to increase costs of production instead of reducing it. It is called internal dis-economies. This may be due to the fact that less efficient factors may have been brought into use. If the firm expands beyond a limit, it may be beyond the capacity of the manager. Hence, the management becomes inefficient and the internal dis-economies set in.

Dis-economies of Large Scale Production

The economies of scale cannot continue indefinitely. A time

will reach when further expansion of a firm or an industry leads to dis-economies instead of economies of scale. Internal and external dis-economies are necessarily the limits to large scale production.

The following are the various internal diseconomies of scale of a firm.

(i) *Financial Dis-economies*: Business firm needs finance to expand business. But the required amount of finance may not be available at the appropriate time. Lack of adequate finance prevents the firm from expanding productive activities which may cause increase in cost of production.

(ii) *Managerial Dis-economies*: Inability to supervise and control the business properly on the part of the management may lead to confusion and chaos in the production fields. There is a limit beyond which a firm becomes unwieldy and unmanageable. Lack of supervision, inefficient working and wastages of production all result in high cost of production.

(iii) *Marketing Dis-economies*: The expansion of a firm beyond a limit may also involve marketing problems. Sufficient quantities of raw materials may not be available due to scarcity. The damand for the product may be adversely affected as a result of changes in the tastes and preferences of the consumers.

(iv) *Technical Dis-economies*: A large sized firm often operates heavy capital equipment. Large scale capital equipment are indivisible. Indivisibility of factors may lead to inefficiency. As a result, cost per unit increases.

(v) *Economies of Small Scale Production*: Small scale production is also one of the distinguising features of modern industrial organisation. Small scale production is carried on present even in developed countries like USA, France, Germany and Japan.

We may now enumerate certain advantages of small scale production—

1. Small scale production is capital light. It requires lesser amount of capital as compared with large scale production. Production on small scale economises the use of capital.

2. Production on small scale is skill light. Small scale production requires smaller techniques of production. Hence skilled

labourers are not necessarily required as compared with large scale production.

3. Small scale manufacturer possesses greater degree of manoeuvrability. He is capable of prompt decision and quick execution.

4. Close supervision is possible in the case of small scale production. Marshall has rightly pointed out that "the master's eye is everywhere". Hence, economical working is possible.

5. Under small scale production, the owner is the sole proprietor. He takes personal interest in the functioning of the business. Self interest motivates him to avoid wastages of raw material and working time.

Even though there are many advantages for small scale production, it is not free from disadvantages. A small sized firm is not in a position to reap technical, financial and marketing economies. Hence, cost of production becomes high. A small firm is not in a position to mobilise adequate capital resources. There is little scope for research, experiment and specialisation. Due to non-availability of better techniques and raw materials and skilled workers, he may not produce quality products. There is little scope for division of labour.

NOTES AND REFERENCES

1. A. Marshall : Principles of Economics, 1936, p. 138.
2. A. Marshall : *op. cit.*, p. 65.
3. Knut Wiecksell, Lectures on Political Economy, Vol, 1. p. 160.
4. Donald S. Watson : Price Theory and its uses, Second Edition, Indian Edition, Scientific Book Agency; Calcutta. (1968). p. 159.
5. George J. Stigler The Theory of Price, Third edition, Macmillan, (1966) p. 122.
6. F. Benham Economics, p. 209.
7. Stonier & Hague A Text Book of Economic Theory, p. 116.
8. Donald S. Watson Price Theory out its uses (second Indian Edition, Scientific Book Agency, Calcutta, 1970) p. 207 (Footnote).

4

THE THEORY OF MARKET BEHAVIOUR

THE FIRM AND THE GOLDEN RULE

The firm is a basic unit of production and independent business organisation that produces goods and services for sale. It directs production, allocate resources and exercises control over its productive activities. Though the firm's legal entity may take a variety of form such as individual proprietorship, partnership or corporation, the pursuit of profit is considered as an underlying motivation behind their engagements.

The economic analysis of the entrepreneurial behaviour is based on the assumption that the entrepreneur acts in a rational way to make the best of the existing market situations. It aims to do the best it can in the circumstances. The essence of the idea is that it would take rational action to maximise profit. That is, the firm always acts in such a way as to maximise profits. Profits of a firm at any time is the difference between revenues and costs.

Some economists have challenged the assumption of profit maximising principle to explain the entrepreneurial behaviour. H.A.

Simon[1] coined the term 'profit satisficing' in place of profit maximising to describe the motivation of firms. He argued that the firm aims at satisfaction profit rather than maximum profit. Since they operate in an uncertain world, they are contented with the realisation of target rate of return where their profit aspirations are satisfied.

W.J. Baumol has further argued that the aim of the firm is not profit maximisation but sales maximisation.

Though alternative goals are there, still, pursuit of profit keeps the key role in the economic theories of the behaviour of the firms.

In order to ensure the best possible achievement in situation, there is a guideline, the golden rule to pursuit. It combines the cost and revenue sides of output since they together determine firm's net income. Costs are the foregone benefits and revenues are the receipts by selling the output. Revenue depends upon nature of demand and market structure.

We may note that there exists a definite relationship between costs and revenue to satisfy the prime objective : maximising profit. This expresses a rule that firm should always equate MC with MR. By equating these two marginal values, the firm would always ensure maximum return and minimum loss. This can be briefly explained with the help of a diagram. Consider Figure 4.1. MC represents marginal cost of the firm and MR the marginal revenue. Assume that the firm is producing 4 units of output. If the 5th unit were to be produced the revenue the firm would receive from the sale of that unit would be greater than the cost of producing it. Hence the firm would produce the 5th unit of output. This is true in the case of any output level below 6 units. However, if the firm is producing, say, 7 or 8 units then the firm should contract its output. Only when 6 units are produced at which MC=MR, the firm should maintain constant rate of output.

Figure 4.1 shows only the upward sloping part of the MC curve since maximising principle only applies to output levels in the range of upward slope of the curve.

For more brevity, equating MC and MR maximises the firm's profit only if the MC curve cuts MR curve from below. If output is maintained at that level where MC curve cuts MR curve from above the profit of the firm would not be maximised since a unit of increase in output would add more to revenue than costs. Figure 4.2 illustrates this.

As shown in the diagram, if the firm maintains its output at the level of 2 units where MC equals MR, when the former is falling at

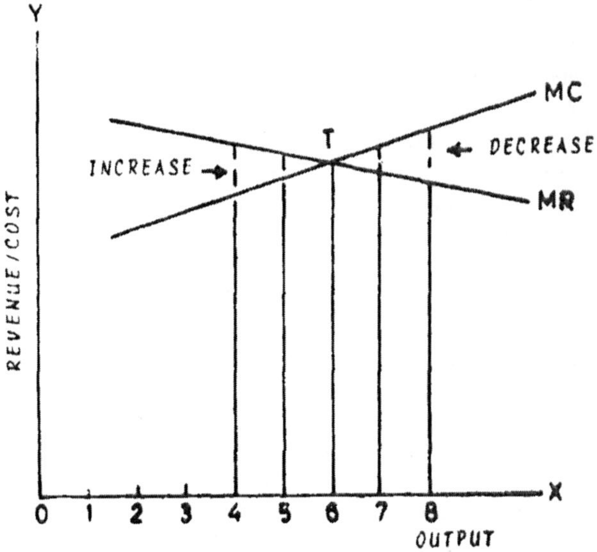

Figure. 4.1 : Profit Maximising Situation.

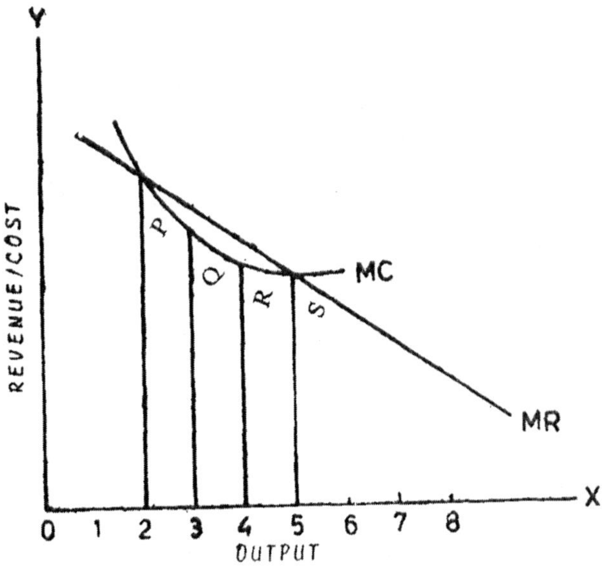

Figure. 4.2 : MC Curve Cuts MR From below.

Point P, it would have to forego the income (revenue) which would be accrued by the sale of next 3 units of output. Each additional unit from 3rd to 5th adds more to revenue than it does to costs. Revenue is being maximised only when 5 units are being produced where MC equals MR and the former is rising at Point R. When the firm reaches this level of output we would say that the firm is in equilibrium.

The equilibrium condition of the firm can also be explained with the simple application of total revenue and total cost curves. This is done in Figure 4.3. Panel A of the diagram represents such a situation and it includes total profits. The corresponding MC curve is traced out in Panel B. TC is the total cost curve, TR is the total revenue curve and TP is the total profit curve derived as the locus of all vertical distances between TC and TR curves. Thus when output is less than ON1 and total revenue is less than total cost, total profit is negative. Total profit is again negative when intented output exceeds N 5 units and in between output levels N1 and N5, total profit is positive. We may see that profit is greatest at output level N3. At this level of output total profit is N3P, equal to the greatest vertical distance between TR and TC curves. At this level of output MC equals MR which satisfies the 'golden rule'.

PRICING UNDER PERFECT COMPETITION

With the theory of production and cost in mind, we may now proceed to analyse the theory of the firm—the theory that helps to understand the price and output policies of the enterprising firm.

It is to be kept in mind that revenue and cost of production together form the price—output policy of the business firm. The conditions of revenue that a firm confronts are largely determined by the type of market in which it operates. Some may face stiff competition from other firms; while others may confront comparatively less competition. Between these, the firm may have an entire market itself which is a market situation called monopoly. So much so that different models of business firms are to be examined. In this chapter we are concerned with the case of pure competition.

Pure Competition

An industry is said to be in pure competition if every buyer and seller is so small relative to the entire market that he cannot influence the market price by changing his purchases or sales. More

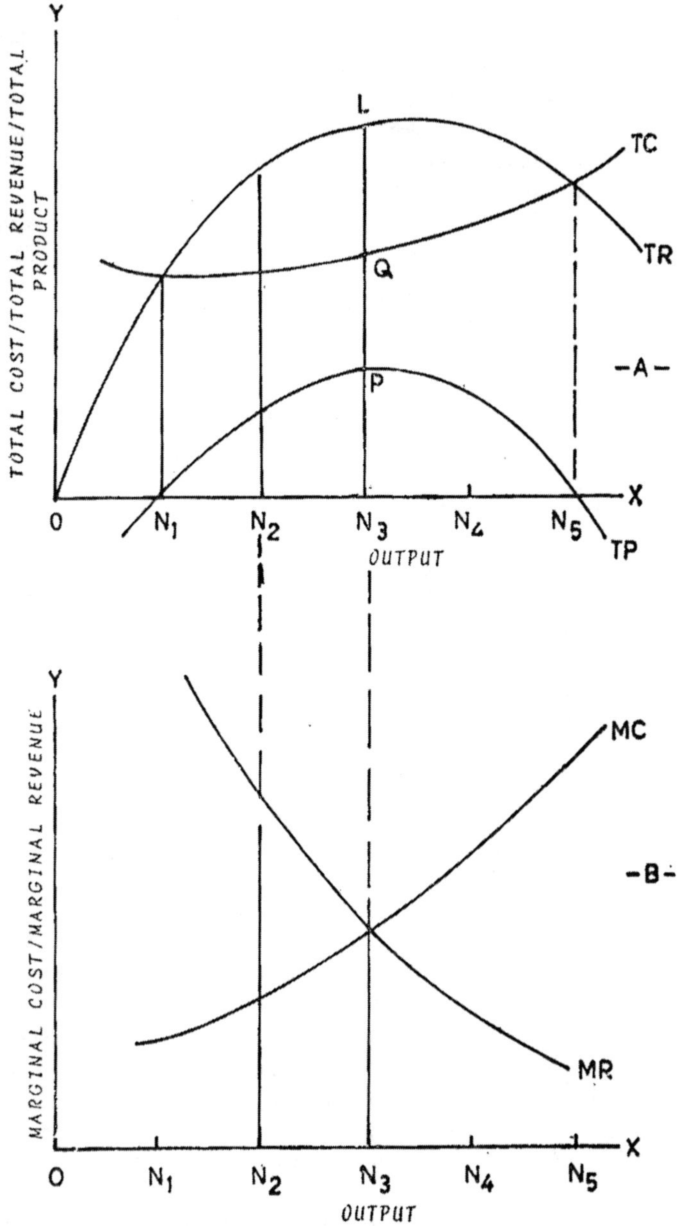

Figure 4.3 : Equilibrium of the Firm.

specifically, pure competition exists where the following conditions are satisfied.

1. There must be large number of buyers, each of whom purchases an insignificantly small part of the total output.

2. There must be large number of sellers, each of whom produces or sells only an insignificant part of the total output.

3. The products produced and sold by the industry must be homogeneous. That is, the commodities dealt with the industry must be indentical in every respect.

4. There must be free and unrestricted entry into and exit from the industry. Anyone who wishes to produce may produce the commodity in question and anyone who wants to leave the industry may do so.

It is clearly known that in a purely or atomistic competitive market, each firm is in stiff competition with many other firms producing identical products. Similarly, each buyer is in direct competition with many others who are purchasing the same product. Further, each of them is so insignificant of influence the ruling market price by changing his individual purchases or output.

Demand and Revenue for the Competitive Seller

As we have seen, pure competition is defined as a market situation in which each seller is so small to influence the market price by changing his output. That is, he could sell any number of output at the existing price level. If he sells his output by lessening the price, he could earn nothing but to loss his profit. And he could not sell for a higher price, for, no buyer would likely to pay more. Consider Figure 4.4. Panel A shows the hypothetical market equilibrium in a competitive industry. DD represents market demand, while SS represents market supply. Their intersection determines the equilibrium price and quantity, OP^1 and Oq^1 respectively. Panel B shows a hypothetical firm in this industry. The competitive seller, the owner of the firm, very well knows that he could not affect the ruling market price. If he charges higher price than the market price, he could sell nothing at all, for, no one should purchase the high priced product. If, on the otherhand, he charges a lesser price for his product, he would lose his profit. Therefore he accepts the equilibrium price P' as the price at which he can sell his output.

Through the point P1 in Panel B a horizontal straight line (D=MR) is drawn. First of all, it is a demand curve. The perfe

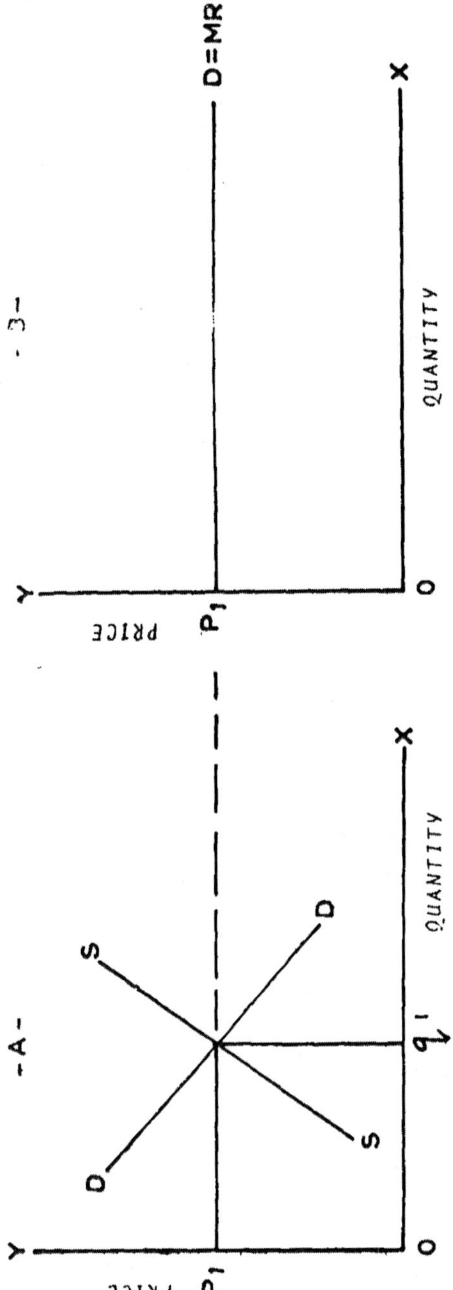

Fig. 4.4 : Demand curve of Firm and Industry in pure Competition.

elasticity of the demand curve for the compentitive seller implies that he could sell nothing at a higher price, but to sell all his output at the ruling market price. An abbreviated example relating to this is given in Table 4.1.

The horizontal straightline in figure is also labelled marginal revenue curve (MR). This is because demand curve and marginal revenue curve are coincided in a purely competitive market.

TABLE 4.1

Demand Schedule for the Competitive Seller

Price	*Sales*
>P1	0
P1	As much as he wishes to sell.
<P1	As much as he can, but to loose.

As already noted, a purely competitive seller can sell any number of output at the prevailing market price. That is, he can expand his sales without reducing price, and the price is always added to the total revenue, and hence price is equal to marginal revenue (P=MR).

Short Run-equilibrium under Pure Competition

There is one basic assumption that each businessman attempts to operate his firm in such a manner as to maximise his profits. Equally, if profit cannot be gained, it is assumed that the entrepreneur attempt to minimise his losses.

In the real world though the firms do not always attempt to earn the absolute maximum possible profit, they do attempt to make substantial profit. We may thus assume that each businessman attempts to maximise his profit from his business operations.

We may be now in a position to absorb the theory of the purely competitive firms and industry. In a broad outline, the theory is simply this. Firms attempt to maximise profit. Profit is the difference between revenue and cost. Consequently, the firms produce the output that maximises this difference. In the case of industry, the market price is determined by demand and supply conditions.

Let us begin with an example. The Table 4.2 given below shows the revenue, cost and profit situation for a hypothetical firm in pure competition. As we have learned, price is at each point equal to MR. Thus price line, demand curve or MR curve is plotted in upper sigment of the adjacent diagram (Figure 4.5) Next, column 3 shows the total revenue. The curve for total revenue is plotted in the lower segment of the figure and is labelled TR. The total cost of production is shown in column 4. The total cost (TC) is also plotted in the lower segment of the Figure. The shaded area indicates profit (TC=TR).

TABLE 4.2

Short-run Cost and Revenue for a Firm under Pure Competition

Quantity SOLD	*Price (=MR) Rs.*	*Total Revenue Rs.*	*Total cost Rs.*	*Average cost Rs.*	*Morginal cost Rs.*	*Profit Rs.*
10	5	50	104	1.04	—	—54
20	5	100	124	6.2	20	—24
30	5	150	149	4.9	25	—1
40	5	200	180	4.5	31	20
50	5	250	220	4.4	40	30
60	5	300	270	4.5	50	30
70	5	350	335	4.7	65	15
80	5	400	420	5.2	85	—20
90	5	450	530	5.8	110	—80
100	5	500	670	6.7	140	—170

Column 5 of the Table 4.2 contains the average cost of production. Average cost is plotted in Figure as AC, The 6th column shows the marginal cost (MC), a curve is also plotted in Figure. Finally the last column in the Table 4.2 gives the profit or loss data.

We are now in a position to determine maximum profit with the aid of these figures. Profit maximising output is determined by finding the point at which TR exceeds TC by the greatest amount. This is 60 on the graph. At this point, total cost is Rs. 270 and total revenue is Rs. 300. The resulting profit is Rs. 30. We may confirm from the Table 4.2 this is the that largest possible profit that the hypothetical firm can earn.

Another method of analysis is given in the upper segment of the Figure. On this graph are plotted D = MR, AC and MC

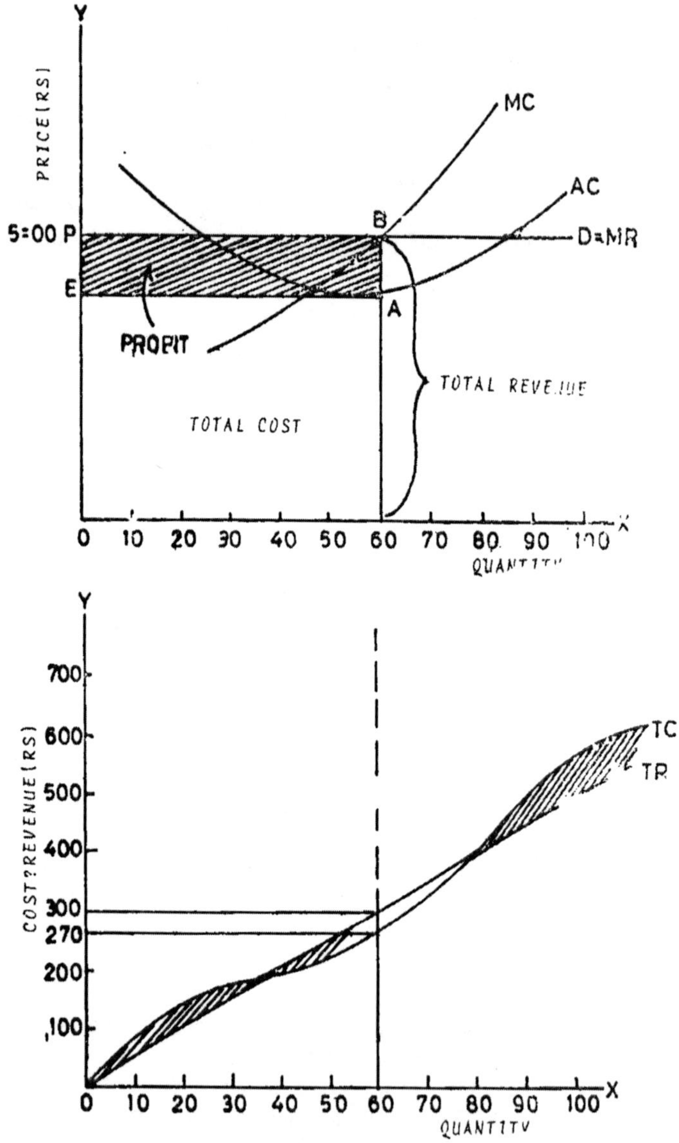

Fig. 4.5: Cost and Revenue under Pure Competition.

curves. It is already known that the profit maximising output is 60 units. The abseissa point corresponding to this output is labelled Q. Draw the line QB till D = MR line is reached. Note that this happens to be at the point where MC equals MR equals price (MC = MR = P). The rectangle OQBP is the total revenue of the firm, since total revenue equals price OP multiplied by quantity OQ. Hence the area OQBP.

Next is to find total cost. Total cost is the average cost multiplied by quantity. For the output OQ average cost (AC) is QA = OE. Multiplying OE by OQ, we obtain the area OQAE = total cost. Since profit is the difference between total revenue and total cost, we can find profit by substracting OQAE from OQBP obtaining the shaded rectangle EABP.

Thus we may note the fundamental theorem that a firm in a purely competitive industry in a purely competitive industry maximises profit or minimises loss by producing that output for which marginal cost equals price.

Long-run Equilibrium under Pure Competition

Though it is possible to distinguish between short-run and long-run equilibrium for the individual firm, equilibrium of the industry can only be a long-run phenomenon. Equilibrium concerning industry is, thus, a state in which the firms are neither entering nor living the industry.

Let us explain the theory of long-run competitive equilibrium with the help of the Figure 4.6. First consider parcel A, which shows the demand and supply conditions for industry. D is the demand curve. At the outset there is relatively small number of firms in the industry. When the market supply curve is S1, the market equilibrium price P1 is determined. Given the demand curve D1 and long-run marginal cost curve LMC, the individual firm comes into equilibrium at Point A on Panel B, producing Q1 quantity of output. The earning profit is represented by the distance between Point A and LAC curve.

This condition, however, cannot remain permanently. Each producer earns profit. The profit is a signal to the producers in other industries tries to shift into this industry. Since entry is free they can shift in the long-run into this industry. Thus new firm enter. This serves to increase the supply shifting the supply curve to S2 and every firm takes a curve D2. Accordingly each firm comes to equilibrium at Point B where D2 = LMC. Each firm produces Q2 quantity.

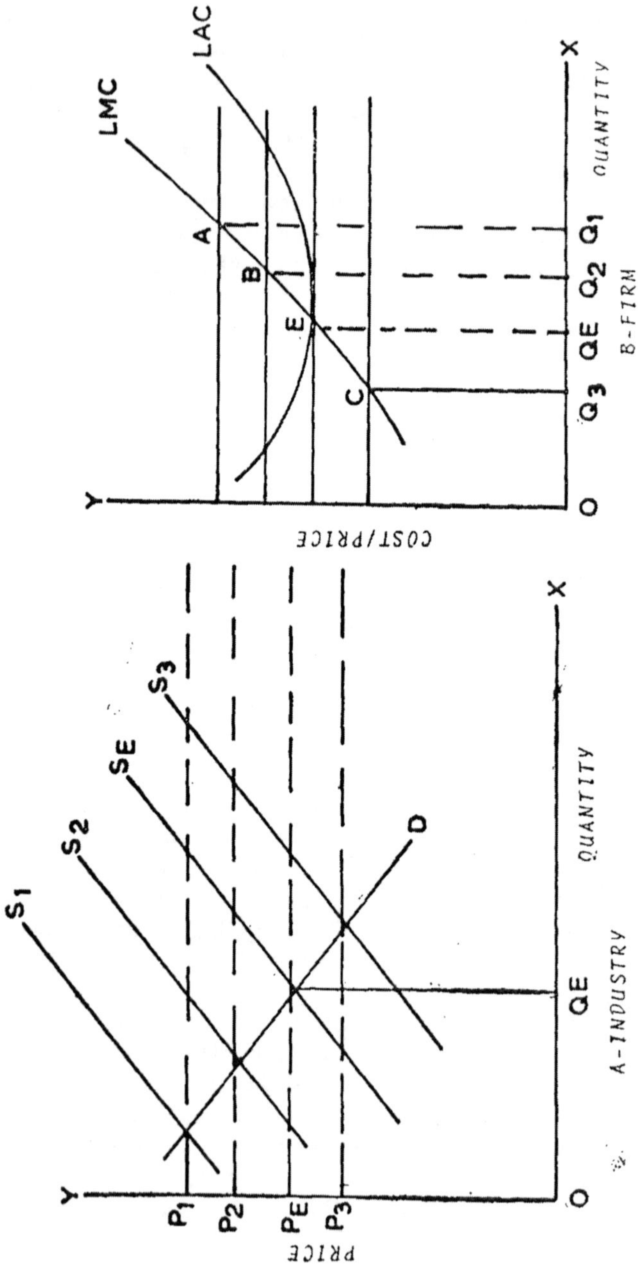

Figure 4.6 Competitive Equilibrium—Long—run.

of output in order to maximise profit. But the Point B is not stable. Suppose that a fairly large number of firms enter the industry shifting the supply curve to S3 and market equilibrium price to P3. D3 becomes the demand curve and Point C the temporary equilibrium where price equals marginal cost. Now the situation is reversed. Each firm is incurring losses. This a signal to leave the industry. Hence firms will leave the industry till long-run equilibrium is attained. The Point E is the long-run equilibrium position and each firm produces QE quantity output and sells at price PE.

We may note the long-run equilibrium theorem thus : In pure competition, the firms attain long-run equilibrium at the point where market price is equal to minimum average cost.

PRICING UNDER MONOPOLY

We now turn to the other end of the market spectrum where competition doesnot exist. In vivid contrast to pure competition, it is one is which all market power is concentrated in one source. It is usually referred to as pure monopoly.

Pure monopoly is defined as a market situation in which there is only one seller of a product for which there are no close substitutes. The monopolist has no competitors but has the market all to himself.

Monopoly is common in public utilities. Electricity supply, post and telegraph, railways are the possible examples. There are no good substitutes for telephone service nor are there competing companies to provide us electricity or railway transport. There are markets which are not lending itself well to competition.

Short-run Equilibrium under Monopoly

Short-run equilibrium for a monopolist is attained when profi is maximised or loss is minimised. Monopolists, unlike purely competitive firms, are not price-takers but price makers. The monopolist can alter the market price and quantity of output he sells according to his whims. Since the monopolist faces the entire market demand if he wants to expand his volume of sales, he must lower his price. Marginal revenue thus lies below price and his demand is not infinitely elastic but is downward sloping.

Let us state a brief comparison between the monopolist and

the pure competitor before we analyse the monopoly case in detail. A producer in a purely competitive industry takes the market equilibrium price as given. He merely adjusts his quantity of output until marginal cost equals the equilibrium price. The monopolist, on the other hand, has a slightly more complicated problem. Since he faces the entire market demand, he cannot merely adjust for a given price. He therefore, must pay attention to both output and price changes.

We may now turn to the monopolist's problem with an example consider Table 4.3 given below. The first-two columns give the market demand situations. The 3rd column shows the monopolist's potential total revenue and 4th column gives his marginal revenue. Columns 5, 6 and 7 give the monopolist's cost situations, total cost, average cost and marginal cost respectively. Finally the last column shows the net profit or loss that would result from each level of sales. It is seen from the Table 4.3 that the monopolist earns maximum profit by producing and selling 700 units for Rs. 4.75 per unit. At this point his total profit is Rs. 350. The various columns of Table 4.3 are plotted on Figures 4.7 and 4.8. The

TABLE 4.3

Short-run Cost and Revenue for a Monopolist Firm

Qty. sold	*Price* Rs.	*TR* Rs.	*MR* Rs.	*TC* Rs.	*AC* Rs.	*MC* Rs.	*Profit loss* Rs.
1	2	3	4	5	6	7	8
0	0	0	0	1500	0	0	1500
100	6.25	625	625	1700	17.00	2.00	-1075
200	6.00	1200	575	1875	9.38	1.75	- 675
300	5.75	1725	525	2025	6.75	1.50	- 300
400	5.50	2200	475	2200	5.50	1.75	0
500	5.25	2625	425	2400	4.80	2.00	225
600	5.00	3000	375	2650	4.42	2.50	250
700	4.75	3325	325	2975	4.25	3.25	350
800	4.50	3600	275	3400	4.25	4.25	200
900	4.25	3825	225	3950	4.39	5.50	- 125
1000	4.00	4000	175	4650	4.65	7.00	- 650

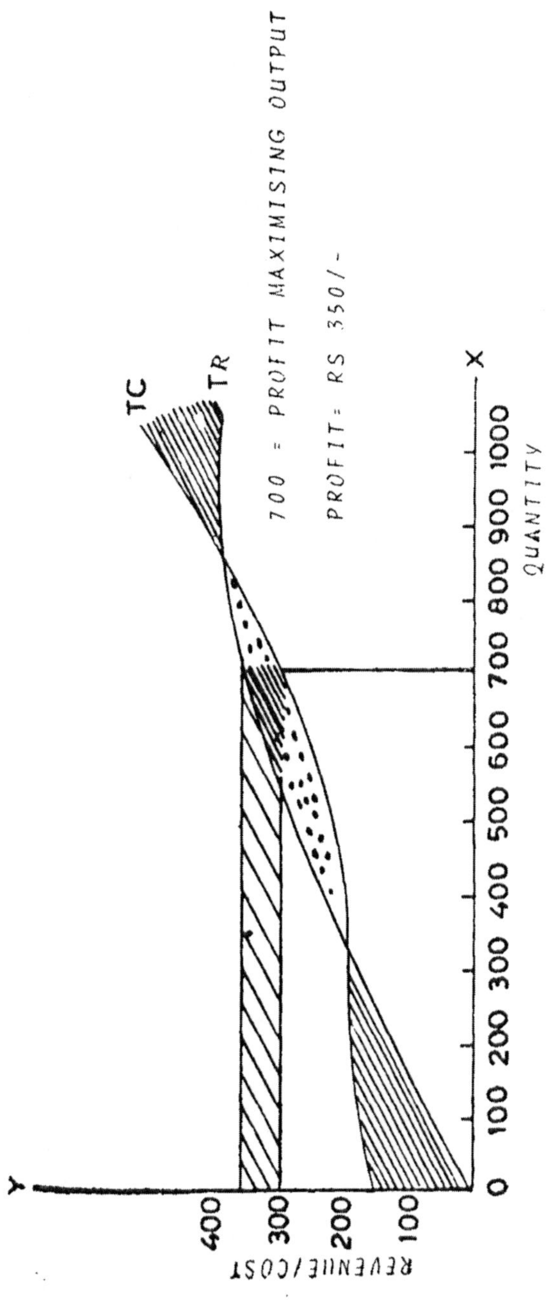

Figure 4.7 Total Revenue and Tolal Cost Under Monopoly.

total cost of operation from column 5 is plotted and labelled TC. Similarly total revenue from column 3 is labelled TR. The greatest distance between TR and TC curves implies the maximum profit and the profit maximising output is seen as 700 units.

Though the total revenue—total cost analysis is helpful, the marginal analysis approach is embodied here, look at Figure 4.8. Demand and marginal revenue curves are plotted on this graph along with AC and MC curves. In terms of the figure we may note that at output 700, total cost is the area of rectangle OQAC. Total revenue is similarly given by the area rectangle OQBP. Finally subtracting total cost rectangle OQAC from the total revenue rectangle OQBP, the profit rectangle CABP is obtained.

In the short-run, thus, the pure monopolist maximises profit or minimises loss by producing that quantity of output for which marginal cost equals marginal revenue.

Long-run Equilibrium for a Monopolist

The monopolist, like the purely competitive firm, will make some adjustments in the long-run. The long-run adjustment process of a single plant monopolist is discussed with the help of Figure 4.9.

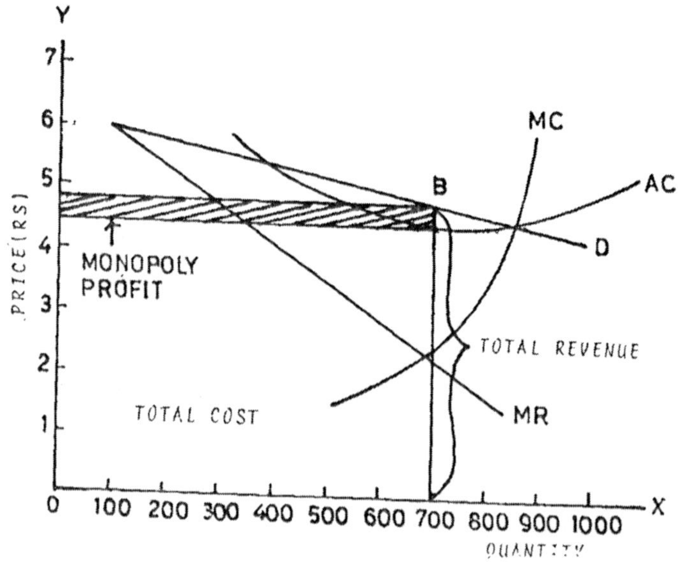

Figure 4.8. Short-run Equilibrium under Monopoly.

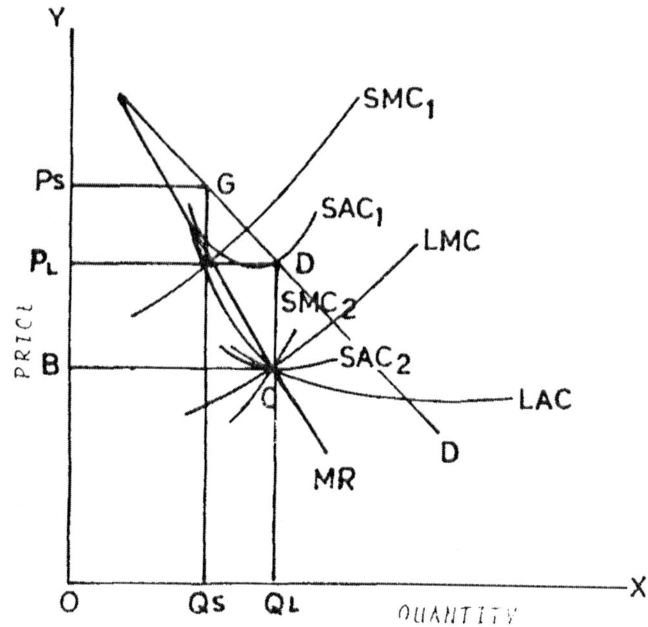

Figure 4.9 Long-run Equilibrium for a single Plant Monopoly.

In the Figure 4.9 D and MR are the monopolist's demand and marginal revenue curves while SAC[1] SMC[1] are the short-run average and short-run marginal cost curves, respectively. Suppose the monopolist begins operation with the plant presented by these short-run cost curves. Equilibriating short-run MC with MR, the monopolist maximises profit by producing OQs units selling them for OPs price.

In the long-run there may be other prospects. The curve LAC represents the long-run average cost while the curve LMC is the long-run marginal cost. As per the rule, monopolist will equilibriate the LMC with MR at profit maximising output OQL.

Given the demand curve, the equilibrium price falls to OPL. In this position of long run equilibrium, price is less and output is greater. Profit is also greater as seen by the rectangle BCDPl.

PRICE DISCRIMINATION

Price discrimination is generally seen in a market where the sellers are monopolists or oligopolists. Price discrimination means the practice of charging different prices for different units of a product or from different buyers. When a firm charges two or more prices for the same thing at the same time, it is called price discrimination. In the words of Mrs. Joan Robinson, "the act of selling the same article, produced under single control at different prices to different buyers is known as price discrimination."[2] It is only possible when a firm sells the commodities in different markets in such a way that it is unable to transfer any unit of the commodity from the cheap market to the dearer market. Price discrimination is possible only when two or more markets are kept separate. That is, price discrimination is not possible under perfect competition and is done only when there are market imperfections.

Price discrimination is an extension of monopoly pricing.[3] A monopolist with a sloping demand curve always prices independently. Price discrimination implies that the differences in the price independently. Price discrimination implies that the differences in the prices of things are greater than the differences in their cost of production. Prof. Stigler considers price discrimination as "the sales of technically similar products at prices which are not proportional to marginal costs."[4]

Forms of Price Discrimination

Price discrimination is seen in many forms and guises. Firstly, there is *personal* Price discrimination, which is based on customer's income and wealth. When a seller charges different prices from different customers on the basis of incomes, it is called personal price discrimination. Doctors, for example, charges different rates from different customers so also the lawyers.

Secondly, there is price discrimination *according to the nature of products*. Different charges are fixed for different varieties of the same product. Relatively lower prices are offered, for example, for the paper back editions than the deluxe editions of the same book. Unbranded produces are sold at lower prices than the branded ones.

Thirdly, in certain cases, price discrimination is also done *on the basis of age, sex and status of the customers*. Hair cut charges are comparatively less for children. Ladies at certain cinema stalls are admitted at lower charges.

Again, price discrimination *based on locality* implies that charging different prices from people of different regions or localities.

Fifthly, price dicrimination is also made on the basis of the use of the product. *Price discrimination according to the use* of the products means that charging different prices on the same commodity for different uses. Electricity is usually supplied at lower rates for industrial purposes than that for domestic purposes.

The principal forms of price discrimination are listed in the following Table 4.4.

Pre-Conditions for Price Discrimination

Existence of separate markets and differences in elasticities of demand between markets are the necessary pre-conditions for the price-discrimination. A possible example is the monopoly that sells at a low price in the foreign market and at a high price in the domestic market. The two markets are kept separate by tariff wall. The domestic buyers can hardly purchase commodity from abroad at a lower price due to import restrictions. Since the demand is more elastic in the foreign market due to competition from similar products

TABLE 4.4

Principal Forms of Price Discrimination

Classes	*Bases of Discrimination*	*Example*
Personal	Income of Customers	Physician's fees
Group	Age, sex and status of customers	Children's haircut charges. Entrance for ladies at low rates for cinemas, lower Admission charges for military personnel.
	Location of buyers	Zone prices, lower export prices.
	Use of products	Rail charges, Electricity charges.
Product	Nature of products	High price for deluxe edition, low prices for paper back.

the price is comparatively low. The domestic market lacks such competition.

Market imperfections form another pre-requisite of price-discrimination. If there is some degree of market imperfections the monopolist can pursue some sort of price discrimination. The monopoly seller can divide and the monopoly seller can divide and keep his market separate only if it is imperfect. The buyers do not move readily from one market to the other because of lack of informations or ignorance.

Degrees of Discrimination

How far a monopolist can go incharging different prices for his product is explained in the concept of degrees of price discrimination, the expression of which is employed by A.C. Pigou, who has developed the three kinds of price-discrimination viz., price-discrimination of First Degree, Second Degree and the Third Degree.

Price Discrimination of the First Degree

The limit of the increase of the net profit of the seller is explained in the concept of the First Degree Price Discrimination. In this form of price discrimination, the monopolist sets his prices for his products in such a way that no consumers' surplus would be available to the customers. Mrs. Joan Robinson calls the phenomenon 'the perfect price discrimination.' Price discrimination of the First Degree means the act of selling each separate unit of the product at a different price. This form of price discrimination is said to exist when every buyer is forced to pay the price which is equal to the maximum amount he is willing to pay rather than go without it. It implies that each consumer is exploited to the maximum possible extent in the interest of the seller's profits. When the consumer is paying the maximum amount he is willing to pay, he could enjoy no consumers' surplus. That is, the seller, instead of setting a few market prices to each unit of the products, makes a separate bargain with each buyer.

We may explain the above concept with the help of the following Table 4.5 and Figure 4.10.

TABLE 4.5

Price of Oranges (Rs. per doz.)	*Quantity demanded (Oranges-doz.)*
1	10
2	9
3	8
4	7
5	6
6	5
7	4
8	3
9	2
10	1

Figure 4.10 represents demand schedule of a consumer for a product, say, oranges. The Figure shows that at Re 1, per dozen, the consumer will buy 10 dozens of oranges, at Rs. 2, quantity purchased would be 9 doz, at price Rs. 3 he would like to buy 8 doz. Under simple monopoly pricing the monopolist's setting the market price is influenced by the relation between marginal cost and marginal revenue. It, for example, under simple monopoly, the seller set the price at Rs. 6 the buyer would take 5 doz. and will pay Rs. 30 as the price of Oranges. The consumer is, therefore, enjoying consumer's surplus of total value of Rs. 10, for the buyer is willing to pay Rs. 10 for 1 doz, Rs. 9 for 2 doz., Rs. 8 for 3 doz., Rs. 7 for 4 doz and Rs. 6 for 5 doz. In sum, he was preparing to pay Rs. 40 (= Rs. 10+9+8+7+6) for the units of

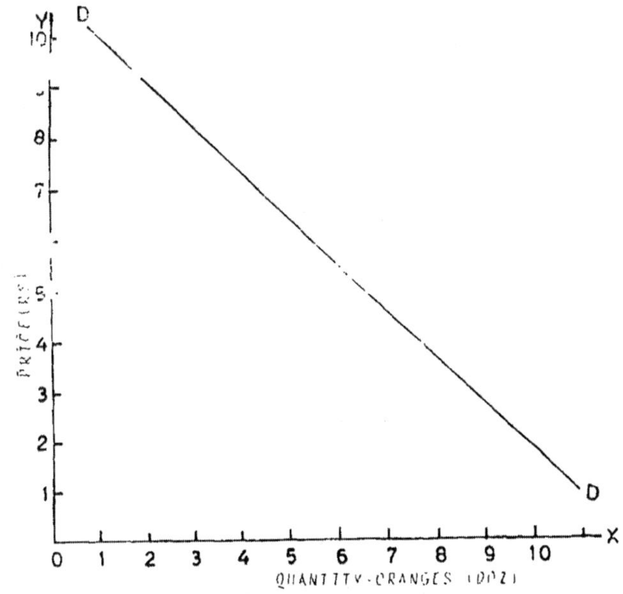

Figure 4.10 First Degree Price Discrimination.

the products rather than go without them. Now the discriminating monopolist can extract all the surplus which the consumer is getting and foreing him to pay the maximum amount. Thus the discriminating monopolist, in the First Degree, will charge Rs. 40 for the 5 doz. which is the highest price that a consumer can pay.

Price Discrimination of the Second Degree

In the Second Degree Price Discrimination, the customers are divided into separate groups and from each group, a different price is charged. This form of price discrimination is possible when each individual consumer had a perfectly inelastic demand for the goods. The monopolist extracts parts of buyer's consumer supluses, but not all of them. Electricity Supply Authority, for example, charges different rates for different slabs. The Figure 4.11 is self explanatory. The curve DD represents the demand of households for electricity. The price schedule shows that high price is charged for the first slab. At the price P_1 (in Figure) the total consumption is OA kwh (1 slab). For the II slab the price is fixed at P_2 at which AB kwh is consumed. Similarly at price P3, BC kwh is consumed. Rate schedules are usually have more than three slabs which are inequal in size.

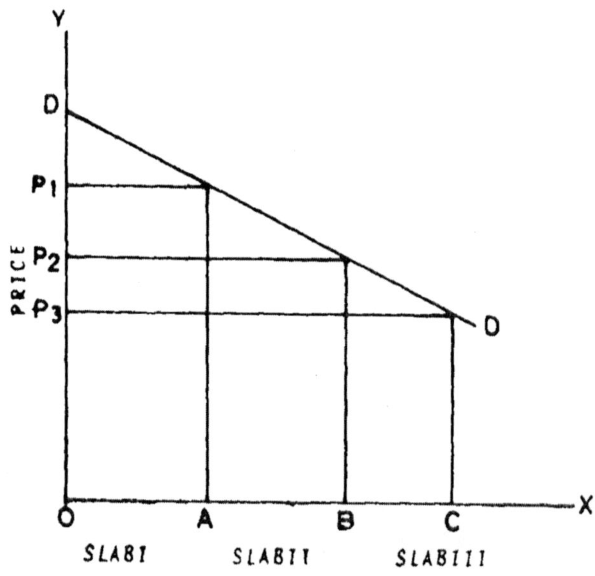

Figure 4.11 Second Degree Price Discrimination.

If the monopolist—the hypothetical electricity supply authority were allowed to charge only one price, and if it sold the among OC at price P3 his total revenue would be the rectangle given by P30 × OC. But with the prices the total revenue is the sum of three rectangles P 30 × OC, P 20 X OB and P 10 × OA. The monopolist in this way snatches parts of consumer's surplus.

Price Discrimination of the Third Degree

When a monopolist divides his customers into two or more

classes or groups, charging different prices to each class or group, it is called Third Degree Price Discrimination. Each class is invariably a separate market. Different rates fixed for different seats in a Cinema Hall are the possible examples. The seats in a Cinema hall are divided as 'Reserved', 'First Class', 'Second Class' and Third Class'.

We may illustrate this common kind of price discrimination by taking the monopolist who sells his products in two separate markets. When he sells in two separate markets, he could adjust the amounts in such a way as to make the marginal revenues equal. That is, the last units sold in each market added the same amount to the total revenue. The monopolist will quantify the amount to be sold in two markets according to the elasticities of demand for the product in each market. If the demand is more elastic, he will sell smaller amount than that in the market where there is inelastic demand.

The Third Degree Price Discrimination is illustrated with the help of the following diagram. In Figure 4.12 there are two markets Market I and Market II for the monopolist with demands D 1 and D 2. The demand in Market I is smaller and more elastic than the demand in Market II. The MR 1 and MR 2 are respective marginal revenue curves. Since the same product is sold in two markets one marginal cost curve is suffice.

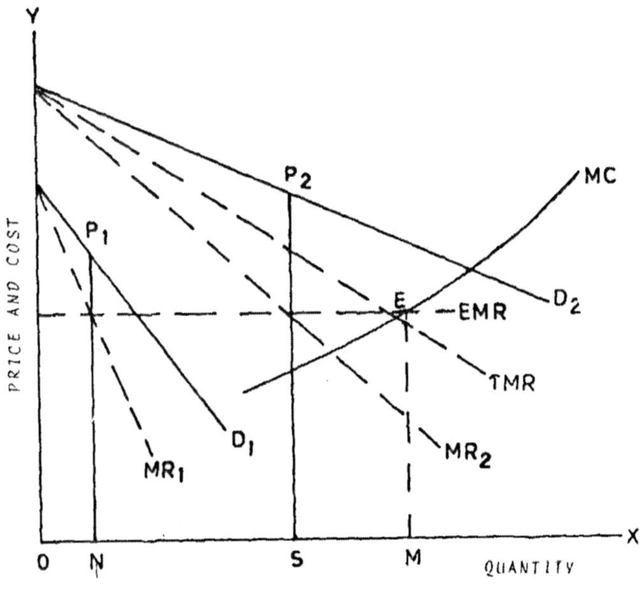

Figure 4.12 Third Degree Price Discrimination.

Knowing the demands in two markets, the monopolist calculates marginal revenue in each and adds them. In Figure the total marginal revenue curve, TMR is the horizontal summation of two separate marginal revenue curves, MR1 and MR2. The TMR and MC curve intersect at Point E which shows the total output, OM. The line EMR is the line of equal marginal revenue. It then shows that ON amount of goods is sold in market I at price P1 and that OS amount is sold in Market II at price P2. The amount ON and OS equal the total amount OM. Both MR1 and MR2 equal EMR which equals the marginal cost of OM.

Dumping—A Special Form of Price Discrimination

Dumping is said to exist when a monopolist is selling in two markets, one a protected home market in which he is the sole monopolist and the other a foreign market he faces perfect competition. Usually the monopolist sells a portion of his output in a foreign market at a low price and the other part of his output in the home market at a high price by which he can enjoy maximum profit. In this form of discrimination, the output is determined by the equality of the total marginal revenue curve and the total marginal cost curve of producing the product. The demand curve for the product in the foreign market is perfectly elastic since the market is under per fect competition, and the demand curve for the product in the domestic market, where he is the monopolist, is downward sloping. Figure 4.13 illustrates the price-output determination under "dumping".

The demand curve for the product in the foreign market is the horizontal straight line DF which is also the MR curve. The demand curve for the product in the home market is a downward sloping one and is represented by DH. The corresponding marginal revenue curve is MRH. The latteral summation of the two marginal revenue curves is ABTDF which is the combined marginal revenue curve. In oder to determine the quantum of output to be produced by the monopolist we take the marginal cost curve MC. At Point T the marginal cost curve equals the combined marginal revenue curve ABTDF. The monopolist will produce ON output for sales in two markets. TN being the marginal cost, equilibrium in the home market is determined at Point B, where MC equals MR and OM amount will be sold in the home market at price OPH and the remaining quantity MN is to be sold in the foreign market at a comparatively low price OPF. Thus, the firm will sell more in the foreign market at a low price and less in the domestic market at a high price.

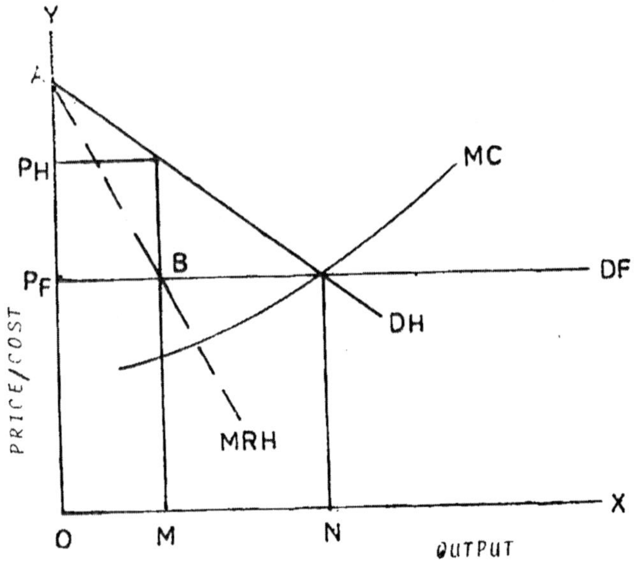

Figure 4.13 Dumping

MONOPSONY

Monopsony is a market situation where there is a single buyer. It implies a monopoly element in buying. In monopsony, the single buyer or purchasing agency purchases the whole amount of a commodity or service. It is important to note that when monopsony refers to a single buyer in the market, on the otherside, there may be a single seller, a few sellers or a large number of sellers. Monopsony may be formed when all the consumers are against together or when a person likes a particular commodity which no one else requires.

The analysis of monopsony pricing is identical with the monopoly pricing. Just as the monopolist's aim is to maximise profits, the monopsonist's aim is to maximise consumer's surplus. Just as the monopolist could influence the supply price of the product by the quantum of supply, the monopsonist tries to influence the supply price of his purchases by the amount he buys. In order to get maximum profiit, the monopolist equates marginal cost with marginal revenue, whereas the monopsonist, to get maximum profits, equates his marginal cost with marginal utility. This is illustrated with the help of Figure 4.14. The demand for the product for the monopsonist is represented by demand curve D/Mu which is also the marginal utility curve. The curve S/AC is the supply curve of the product which is same as average cost to the monopsonist. At Point R, the marginal cost is equivalent to marginal utility. The monopsonist buys OM amount of the produce and the price is set as OP. As per the figure, the total expenditure incurred for the monopsonist is given by the area OMP1P, but the total amount that he is willing to pay is given by the area OARM. The consumer's surplus is therefore, given by the area OARM-OPP1M=ARP1P.

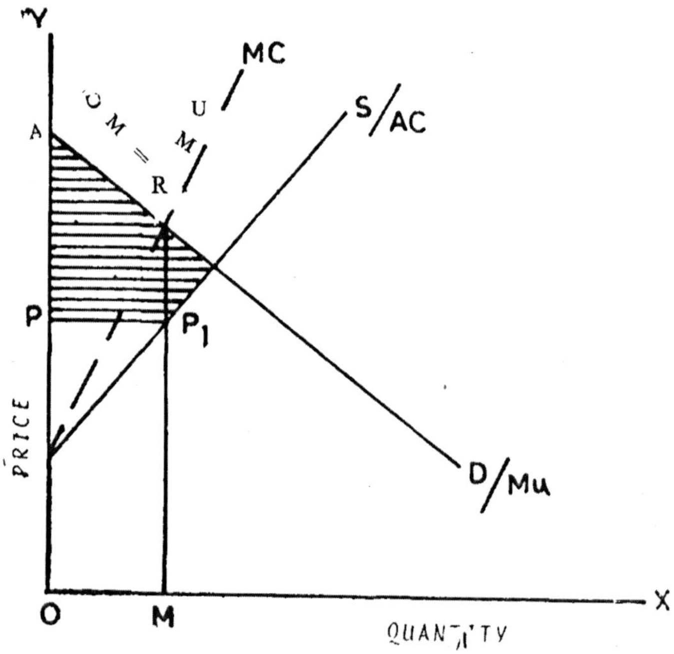

Figure 4.14 Monopsony.

Bilateral Monopoly

Bilateral monopoly refers to a market situation in which a monopolist faces a monopsonist. There is only a single seller to sell the commodity and a single buyer to purchase the same. A possible example of bilateral monopoly is a sugar factory, in an isolated region, offering employment for labour and with a trade union controlling the entire labour supply. The trade union that controls the supply of labour is the monopoly and the sugar factory which is the sole buyer of labour service is the monopsony.

The bilateral monopoly has two dimensional problems. The first relates to *isolated exchange between* two individuals. The problem of pricing under this form of bilateral monopoly is an insoluble one. As Edgeworth points out, "price formation in the case of isolated exchange is essentially an indeterminate problem, which is not soluble because there is an undecidable opposition of interests as each aims at the maximisation of his money gain."

The second problem refers to the case of a single seller selling raw materials to a single buyer who is also a monopolist in selling the final products. The pricing under this kind of bilateral monopoly is illustrated with the help of Figure 4.15.

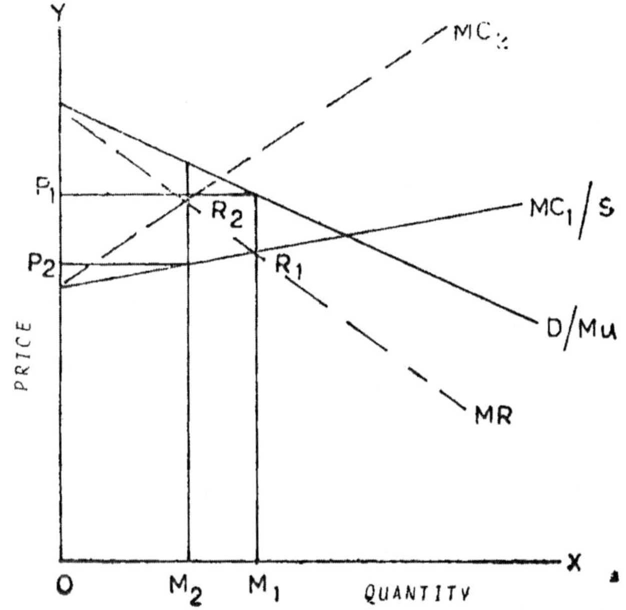

4.15. Bilateral Monopoly.

Suppose, we assume that the monopoly seller is a Bamboo Corporation, the only one in the locality, which is selling bamboos to the lone Rayons Factory in the region, which is in a position of the monopsony. The demand for bamboos comes from the Rayons factory and is based on marginal utility of bamboos to them. In

Figure 4.15 the demand curve D/Mu is given, The monopolist, the Bamboo corporation, calulates the marginal revenue for its product. Then it wants to deccide how much bamboos to sell and at what price. This will depend up on the monopoly seller's marginal cost of production. The marginal cost of production of bamboos to the monopoly seller is given by the curve MC1 in the figure. The equality of MC1 and MR are shown by the Point R1 and the monopolist will like to produce OM1 quantity of bamboos and will sell at the price OP1 at which the monopolist will maximise his profits.

Let us now examine the position of the monopsonist of bamboos viz., the Rayons Factory. The demand of this firm is represented by D/MU curve. It is assumed that at higher and higher prices of bamboos the monopsonis will get more and more bamboos, for at higher price more bamboos are supplied. MC1 is also the supply Curve of the product. When supply is more at higher prices, the monopsonist will calulate his marginal cost of production which is represented by the curve MC2. The monopsony buyer will like to buy that amount and at that price at which marginal cost (MC2) is equal to its marginal utility (D/Mu). This equility is drawn by the Point R2. The monopsonist will therefore, buy OM2 amount of bamboos but at price of OP2.

We may note an interesting situation here that the monopoly seller likes to sell OM1 quantity of bamboos while the monopsony buyer will like to buy only OM2 amount of it. In the meanwhile, the monopolist is willing to sell at the price of OP1 while the monopsonist will be willing to offer the price of OP2. There is, thus, an indeterminateness in pricing under bilateral monopoly and no theoretical conclusion has been made on this problem. The price may likely to be formed in between OP1 and OP2.

MONOPOLISTIC COMPETITION

Pure competition and pure monopoly are two extremities that seldom exist in the real world. What we observe in the real world are industries that are more or less competitive, that have fairly large or fairly small number of firms, and that produce more or less similar products. Consequently, the types of business with which we are familar are not likely to fit conveniently into the format of either pure competition or pure monopoly. For this reason, the present discussion is devoted to intermediate type of market called monopolistic competition.

Monopolistic competition is a market situation where there are substantial number of firms, each producing similar but not identical products.

We have seen that product homogeneity is a pre-requisite for pure competition. Unless the producers sell identical products, the consumer can identify a particular product that he prefers to buy. The consumer may, then, develop a preference for one variety over others, thus making competition imperfect. When products are closely related but not identical, we say that there is product heterogeneity or product differentiation.

Products may be differentiated in a variety of ways. There may be real quality differences among related goods. Technical differences and appearance may also make products heterogeneous. Some products are differentiated exclusively by advertising. Product heterogeneity leads to quality competition in general which is likely to stimulate improvements in products over time.

Prof. E.H. Chamberlin of Harvard University has made a valuable contribution to the theory of Monopolistic competion[5] though a related approach was also developed simultaneously by Mrs. Joan Robinson in 'Economics of Imperfect Competition'.

We may repeat the definition of monopolistic competition as a market situation in which there are many sellers of a product, and although all sell the same general type of product, that of each seller is in some way differentiated from that of others.[6]

The retail and service industries in cities are the best examples of monopolistic competition. There may be many grocery stores selling many brands of each of a wide variety of products. Each store has its group of steady customers who like its convenience, its special kinds of service, its credit arrangements or other features. Each one has also a fringe group of customers who are just on the verge of trading elsewhere. Since there are many number of stores in the city, most of the customers are not affected if one store goes out of business or if a new store is established. The same general situation is true of restaurants, coolbars, medical service establishments and others.

Price-Output Determination under Monopolistic Competition

To analyse the price-output determination under monopolistic competition, let us begin with demand. In our discussion of pure competition and monopoly, the firm's demand occasioned no particular difficulty. In monopoly the firm and industry are one and the same. Thus, the industry's market demand curve form the firm's also. Under pure competition, there is a market demand curve for the homogeneous products produced by the industry. Each firm is so small relative to the industry that it regards market price as given. Hence. the individual demand curve of each firm is infinitely elastic.

In the case of a monopolistic competition, the members of a group of producers do not produce homogeneous products so that there is no market demand curve. However, there is presumably a general demand for the particular items of goods produced by the group. Each firm has a market demand curve. Since there are many competitors producing closely related goods, the demand for the product of any one firm depends upon the price and output of others.

Le us see the nature of demand curve facing a single firm in monopolistic competition. We may conveniently start with the demand curve facing a purely competitive firm. Since, the primary difference between the two kinds of market is product differentiation, it is our main task to examine the effects of this factor.

Look at Figure 4.16. Suppose we start with DD, a hypothetical demand curve facing a purely competitive firm. Consider now the impact of product differentiation on it.

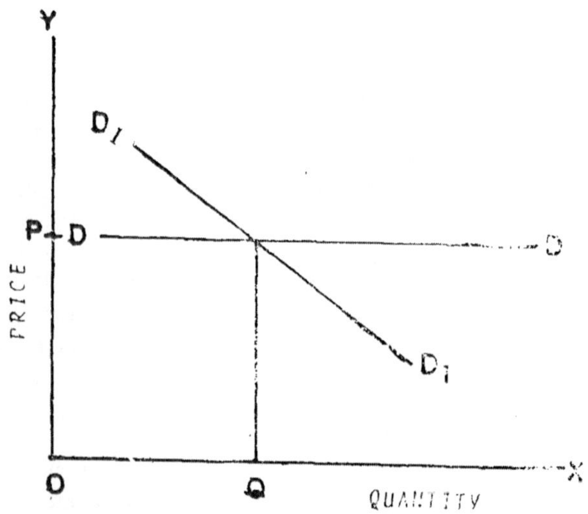

Figure 4.16. Demand Curved under Product Differentiation

Where product differentiation occurs, different customers tend to develop preferences for the kind or brand of goods sold by particular sellers. Some customers have stronger preference than others for a particular firm's product or service still, under monopolistic competition, the products sold by different sellers are good substitutes for one another and at any given time any one seller will have fringe customers just on the verge of trading elsewhere.

Suppose a firm is selling quantity at price P and that product differentiation occurs between the products sold by this firm and others. If there is a slight increase in price, fringe customers find the products sold by other firms more attractive because of thier relative lower price. They desert the firm and sales fall off rapidly product differentiation, thus, tips the demand curve from the horizontal DD curve to the downward stopping D1D1.

Short-run Equilibrium under Monopolistic Competition

The monopoly element of monopolistic competition comes to the fore front when we consider the short run equilibrium adjustment of the firm. Each entrepreneur attempts to maximise profit. As we have already learned the firm mixmises profit when it produces that quantity for which MC and MR are equal.

The process of short-run equilibrium analysis is shown in Figure 4.17. Since the firm faces a downward slopping demand curve DD, the marginal revenue curve MR lies below it. SMC and SAC are short-run marginal cost curve and short-run average cost curve respectively. By producing and selling OQ quantity at a price of OP per unit the firm maximises profit. At this point average cost is C per unit and profit is equal to the shaded rectangle PABC.

Long-run Equilibrium under Monopolistic Competition

The long-run equilibrium adjustments in monopolistic competition are basically as they are in pure competition. As such, important competitive assumptions underlying monopolistic competition may be specified.

First, members of the product group are so numberous that each feels that his actions will have little effect upon his rivals.

Second, there is active price competition among the members of the group. Each firm may attempt to gain customers and sales by bidding down prices.

Third, free and easy entry into and exit from the product group. If profits occur in an industry, new firms will have an

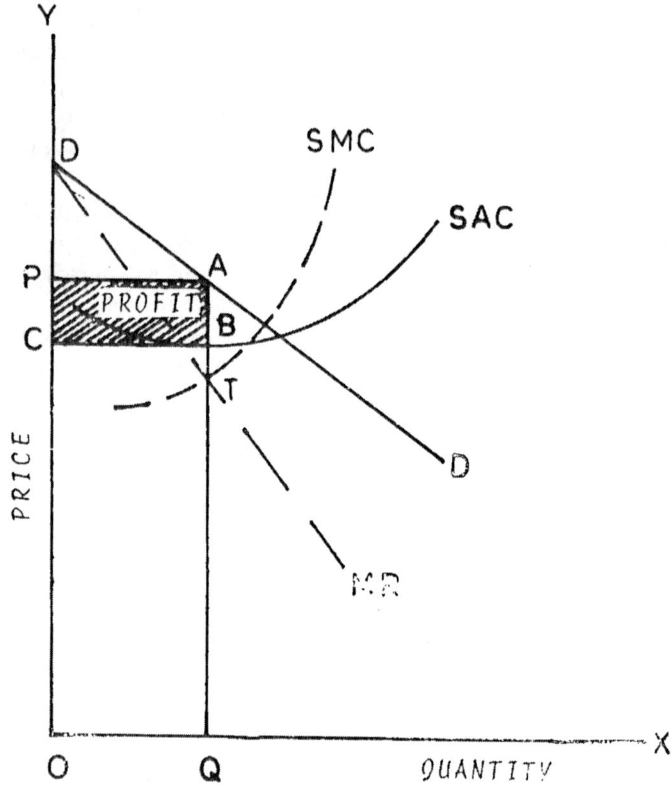

Figure 4.17 Short Run Equilibrium Under Monopolistic Competition.

incentive to enter, and if losses are incurred firms are pressured into leaving.

In Figure 4.18 the firm with demand curve DD and marginal revenue curve MR maximises profit by producing OQ amount of goods X for which LMC is equal to MR. The profit is to the tune of shaded rectangle PABC. At this level new firms would enter as entrepreneurs seek higher return on their investment.

The entry of new firms will push down the profits. The productive capacity and the total output of industry are expanding. As a result the demand curve facing the individual firms shift downward. Finally, all the firms in the industry will reach a position like that of Figure 4.19. Long-run equilibrium for the industry will thus exist.

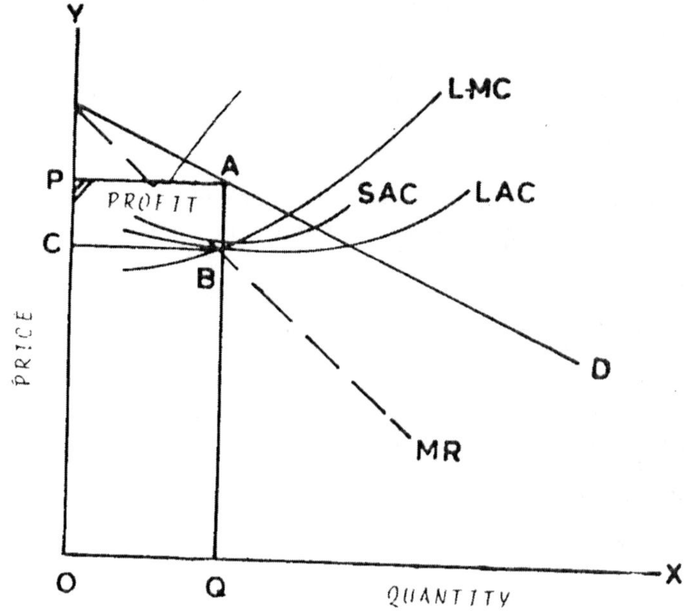

Figure 4.18 Profit Maximising Firm

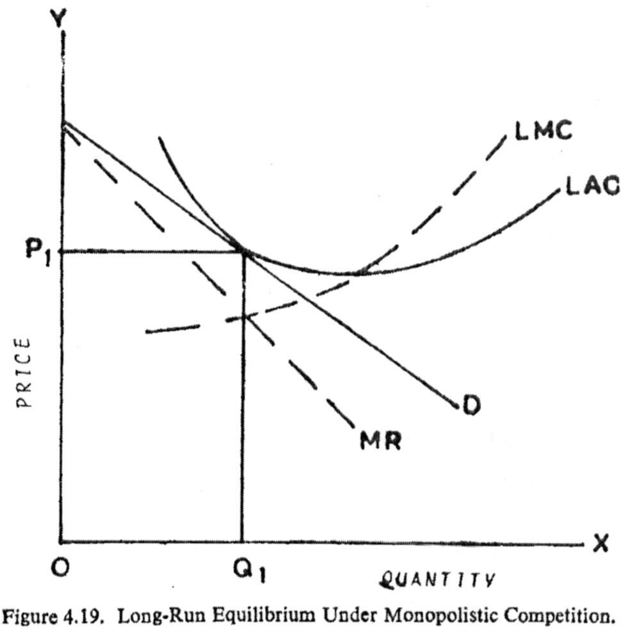

Figure 4.19. Long-Run Equilibrium Under Monopolistic Competition.

Long-run equilibrium under monopolistic competition attains when the number of firms in the group is such that no firm earns pure economic profit or sustains a pure economic loss. At this point, the firm's individual demand curve will be tangent to its long-run average cost curve.

Product Differentiation

We may know that the theory of monopolistic competition explains the price and output in market structures where sellers are many and each seller has a product differentiated from those of rivals. Products are differentiated by brands, trade marks, designs or by any other means.

Product heterogeneity shapes the demand for a firm's output. Figure 4.20 contains two demand curves d1d1 and d2d2. Except at very low prices, both the curves are elastic since both products are in close competition with other makes of the same thing. Demand curve d1d1, however, is much more elastic than demand curve d2d2. Product B is less strongly differentiated than product A.

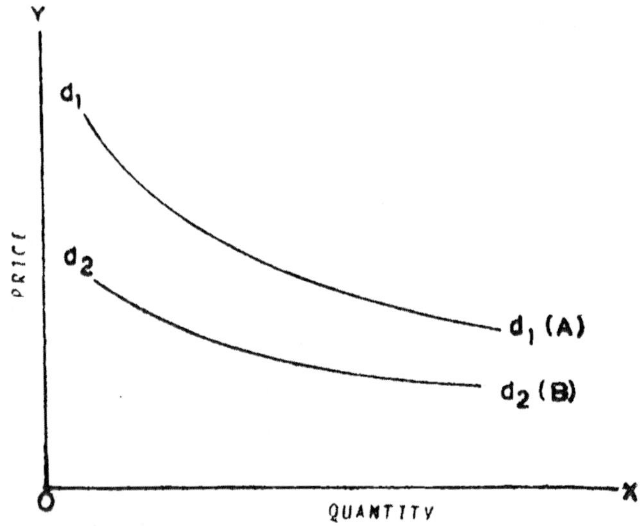

Figure 4.20 : Demand Curves Under Product Differentiation

Selling Costs

Selling costs are advertisement costs. They are incurred to increase the demand for a product. It includes not only advertising costs but also the cost of sales promotional activities. Selling costs are, infact, the costs of changing consumer's wants.

Let us study the effect of competitive advertising on sales of the firms under monopolistic competition. A firm seeks to increase its own sales by spending more on advertising. Sometimes the effect is to add to the sales of the firm's rivals.

A simple model of advertising competition as adopted from Chamberlin is appended here. Suppose, the firms in a group are in equilibrium. To begin with none of them does any advertising. Suppose, that one of them thinks that he can earn some profits by advertising and he does so.

Figure 4.21 shows what happens. The production cost curve of the firm is PC. The price is OP. The initial equilibrium output is OA. One of the firms draws up an advertising plan, shown by the curve SC1. If he is the only one to do so he would definitely increase his sales to the extent of OB1 which is an optimum output. But the firm does not achieve the desired output OB since his rivals follow suit and advertise their products. The sales of each firm increases only a little just as they do when all firms cut their prices. Now, all the firms are advertising with some amount. Thus, the new selling cost curve is SC2. Stable equilibrium comes only when all firms produce and sell the amount OC and have selling cost curves SC3.

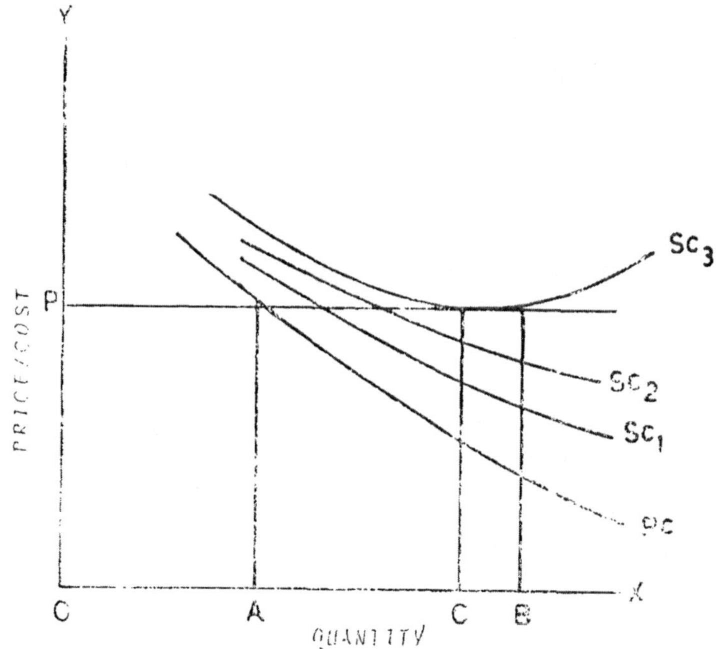

Figure 4.21 : Advertising Competition.

OLIGOPOLY

Oligopoly refers to a market situation in which there are few sellers. The prices and volumes of production of several products such as automobiles, electrical equipments, types, household utensiles are determined by the few firms in each of the industries that produce them. Oligopoly is, therefore, said to exist when there are two or few firms or sellers producing or selling a product. Products produced by the oligopolistic firms may be either homogeneous or differentiated. When products of few sellers are homogeneous it is called pure oligopoly. While the firms are producing differentiated products they are known as Imperfect Oligopoly.

The fewness of sellers is the basic characteristic of an oligopolistic market. Oligopoly is often referred to as 'Competition among few'. When the firms are a few, each produces a considerable portion of the total output of the industry. Each firm can have a noticeable influences on market situations. Each seller is aware of the price-moves of the rivals and the rival firm's price-output movements place an impact on his profit. There is, therefore, complete interdependence among the sellers.

The Theory : Group Behaviour

For the theories of perfect competition, of monopoly and of monopolistic competition we could have no problems of appropriate assumption of human behaviour. In perfect and monopolistic competitions the mass behaviour is handled with profit maximisation assumption. At the other extremes there exists the sole producer, the monopolist, whose main aim is also maximising profit.

The theory of oligopoly is a theory of group behaviour.[7] There can be two or more than two, but not too many firms as in a perfect or monopolistic competition. It is few and each one knows that anything he does will have some impact upon the group. Since the members of a group never agrees a common goal, there is no generally accepted theory of behaviour of a group. Even if they agree, an individual's goals never tie in with the common objectives. Groups have seldom a recognised organisation nor they have the recognised rules of conduct. Therefore, we may note that there is no unique pattern of pricing. Each firm wants to remain independent and to maximise profit. Towards this end, each acts and reacts on the price-output movements of the rivals under a continuous effect of uncertainty. All rival firms, therefore, enter into a tacit or formal agreement regarding price-output setting.

Pricing under Oligopoly

As already noted oligopoly is mainly of two types—Pure oligopoly where a few firms produce homogeneous product and imperfect oligopoly where few firms produce differentiated products. Imperfect oligopoly, also known as differentiated oligopoly, is a situation that lies in between pure oligopoly and monopolistic competition. Since pure oligopoly is only a theoretical concept and differentiated oligopoly is a real situation, we may now concentrate on differentiated oligopoly pricing under three major heads :

(i) Independent pricing,
(ii) Pricing under collusion, and
(iii) Pricing under Price leadership

1. Independent Pricing

Independent pricing relates to individual action of each oligopoly seller independent of others within the industry. The independent action of each seller stems from the mutual distrust among rivals. A seller who reduces his price to boost up his sales will always be looking on the price move of his rivals as a result of his price cut. Since each seller is tempted to raise his profit, there is the fear of the counter moves of rivals. This results in independent pricing.

Independent price setting on the part of sellers invariably leads to price wars. That is, when a firm resorts to price-cut to attract more customers so as to get more profits, the rival firm also follows the same. A retaliatory price cut would be the result. As a result of independent action of each individual seller price stability would be maintained in the long-run.

Let us now examine the problem of price-war and then how price rigidity is maintained. Price war is said to exist when one seller in order to maximise his sales, reduces price of his product and the rivals also try to follow him. The rival firm fearing a reduction in his sales as a result of former's price-cut retaliates and tries to under cut the other. This in turn unleashes a price-war throughout the oligopolistic industry till it reaches an equilibrium price which will remain stable over a long period of time.

Price rigidity refers to a situation of stable price level in oligopolistic market. Despite changes in cost or demand conditions, the oligopolistic sellers are hardly inclined to price changes.

Price rigidity occurs in oligopolistic markets for a number of reasons. First, price stability is preferred to the firms after the bitter experience of price wars. Second, oligopoly firms like to avoid unnecessary insecurity and uncertainty and are satisfied with the current prices output and sales. Third, oligopoly seller may prefer to maintain the present level of prices so as to obstruct the entering of new firms. Lastly, oligopolistic firms resort to advertisement campaigns rather than reducing prices to promote sales.

Kinked Demand Curve Analysis

The theoretical conclusion of price rigidity in oligopolistic markets can, very well, be explained with the help of the kinked demand curve analysis. In many of the oligopolistic industries, we may observe a considerable degree of price rigidity. Even if there is a change in the economic structure, the oligopolistic firms have no tendency to change the price. Many explanations have been given on the causes of price rigidity of the oligopolistic firms and the kinked demand curve hypothesis forms the most popular explanation which was formulated independently by the American economist Paul M. Sweezy[8] and the Cambridge economists Hall and Hitch.[9]

The kinked demand curve analysis hardly explains price determination under oligopoly but only examines how the price remains rigid or unchanged. The analysis is based on the following assumptions—

1. There is a prevailing market price for the product of the oligopolistic industry.
2. Each seller's attitude has an impact on his rivals.
3. Any seller's attempt to raise his sales by reducing prices will be retaliated by his rivals who follow the same.
4. If any seller tries to increase price, the others will not follow him and will stick to the prevailing price to attract more customers.
5. Changes in marginal cost do not necessarily affect price and output of the oligopolistic firms. Figure 4.22 shows a kinked demand curve DPd and P1 the prevailing price in the oligopoly marked for the amount of the product OM of one seller. The firms attempt to raise price above P1 will necessarily reduce his sales, for the other sellers are not expected to raise price. This is so because the DP segment of the kinked demand curve is elastic and the corresponding segment of the MR curve (DS) is positive. Therefore any price increase will adversely affect his total sales so also to his total revenue and profit. Consider the other way round. If the seller reduces the price of his product below P1 his rival firms will follow him and reduce prices. Since the Pd segment of the kinked demand curve is inelastic the volume of his sales will definitely be

increased, but his profit would be less than before. Thus, in both the cases of price-raising and price-cutting actions, the seller is a loser. He would, therefore, stick to the prevailing market price P1 which remains rigid or stable.

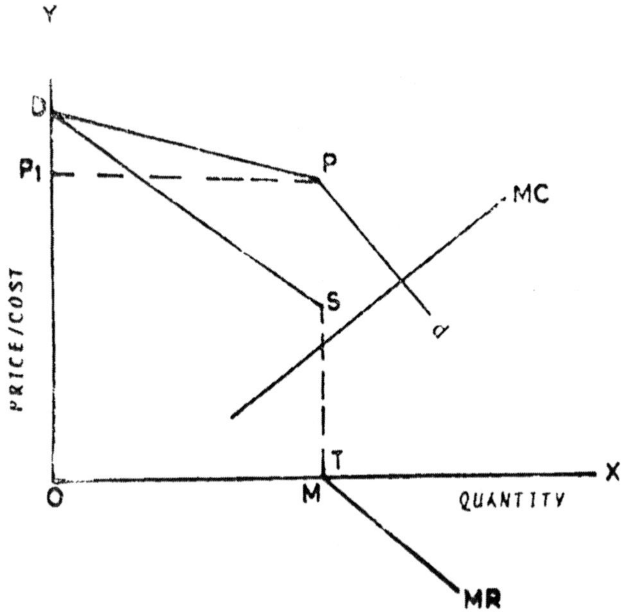

Figure 4.22: Kinded Demand Curve.

2. Pricing under Collusion

Collusion simply refers to the co-operation of rival firms. The firms are said to engage in collusion when competitors co-operate in pricing their products. Under collusive oligopoly, different oligopolisticfirms arrive at formal agreement on common policy to be pursued by them. When the firms reach a formal agreement it is referred to as cartel. A cartel is an organisation of independent firms within the same industry formed for the common benefit of its members. Common policies relating to price, output and sales are followed so as to increase joint profits of the organisation.

Cartel agreements may take various forms. An extreme form of cartel agreement is occured when the firms surrender all their rights to a central agency whose main functions consist of setting prices, determining output quotas and distributing profits. Such a form of formal collusion is commonly designated as 'perfect cartel,' which may set uniform or related prices for the products of member firms but are allowed to compete among themselves in relation to sales or sales promotion activities.

Under perfect collusion price-output determination of the industry and each of the member firms is done by the central administrative agency which aims at maximising joint profits of all the member firms. Since the entire industry is under a central control, the pricing under perfect collusion will be synonymous with monopoly pricing. Price and output will be determined in such a way as to get maximum joint profits and it is done by calculating the cartels' marginal cost and marginal revenue. Let us assume a cartel consists of two firms—Firm I and Firm II. Figure 4.23 illustrates the pricing under collusion. The industry's demand and marginal revenue are represented by D and MR curves. The curve ≷MC is cartel's marginal revenue curves of two rival firms. Since the aggregate marginal cost curves and the aggregate marginal revenue curves are equal at T, the cartel will naturally fix MP price and produce OM quantity at which cartel will realise maximum possible profits. Having decided the total output OM to be produced the cartel will allot output quota to be produced by each firm so that marginal cost of each firm is same. It is seen from the figure that when Firm I produces OM1 and Firm II produces OM2 amount of the products, the marginal cost of two firms are equal. Thus output quota of Firm I will be OM1 and of Firm II will be OM2. We may note that the total output OM will be equal to OM1+OM2.

The formation of perfect cartel as described above is quite rare in the real world. In the actual collusion, the firms are generally arrived at agreement only on the price front and the member firms are free to produce and sell their products in such a way as to maximise their individual profits. Each firm will therefore, earn profits according to the output produced and sold and the cost incurred on it. As per our diagram, the price fixed is the joint profit maximising-price which is determined at Point T, when MC equals MR. Now, each firm will maximise profit by producing that amount at which its own MC equals the collusive marginal revenue. As in perfect cartel, the Firm I produces OM1 and the Firm II OM2 for their individual marginal costs are equal to the collusive MR—at their output respectively. It is seen from the figure that Firm II will realise maximum profits since it produces and sells largest output.

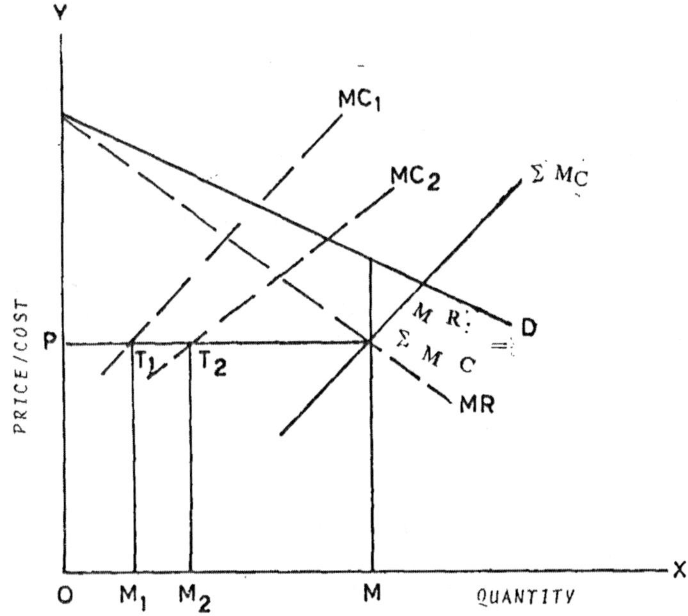

Figure 4.23 Collusive Oligopoly.

3. Price Leadership

Independent price setting is a rare phenomenon in oligopolistic markets. Some form of understanding or agreement among oligopoly firms usually exists in any kind of industry. There may be tacit or formal agreement among oligopolists. A formal agreement is usually refers to a written agreement among oligopolists to observe certain common rules of conduct regarding price, sales, or output determination. A tacit agreement, on the otherhand, refers to a form of understanding among themselves and pursues a uniform policy regarding price, output or sales. Price leadership is a form of tacit agreement among oligopolists. Price leadership does not involve any formal agreement and there is not a controlling agency to regulate or co-ordinate their activities.

Different types of price leadership which are generally found in oligopolistic markets are ;

1. Barometric Price Leadership

Barometric price leadership is said to exist when an old, experienced or a largest single firm assumes the role of a price setter. It announces the price changes from time to time and the other firms follow it.

2. Dominant Price Leadership

Dominant price leadership is one in which a largest firm in the industry dominates the market. There are other few firms which are so small and are unable to influence the market unlike the dominant firm. The dominant firm after estimating or calculating demand and cost conditions, independently set prices and the small firms follow the dominant one and accept the price set by it.

3. Aggressive Price Leadership

The third type of price leadership is exploitative or aggressive price leadership in which the largest or dominant firm establishes its leadership by pursuing aggressive policies and other firms are compelled to follow it regarding price policies.

Pricing Under price Leadership

Various models are developed in determining prices under price leadership. We may now examine a case of dominant price leadership to explain a simple theorem of pricing under price leadership. For the analytical purposes, the following assumptions may be made.

1. There are two firms producing homogeneous/identical products and hence consumers have no preference between them.
2. One of the firms has a lower cost of production than that of the other, say, Firm I has lower cost of production than Firm II.
3. Each firm influences market and has been assigned equal share in the market.

Pricing under price leadership is illustrated in Figure 4.24. DD is the market demand curve for the product and MR is the marginal revenue curve of each firm. MC1 is the marginal cost curve of Firm I and MC2 is the marginal cost curve of Firm II. MC1 lies below MC2 since we assume that Firm I has lower cost of production than Firm II.

The Firm I will be maximising profit by selling OM amount of output and setting price M1P1, as at output OM1 its marginal cost is equal to the marginal revenue. Firm II's profits will be maximum when it sets price MP2 and sells output OM2. It is seen from the figure that profit maximising price M1P1 of Firm I is lower than the profit maximising price M2P2 of Firm II. Since they are producing homogeneous products they cannot sell their products at different prices. Since the profit maximising price of Firm I is lower than that of Firm II, Firm I will dictate price to Firm II. The Firm II

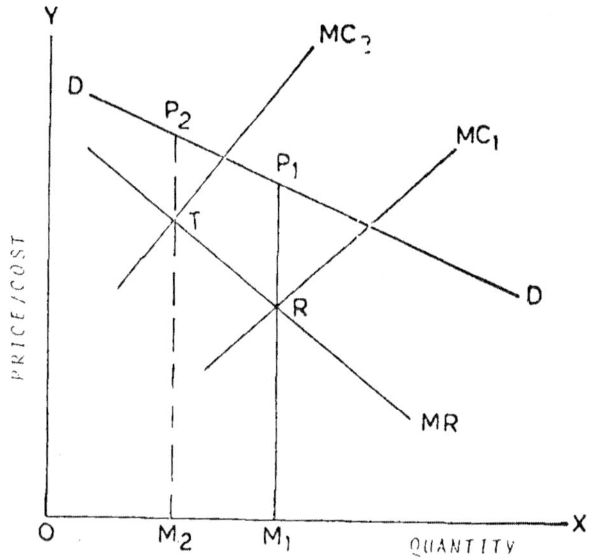

Figure 4.24 Price Leadership.

will, therefore, be forced to sell his products as the former does and the Firm I will emerge as the price leader.

Duopoly

Duopoly is a special form of oligopoly in which there are two sellers. Since it is a limiting form of oligopoly, more often duopoly and oligopoly are considered together. Both the sellers are absolutely independent and any agreement hardly exists between them. Though they are independent firms, any change in the price and output of one may affect the price and output of the other. As there are only two seller in a market, each seller is fully informed of his rival's policies. Any action benefiting one will be adversely affecting the other. Therefore, an action of one firm will have the reaction from the other. The problem of duopoly pricing was examined by the two prominent classical economists Cournout and Edgeworth. Let us consider each.

Cournout's Solution

The French economist Augustin Cournout discussed the problem of duopoly pricing and gave a solution in 1838. His explanation is based on the following assumptions :

1. There are two sellers producing and selling homogeneous products.
2. There are large number of buyers.
3. Each seller is fully informed of demand curve of the product.
4. The cost of production to each firm is assumed to be zero.
5. Each seller is ignorant about his rival's plan and policies.
6. Each seller takes the supply of his rival as constant, and
7. The aim of each seller is to obtain maximum possible net profit.

In order to explain Cournout's solution let us consider his classic example of mineral springs exploited by the two sellers A and B. They have no cost of production i.e., average costs and marginal costs are assumed to be zero. The demand for the mineral water is given by the curve DD1 in the Figure 4.25. The total daily output of mineral water is OD1, which is equally attributable to two sellers, so that OM=MD1. Since total cost is zero, marginal cost is also zero. Therefore, at OM output MC=MR-at zero price. Suppose, the two

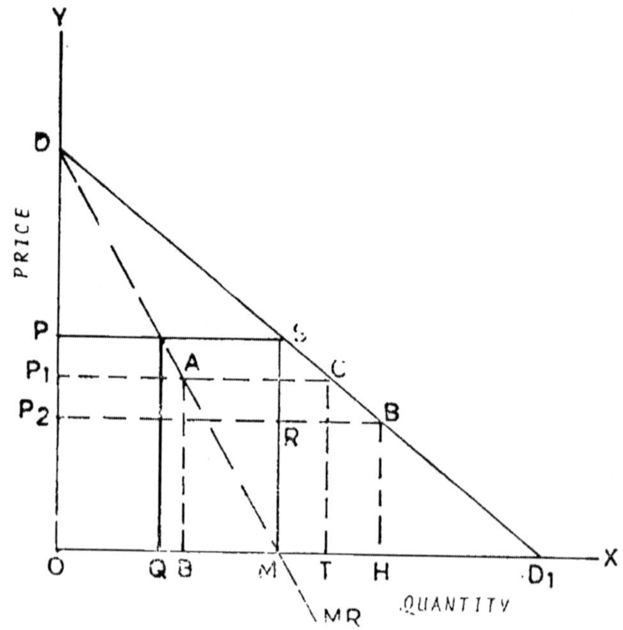

Figure 4.25 : Duopoly-Cournout's Solution.

producers combine, then they would supply OM amount at MS price and their joint profit will be formed by the area OMSP. But we assume that each seller is independent and there is no mutual dependency. Let the seller A be the first to produce and sell the amount OM at MS price and he earns the monopoly profit OMSP. Then Cournot solution begins. The seller B starts production and he knows that A will not change his volume of output from OM. B's demand curve is given as SD1. He produces MH amount of product. As the demand curve is SD1 its corresponding marginal revenue curve will pass through half way between MD1. When each seller sells his product at the ruling price, the total supply OH will be sold at HB price. Total profit, therefore, falls to OHBN of which OMRN is A's profit and MHBR is B's profit.

Now, in an attempt to restore profit, seller A reduces his supply to $\frac{1}{2}$ (OD1-MH). It will incite B to raise his output by $\frac{1}{2}$ (OD1-B's supply). This process will continue till both the firms are reaching at equilibrium at which each is supplying exctly equal quantities of output, that is OT=OB+BT.

Edgeworth's Solution

Edgeworth gave his solution of the problem of pricing with the help of the Figure 4.26. The market is equally divided between the two sellers A and B. The curve DA and DB are the respective demand curves and ON2 and OM2 are the maximum output of each. Price axis is OD. At the first instance, the seller A is selling ON1 units at NIT =OP price. Now, believing that A will not change

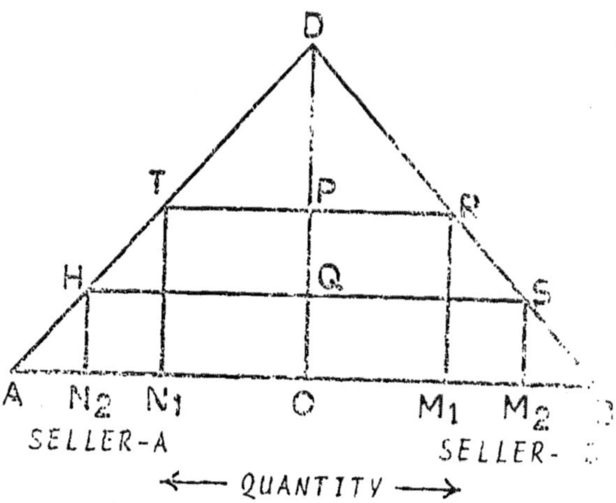

Figure 4.26 : Duopoly-Edgeworth's Solution.

price at any case. He, therefore, fixes a slightly lower price than OP so as to attract A's customers. By seeing that his sales are being reduced the seller A will reduce his price. This will lead to a price war between the two sellers and will continue till the price reaches at OQ at which both A and B sell the entire amount of output.

NOTES AND REFERENCES

2. The Economics of Imperfect Competiton, p. 179.
3. Donald S. Watson : Price Theory and Its Uses, Indian Edition, P. 324.
4. G. J. Stigler : The Theory of Price, revised edition, 1952, p. 215.
5. See E.H. Chamberlin : The Theory of Monopolistic Competition.
6. Richard H. Leftwich : Introduction to Micro-economics, p. 194.
7. Donald Watson : Price and Its Uses, Indian edition, p. 364.
8. "Demand under conditions of Oligopoly", Journal of Political Economy, Vol. XL VIII, August 1939.
9. "Price Theory and Bussiness Behaviour", Oxford Economic Papers, No. 2, May 1939.

5

THE THEORY OF FACTOR PRICING

THE MARGINAL PRODUCTIVITY THEORY

Theory of distribution is the theory of factor pricing. It explains how the prices of factors of production are determined. So far we have discussed how the prices of products are determined in various market conditions. Let us now analyse how the prices of factors of production are determined or how they are rewarded for their services rendered in producting national output.

In economics distribution implies sharing of national income among factors of production such as land; labour, capital and entrepreneurs as their rewards such as rent, wages, interest and profit respectively. 'Distribution' refers to personal distribution and functional distribution. Personal distribution relates to the distribution of national income among various individuals or families. In this process we consider each individual and determine how much income he receives from his work and property. We may not enquire about the type of work he has done. He may receive certain amount of income by way of wages, certain amount of income by way of rent, certain amount by way of interest and so forth.

Functional distribution, on the otherhand, relates to the distribution of national dividend among factors of production as their rewards. Productive activity requires co-ordinated effort of factors of production. They render their services for producing products for which they are rewarded. Rent, wages, interest and profits are the rewards for the services of land, labour, capital and entrepreneurs respectively. Functional distribution studies the forces underlying the determination of these rewards.

It is the functional distribution which forms the subject-matter of the theory of distribution. Theory of distribution is the theory of functional distribution. In the functional distribution, the whole national dividend is distributed among factors of production as factor prices. In other words, all factor owners receive their respective factor incomes such as rent, wages, interest and profit as shown in following diagram. (Figure 5.1).

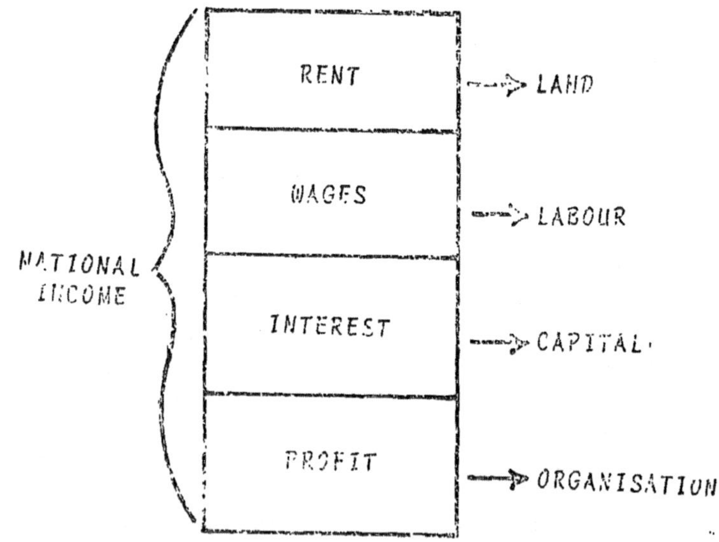

Fig. 5.1 National income

Marginal Productivity Theory

The Marginal Productivity Theory of Distribution provides a simple explanation of how prices of factors of production are determined. The theory was developed by J.B. Clark, Wicksteed and a host of others during the last quarter of the 19the Century.

The essence of the marginal productivity theory is that the price of a factor of production depends upon its marginal productivity. It also seems to be very fair that a factor of production should be rewarded according to the contribution it makes to the total output i.e., its marginal productivity.

We may note that the demand for a factor of production is not direct but derived demand. A factor is hired not for the purpose of producing something. They are demanded because they are productive and they are paid for their productivity

Let us now consider marginal productivity of a factor, say, labour. Marginal product of any factor is the addition to total output or income by employing an additional unit of that factor. If perfect competition is assumed a large output it can be sold at the same price as a small output, and so if employment of one more worker in an enterprise results in the production of 40 units per week that can be sold for Rel each, then the marginal productivity of the factor, labour in this enterprise is Rs. 40 per week. The employment of more workers will reduce the marginal productivity of labour. The more labour (or any other factor) the entrepreneur employs, the lower will be the marginal productivity of that factor. The Table 5.1 given below shows the marginal productivity of labour when different number of men are employed.

When 41 workers are employed the marginal physical productivity of labour is 40 units of the commodity and the.

TABLE 5.1

Marginal Productivity of Labour

Price = Re 1 per unit

Number of men	*Units of Output*	*Total Revenue*	*Marginal physical Productivity*	*Marginal Revenue Productivity*
40	500	500	—	—
41	540	540	40	40
42	575	575	35	35
43	606	606	31	31
44	634	634	28	28
45	660	660	26	26
46	685	685	25	25

marginal revenue productivity is Rs. 40. If 42 men are employed marginal productivity falls to 35 units or Rs. 35. How much a consumer will buy of a commodity depends on its price, more being demanded at lower price, so that the demand curve for the commodity slopes downwards. Similarly, how much labour the entrepreneur will employ will depend up on the price i.e., wages-of labour. If he has to give a wage of Rs. 28 per week, in the above example, he will employ 44 men, but if the wage is Rs. 40 per week, he will employ 41 men.

Under perfect competition, then, according to this theory, no facter will receive more than the value of its marginal product, and in fact the price paid by the entrepreneur will be equal to its marginal productivity.

The marginal productivity theory can be illustrated with the help of the Figure 5.2. The curve MPL represents diminishing marginal product. It implies that as more and more labourers are employed with given other factors of production, marginal productivity of labour diminishes. Now, if the available quantity of labour force is OL in the whole economy, the marginal product OL quantity of labour force is PL. The wage-rate is determined by this marginal product PL and therefore equilibrium wage rate will be settled at OW. At a higher wage rate OW', the employer will employ OL' amount of labour leaving LL' amount of labour unemployed. Unemployed workers in their.

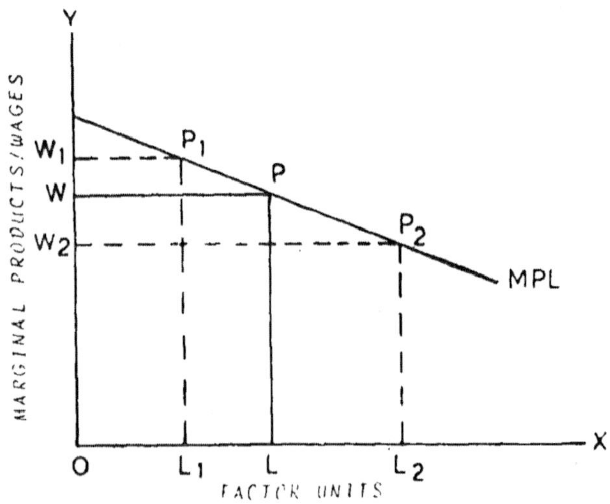

Figure 5.2. Diminishing Marginal Productivity.

attempt will bring down the wage rate to the level of PL at wihch all are employed. On the otherhand, at a lowers wage rate OW2, the employers will demand OL2 amount of labour since their profit will be greater than the available quantity of labour. In their bid to get more labour, competition among employers will push up the wage-rate to OW at which the employers' demand just equals the amount of labour available. The employment of more or less labour will not be desirable for the employer. This shows that each labourer will be employed till its marginal productivity becomes equal to the given wage-rate.

The aforesaid theory of marginal productivity rests on the following assumptions. First, it assumes that all units of a factor are homogeneous, so that we can substitute various inputs without any discrimination.

Secondly, the different factors, though co-ordinated with each other in producing a commodity, can be substituted for each other.

Thirdly, it presupposes the free and perfect mobility of factor units.

Fourthly, there must be full employment in the sense that the existing factors in the economy are fully employed.

Fifthly, it assumes perfect competition among factors' markets.

Sixthly, entrepreneurs are motivated by profit maximisation.

Finally, the theory applies only in the long-run.

The marginal productivity theory has been subjected to much criticism. The concept is certainly highly theoretical, since the employment of one unit of a factor may be impossible, so that in practice the value of its marginal unit cannot be calculated.[1]

Again, all factor units are not homogeneous in real world. Hence, the assumption that all units of factor service are homogeneous is unrealistic. We may know that the labour efficiency differs from worker to worker. Similarly, one piece of land in fertility differs from others. That is, factors are, in fact, heterogeneous and not homogeneous. Since no two factor units are homogeneous they are hardly substitutable for each other. A doctor cannot be put in place of an advocate and a chemical engineer cannot be put in place of a civil engineer.

The theory of marginal productivity assumes perfect mobility of factor units as between different employments and places. But in reality factors are imperfectly mobile.

We all know that there is no perfect competition in the real economic world. The marginal productivity theory holds good only in a perfectly competitive factor market which is an extremity. It also assumes that the entrepreneurs are motivated by maximisation of profits. But as pointed out by Schumpeter, the entrepreneurial action is guided by the desire to find a commercial kingdom, the will to conquer, the joy of creating and getting things done.

Further, the theory is applicable only in long-run, when the rewards of the factor units tend to equal their marginal productivity. But in the real world, we are concerned with short-run problems. As keynes remarks, "in the long-run we are all dead."

RENT

In every day speech the term "rent" is used to mean the hiring charge. It is often referred to as payments received by the owners of all kinds of private property that is leased for a fixed sum. When a person hires a taxi, or anything else, he has the use of it for a specified period on payment of an agreed sum of money ; when we hire a house or a piece of land we are said to rent it, and the periodic payment is called rent. In the ordinary language, the rent is simply a price for the use of factor services.

At certain time economists restricted the term rent to land, but now it is used in relation to any factor. Rent can be defined in a variety of ways, but its main characteristic is that it is a surplus, that is, additional income accruing to a factor. The Italian economist Pareto considered economic rent to be the surplus received by any factor of production above its opportunity cost—that is, any surplus over and above what was necessary to keep that factor in its present employment. Rent can, thus, be received by labour, capital or the entrepreneur, as well as by land.

Ricardian Theory of Rent

David Ricardo, the English economist, published his master piece treatise.—'The Principles of Political Economy and Taxation' in 1817. He propounded a systematic theory of rent which is considered as the basis of the modern concept of rent.

Ricardo defined rent as "that portion of the produce of the earth which is paid to the landlord for the use of original and indestructible powers of the soil". Two inferences are clear from this definition : First, land possesses original and permanent properties with reference to its nature, situation and environment and second, rent is paid for the use of land alone.

Ricardo believed that rent rose on account of differences in fertility of land. All lands are not equally fertile. Certain lands are superior while others are inferior in one way or other. Superior lands, therefore, command certain advantages over inferior ones. The advantages commanded by superior lands over inferior ones are called rent. Hence, rent is a differential surplus.

The Ricardian theory of rent is explained as follows. If a country has an "abundance of rich and fertile land", there will be no rent, because no one will be willing to pay for the use of land if its supply is unlimited. Rich and fertile land, however, is not unlimited in supply and is not uniform in quality. According to Ricardo it is for this reason that rent arises. Ricardo states, "when land of the second degree is taken into cultivation, rent immediately commences on that of the first quality, and the amount of that rent will depend on the difference in the quality of these two portions of land". Land at the margin of cultivation yields no rent. More fertile land will yield a greater return, and the value of this excess yield over that of marginal land is its rent.

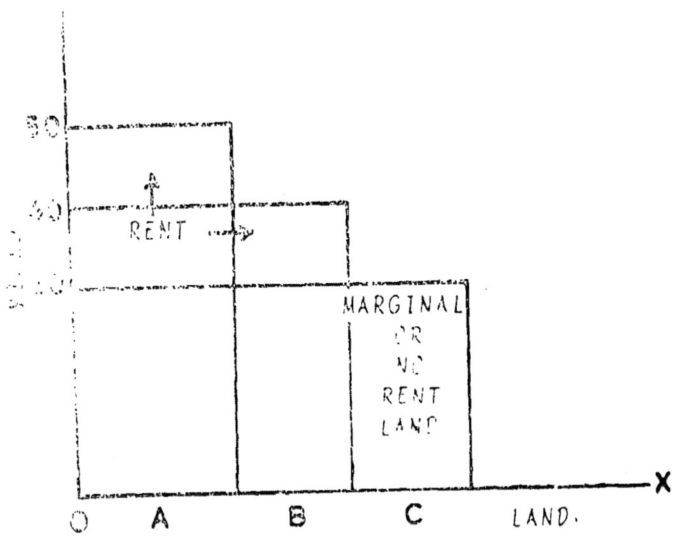

Fig. 5.3 Ricardian Theory of Rent.

Suppose, the value of the crops from three pieces of land of equal area to be Rs. 45, Rs. 40 and Rs. 35. Assuring that the yield worth Rs. 35, comes from the marginal land will be the excess yield over Rs. 35, that is Rs. 10 and Rs. 5 respectively. The operation of Ricardian theory of rent is graphically shown in Figure 5.3 depicting our given example. As population increases, the less fertile land will be drawn into cultivation and the rent of previously cultivated land will rise and the previously cultivated marginal land will become the rent land.

The Ricardian theory of rent rests on the following assumptions:

1. Land is a free gift of nature and any earning on land is a surplus.
2. The supply of land is fixed.
3. Land possesses original and indestructible powers and rent is paid for these powers of the soil.
4. Land differs in fertility. That is, all lands are not eqally fertile.
5. Order of cultivation assumed in the sense that the superior grade lands are cultivated first and the inferior ones later.
6. Land is subject to the operation of the law of diminishing returns.

The essence of the Ricardian theory of rent is that with every increase in population, demand for agricultural products will increase. As a result inferior lands will be put under cultivation. As inferior land brought under cultivation, the superior lands will yield surpluses. These surpluses of superior lands over inferior lands are called rent.

According to Ricardo, price of the product-yields determines rent of land. He maintains that high rent is not the cause of high price. High price, he argues, is responsible for high rent. With every increase in population, demand for agricultural products rises resulting in higher prices. When prices of agricultural products rise, more and more inferior lands will be put under cultivation. Consequently, the superior grade lands go on yielding greater and greater surpluses over the inferior grade lands. It means that with every increase in prices of agricultural crops, rent of land goes on increasing. Hence, according to Ricardo, rent does not determine price, but it is determined by price. Rent is not price-determining, but it is price-determined.

Ricardian theory of rent has been subjected to scathing criticisms. Firstly, it has been pointed out that there are no original and indestructible powers of the soil. Fertile lands, after a few years of cultivation, may lose its fertility, since chemical composition compounding fertility is exhausted due to continuous cultivation.

Ricardo assumes that the best soils are cultivated first. But it is not borne out by historical facts. H.C. Carey points out with his Survey on American Settlements that the order of cultivation was not as per the Ricardian formula.

Ricardo points out that rent arises on account of fertility but in the real world it arises because of scarcity of land. Rent, therefore, paid for land is scares in relation to its demand.

Further, the Ricardian contention that rent does not enter into price is unwarranted. According to Ricardo, rent is determined by prices, but in reality price is determined by rent together with other factor prices. Hence, rent is not price-determined, but price-determining.

Modern Theory of Rent

In a broader sense and consistent with the general interpretation of economists, rent is the return received by the owner of any factor that has an absolutely inelastic supply. So much so that economic rent is the price paid for any factor of production whose total supply is completely fixed.[2] Thus, rent is certainly the return to the land owners.

Since, supply of land is fixed and demand for land is a derived demand, economic rent is susceptible of demand and supply analysis. We emphasise that supply of land is absolutely fixed and as a result, rent is demand determined.

The modern theory of rent, which is the refinement of the Ricardian theory, explains rent in two ways—

1. It is a payment made for the use of land; and
2. It is a surplus over and above the transfer earnings.

Let us analyse the theory of rent in these two senses—

1. Rent : Payment for the Use of Land

According to Ricardo, rent arises due to differences in fertility of land. But the modern economists reject the Ricardian concept of rent as differential surplus. They point out that rent arises due to the relative scarecity of land in relation to its demand. The higher the demand, for land, the greater will be its rent. Therefore, rent of land is determined by the interaction of the forces of demand for and supply of land.

Demand of Land

Like any other factor of production, the demand for land is a derived demand. Land is demanded not for direct consumption but for the purpose of producting consumpion goods. It is derived from the demand for products. If the demand for these products changes, the demand for land also changes. If the demand for these products rises, the demand for the use of land will correspondingly rise leading to an increase of rent. If, on the otherhand, the demand for these products falls, there is a corresponding fall in demand for land tending to fall rent. For example, if the population of a country increases, the demand for food will increase, the resultant of which is increased demand for land and a rise in rent, and *vice versa*.

We have seen that the demand for a factor of production depends on its marginal productivity since the productivity of factors of production is subject to the law of diminishing marginal productivity, the demand curve for land is seen downward sloping from left to right.

Thus, on the demand side, rent of land is determined by its marginal productivity.

Supply of Land

The supply of land is fixed for the whole society, though individuals can increase their supply by acquiring more land from others paying higher amount of rent. The fixity of the supply of land implies that the supply curve of land is perfectly inelastic. It is for this reason that land is having no supply price. Whatever may be the rent, the supply of land cannot be increased or decreased.

Determination of Rent

The rent of land is determined, according to modern theory, by the interaction of the forces of demand for and supply of land. This can be easily illustrated with the help of the Figure 5.4.

Suppose that all arable land in a given geographical area is of uniform quality.

Each piece of land will produce exactly the same yield per acre. Further, assume that only one agricultural crop, say, wheat, is grown in this area. If there are S acres of land available, we may show this in Figure 5.4. by inelastic supply curve SS. Next demand, for land, as we have noted, like any other factor

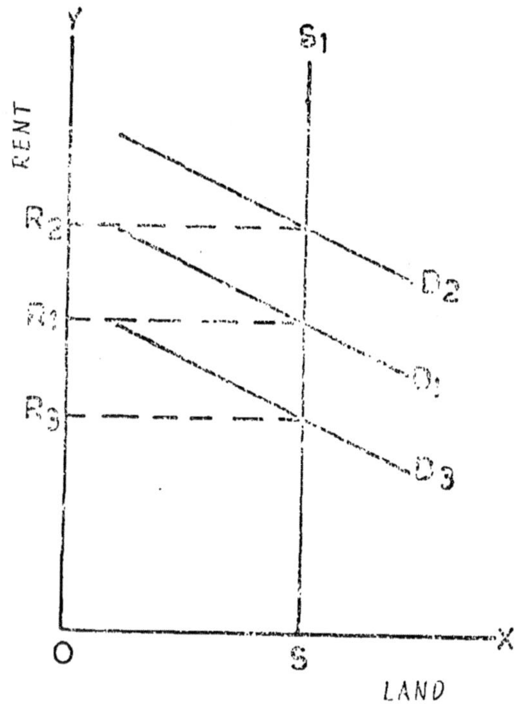

Figure 5.4. Demand for and Supply of Land.

of production, is determined by its marginal productivity. Let D1 be the original demand curve for land. As seen in Figure SS1 is the supply curve of land. Since rent is determined by the interaction of demand for and supply of land, it is determined as R1 per acre. Now, if for some reason, demand increases to D2 or falls to D3, there would be a corresponding rise or fall to R2 or R3, as the case may be.

We may thus repeat the theorem : the interaction of demand, for a land with the supply of land determines rent.

2. Rent : Surplus Over Transfer Earnings

So far we have discussed rent as a payment made for the use of land. There is a modern concept of rent which considers it as a surplus accrued to any factor of production. This theory has been systematically developed by Mrs. Joan Robinson. She contends that rent is a surplus earning over and above the minimum earnings necessary to induce, a factor unit to work. The minimum earnings necessary to induce a factor unit to work is called "transfer earnings."

According to Robinson, "the essence of the conception of rent is the conception of surplus earned by a particular part of a factor of production over and above the minimum earnings necessary to induce it to do the work". That is, rent is a payment in excess of transfer earnings. Transfer earnings imply the amount of money which any factor unit could earn in its next best alternative.

Suppose that a given piece of land is used for growing paddy or wheat. These are alternative uses of a given piece of land. If the land is used for growing paddy, it is prevented from being used for growing wheat. Suppose, further, that the piece of land yields paddy worth Rs. 100. and its next best use wheat fetches Rs. 80. The transfer earning is Rs. 80 in this case and, therefore, in the present circumstance, the rent is Rs. 20, the surplus over transfer earnings.

Quasi—Rent

Quasi—rent is a Marshallian concept. It was Alfred Marshall who first introduced this concept in Economics. Quasi-rent, according to him, is the surplus earning on instruments of production other than land. The term 'rent' is used to denote the income on land and other free gifts of nature, while 'quasi-rent' is used to denote income on man-made appliances. As George Stigler[3] defines, "a quasi-rent is the return to a durable specific productive instrument". Quasi-rent stands for the whole earnings which some agents of production yield when demand for them has suddenly increased. It is earned during the period when their supply cannot be increased in response to its increase in demand, hence, is a short-run concept.

Quasi-rent may, thus, be defined as a temporary surplus earnings on man-made appliances. We may distinguish between rent and quasi-rent on the fact that while the supply of land is fixed, that of the other instruments of production such as machinery, equipments, etc., are fixed only for a short period and can be increased after sometime.

Hence, we repeat that quasi-rent is only a temporary surplus earning. With the increase in the supply of machines or materials, this surplus earning will disappear.

We may illustrate the concept of quasi-rent diagramatically with the help of the Figure 5.5. Let SS be the inelastic supply curve of machines. The demand curve DD intersects the supply curve at Point E. At price OP (=SE), OS number of machines are supplied. Suppose that the demand for machines increases suddenly shifting the demand curve to D1D1, but the supply of machines remains unchanged; it is fixed in the short-run. As a result, the price rises suddenly and the whole price is quasi-rent. The price of machines was OP before and it has become OP1. The surplus, the difference between OP and OP1 (i.e., PP1) is the quasi-rent. But in the long run, the supply of machines can be increased, say, to OM. The price will then come down to OP (=ME2). Now, the quas-rent vanishes, since the price ME2 just covers the supply price which is OP.

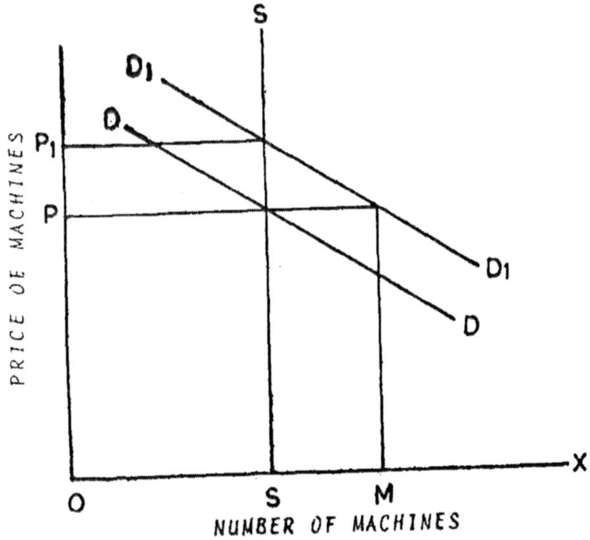

Figure 5.5. Quasi-rent.

It is clear from the above analysis that capital goods earn quasi-rent in the short-run, since their supply is fixed; but in the long-run it disappears when their supply becomes more elastic.

WAGES

Labour is the most important productive service. Labourers are rewarded for their services rendered in productive activities. And the reward for the services of a labour is called wage. According to Benham, "a wage may be defined as a sum of money paid under contract by an employer to a worker in exchange for services rendered."

It is worthwhile to distinguish between real and nominal wages. Nominal wages are wages in terms of money. Real wages, on the otherhand, refers to the amount of goods and services that the money wages can purchase. In addition, real wages include all the benefits that a worker can enjoy by working at particular kind of job. Real wages are, therefore, considered as the best index of the economic welfare of the workers.

Let us now enumerate the factors determining real wages—

1. Purchasing Power of Money

Purchasing Power of Money refers to the capacity of money to command other goods and services. The purchasing power depends upon the general price level. The purchasing or the value of money is inversely related to the price-level. If price rises, the purchasing power of money falls and *vice versa*. The workers are interested not in the amount of money they receive, but in the amount of goods that he can purchase with the amount of money. When the prices of goods and services increase, the real wage is reduced. Hence, real wages depend on prices of goods and services.

2. Supplementary Benefits

A worker, apart from money wages, may get certain additional benefits such as free medical aid, subsidised or free housing facilities, provision of gratuity or pension, free schooling to children etc. Such facilities will increase the real wages of the workers automatically.

3. Scope for Extra-Earnings

If there is enough scope for extra earnings in the work, the real wages increase. A doctor can earn extra income by offering private practice, hence his real wages are higher.

4. Nature of the Job

Certain works are seasonal, irregular and uncertain, while others are regular, permanent and certain. In the case of permanent jobs, even if the money wages are comparatively lower, the real wages are higher. In the case of seasonal or irregular jobs, on the otherhand, even if money wages are higher, real wages will be lower. Hence, the real wages depend on the nature of work.

5. Condition of Work

Conditions of work also influence the real wages of workers. Working conditions refer to the hours of work, nature of work, surroundings of the work, recreational facilities and so on. Eventhough there is less scope for higher money income, if the conditions are good, environment is healthy and congenial and work is comfortable, the real wages of the workers, will be higher.

6. Future Prospects

Even if there is little money wage for a job, the real wage for a job, will be higher if there is good future prospects for promotion to a higher grade. In the absence of future prospects a job with a higher intial salary may not be considered as good as the job with a humble start but with a better future prospect.

THEORIES OF WAGES

1. The Subsistence Theory of Wages

Subsistence theory of wages is one of the earliest theories of wage determination. This theory, also known as Iron Law of Wages, was propounded by the French School of Economic thought, Physiocrats. The theory states that the value of labour, like any other commodity under free competition, is determined by its cost of production, i.e., minimum subsistence earnings required for the support of the labourer and his family and also to ensure the continuous supply of labour. It means that wages paid to the workers must be sufficient for the bare maintenance of life and not more than that.

This theory is based on three propositions. First, labour is like a commodity. Ricardo strongly supported this theory and regarded labour as a commodity whose value must be determined in the way as that of any other commodity. Its natural price is the price which is necessary to enable the labourers, one with another to subsist and to perpetuate their race, without either increase of decrease.

Secondly, subsistence depends upon quantity and quality of food, necessaries and conveniences of life which will become essential to the labourer to lead the life. It implies the bare minimum necessities to eke out a life.

Thirdly, if wages are paid beyond the subsistence level, labour supply would increase. This would reduce the wage rate to the subsistence level. On the otherhand, if wages are less than the amount necessary for the subsistence level of living, workers will be unable to maintain even their families. As a result, population would tend to decline which would push up the price level to the subsistence level.

The theory assumes that an increase in the wage-rate would

tend to increase population. It is proved to be wrong and the modern condition have disproved this fact.

2. The Theory is One-sided

The theory attempts to explain the determination of wages from the supply side of labour. It is a supply theory of wages. The theory does not take into account the demand for labour. It kept undiscussed why labour is demanded.

3. Impact of Higher Wages Neglected

The theory does not consider the impact of higher wages on the efficiency of labour. If wages increase, the level of efficiency would also increase which would tend to further rise in wages.

4. Neglects Wage Differences

The theory assumes that the snbsistence level is more or less uniform for all kinds of workers. Therefore, the theory does not explain why there are wages differences in different occupations.

5. Influence of Trade Unions Neglected

The trade unions can influence the existing rate of wages by their collective bargaining. They can even increase the wages beyond the subsistence level. Therefore, a satisfactory wage theory would consider the influence of trade unions on wage determination. But the subsistence theory of wages ignored this fact.

2. The Wages-Fund Theory

J.S. Mill was the propounder of the wages fund theory. According to him, wages depend upon "the proportion between population and capital". By population, he meant, "the number only of the labouring classes or rather of those who work for hire, and by capital, only circulating capital and not even the whole of that but the part which is expended on the direct purchase of labour."

According to this theory, wages are determined by two quantities viz; (i) the wages-fund or circulating capital set aside for the purchase of labour and (ii) the number of labourers seeking employment. Hence, the general level of wages can be ascertained by way of a simple arithmetical formula. : dividing wages-fund by the number of workers.

$$\text{Wages rate} = \frac{\text{Wages—Fund}}{\text{No. of Workers.}}$$

The wages-fund theory is based on the three fundamental propositions :

(i) Wages are paid from wages-fund.
(ii) Wages-fund is fixed and pre-determined; and
(iii) Wage rate depends upon tbe number of workers and the capital set aside for payment of wages.

According to this theory wage rate can be raised either by increasing the wages-fund or by reducing the total number of work ing population. But, since the wages-fund is assumed to be fixed and pre-determined wages could be risen only by reducing the number of workers.

The following criticisms are levelled against the wages-fund theory. First, the theory states that the wages are paid out of circulating capital alone. There is no hard and fast rule stating whether wages are paid out of capital or from present products. In the case of short-run production processes, wages are paid out of present production. In certain other cases, say, in the long-run production process where there is a long gestation period, wages are, mainly, paid out of capital.

Secondly, J.S. Mill argued that the wages-fund or circulating capital is fixed and pre-determined. But, we all know that part of capital which can be set apart for payment of weges is neither in a fixed proportion nor is pre-determined. Its volume changes according to the prospects of profitability.

Thirdly, the theory does not tell us about the sources of wages fund and method by which it is estimated. It simply states that wages are paid from wages-fund and the rate of wages can be ascertained by dividing the wages-fund by the number of workers.

3. Marginal Productivity Theory of Wages

According to marginal productivity theory, labour is paid exactly equal to its marginal productivity. That is, the wages of the workers will be just equal to the value of the marginal product. The theory states that the producer will pay for labour no more than the value of its marginal product, because by doing so the cost of production will be increased.

The marginal productivity theory of wages has been criticised for the following reasons.

First, marginal productivity and its **equivalent** of wage-rate is a theoretical concept. It will never be possible in the real world.

Secondly, it is practically impossible to calculate the amount or the value of the marginal product of labour.

Thirdly, the employment of one more labourer may upset the method of production itself. Employing an extra worker simply means that there will be more labour than are required.

Fourthly, productivity of labour not only depends upon its own effort and efficiency, but an other factors such as quality of other factors of production, working conditions etc.

Finally, marginal productivity theory is applicable only under perfect competition which are seldom seen in the real economic world.

4. Market Theory of Wages

Market theory of wages ascertains that wages are determined by demand for labour in relation to its supply.

Labour is demanded because it is productive. It means that labour is capable of producing certain commodities or services. Hence, we may note that the demand for labour is a derived demand. It is derived from the demand for the commodities or service it helps to produce. Greater the demand for consumption goods, greater will be the demand for labour producing these items.

We may note that it is the anticipated demand and not existing demand for products that determines demand for labour. Since commodities are generally produced in anticipation of future demand for them, the demand for labour is derived from the anticipated demand for them.

Supply of Labour

There is some ambiguity in the concept of a supply of labour, since supply of labour means either the total number of people available for employment or the total number of hours worked. In the case of a commodity its supply depends upon its cost of production. Though it may be difficult to conceive of cost of production being applied to labour in general, the term supply of lobour can be related to those forms of specific labour which require earnings to be sacrificed during a period of time.

Market Mechanism and Labour Market

Through the price mechanism, supply is brought into equality with demand. A rise in demand for labour in relation to its supply should increase the wages, while a fall in demand in relation to its supply should decrease the wages. It is generally true that a rise in its price (wages) can be expected to increase the supply of a factor coming into the market, but it is uncertain that the supply of labour can always be increased by offering higher wages.

Trade Unions and Wages

Trade unionism has developed gradually from the last quarter of the 19th century and has become a powerful force in the industrial sectors since the 2nd World War. Webbs defined trade union as "a continuous association of wage-earners for the purpose of maintaining or improving the conditions of their employment."

Labour has no reserve power. It is most perishable. Since labour is inseparable from labourer, he is less mobile than a commodity. A day's labour withheld is lost for ever. Isolated workers usually face a limited number of employers who are generally in stiff contract with one another. Owing to the weak bargaining power, the labourers get much lower wages. Employers were likely to exploit the labouring classes by paying lower wages. It was found by labouring classes that unless they unite and improve their bargaining position, they were in danger of serious exploitation by the employers. Thus, trade unionism has become on incessant necessity to save the interests of the working population.

Trade unions play a crucial role in safeguarding and promoting the interests of the workers. Trade unions, in modern times, generally perform two kinds of functions viz; (i) Militant functions and (ii) fraternal functions.

Trade unions are militant organisations in the sense that they are fighting for the rights of the workers. They aim at ensuring adequate wages for workers, better conditions of work and, more recently, securing adequate share in the control of industrial organisations. As Edward T. Nevin points out, "the basic aim of trade union is that of strengthening the bargaining power of workers in relation to that of employers, so as to ensure that the worker obtains his fair share of the product to which he contributes and that he is given decent conditions of work[4]." For the achievement of these objectives. trade unions have to fight by strikes and boycotts.

Recently, trade unions are actively acting as welfare organisations as well. They aim at securing sickness benefit, old-age pensions, maternity and educational facilities, etc 'to the' working population. They also provide financial help to the members in the form of sickness and accidents benefits.

Trade unconism introduces an element of monopoly in the labour market. Instead of individual negotiations, trade unions bargain on behalf of the workers as a whole. It is a case of bilateral monopoly.

The primary function of a trade union is to raise wages and ensure better working conditions of its members. They raise their wages by collective bargaining.

The classical economists, believed that wages could be raised only at the expense of profits. Fall in profits would adversely affect the industrial activity which, in turn, would reduce the demand for labour. Some others maintained that wages are determined by marginal productivity and trade unions cannot raise it above marginal productivity. Hence they concluded that trades unions cannot raise wages.

But it is wrong to believe that trade unions do not have any influence on wages. They can raise wages under certain circumstances.

When wages paid to the workers are below the marginal productivity trade unions can raise wages up to the level of marginal productivity through collective bargaining.

Further, it is possible for trade unions to raise marginal productivity of labour itself by various means. The productivity of labour depends upon many other factors such as working conditions, hours of work, wagerate, etc. They can force the employers to use modern and up-to-date a machinery in production processes so as to increase the labour productivity. By fostering habits of sobriety, thrift and honesty the labourers can themselves raise their efficiency. Trade unions can also restrict the labour supply so as to raise marginal productivity.

Again, trade unions can also raise wages by fighting for standard wage-rates. Once a group of industry adopts uniform or standard wagerates, the individual firms will also follow suit.

4

INTEREST

An economy's tangible resources consist of its labour force

and its stock of useful things which are called capital. Capital includes all economic goods except people and perishables. We may thus define the capital as "anything (other than a free human being) which yields valuable services over an appreciable period of time."[5] Capital is inevitable for productive activities. It may be made available either from cash at hand or from borrowed money. Since, it helps to produce consumption articles, it should be rewarded. And the reward for capital is called interest. More precisely, interest is the price paid for a loan.[6]

Interest is, thus, the payment for the use of capital. Marshall defines interest as "the price paid for the use of capital in any market". Capital is the essential pre-requisite of investment or productive activities. Capital is demanded because it is productive. Knut Wicksell defines interest as a "payment made by the borrower of capital by virtue of its productivity.

THEORIES OF INTEREST

1. Classical Theory

According to classical theory, interest is the reward for savings. Rate of interest is thus determined by the demand for savings to invest in capital goods in relation to its supply.

We may repeat that capitals are demanded because they are productive. They are used to produce goods and services. The demand for capital comes from entrepreneurs who desire to invest. Thus demand for savings in the form of capital arises from investments. The demand for capital goods, thus, depends upon rate of interest. Demand for capital goods and the rate of interest are inversely related. Lower the rate of interest, higher will be the demand for capital for investment and higher the rate of interest lower will be the demand for it. Hence, the demand curve for capital slopes downward to the right.

Capitals are provided by the household in the form of savings. Savings imply postponement of consumption. It involves sacrifice in the form of waiting or abstinence. The price for postponement of present consumptiôn to future consumption is called the rate of interest. Therefore, the rate of interest and savings are directly related. The higher the rate of interest, more will be the supply of savings, and *vice versa*. Hence, the supply curve of capital is positively sloped.

We may repeat that rate of interest, according to the classical theory, is determined by the demand for capital in relation to its supply. In technical terms, the rate of interest is determined by the interaction of demand for capital and supply of capital i.e. savings.

This is illustrated in Figure 5.6.

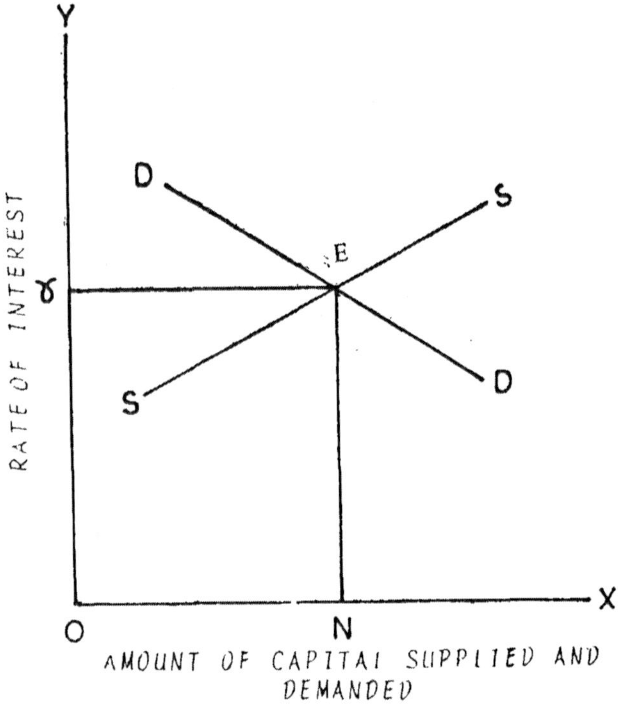

Figure 5.6. Determination of Rate of Interest.

DD is the demand curve for capital and SS is supply curve of savings. These two curves intersect at Point 'E' where the equilibrium rate of interest Or is determined at ON level of capital.

The classical theory of interest has been critic sed on the following grounds. First, the theory is based on the assumption of full-employment of resources, and interest is regarded as the price for abstinence or waiting, "Within the framework of a system of theory, built on the assumption of full-employment, the notion of interest as a reward for waiting or abstinence is highly plausible. It is the premise that resources are typically fully-employed that lacks plausibility in the contemporary world."[7] If there are unemployed resources in an economy, there is no need for paying people to abstain from present consumption to future consumption.

Secondly, classical theory of interest assumes, further, that more investment is caused by curtailing consumption. But fall in consumption expenditure causes for low demand for consumer goods, which in turn affect investment adversely.

Thirdly, the classical theory states that both saving and investment depend upon the rate of interest. But keynes refuted this reiterating the fact that savings depend upon the level of income and investment is determined by the rate of profitability. Therefore, it is concluded that both saving and investment are not interest elastic.

2. Neo-Classical Theory of Interest (Loanable Funds Theory of Interest)

Loanable Funds theory of interest is a refinement of the classical theory. It takes into account monetary factors like hoarding, dishoarding, credit creation by banks, etc., in determining the rate of interest. Though the loanable funds theory was first formulated by Knut Wicksell, it was developed by a cost of Sweedish and English economists.

According to the Neo-classicists, interest is the reward for loanable funds. Loanable funds are those amount of which are demanded and supplied in credit market. This theory explains that the rate of interest is determined by the demand for loanable funds in relation to its supply. In technical terms, the rate of interest is determined by the interaction of the demand schedule for loanable funds with the supply schedule of loanable funds.

Let us briefly analyse the demand for and supply of loanable funds in the credit market.

Demand for loanable funds arises for three important purposes viz. ; consumption, investment and hoarding. The demand for loanable funds mainly comes from business entrepreneurs. They borrow money for purchasing raw materials or for building up of inventories. Investment demand for loanable funds is an important constituent of total demand for loanable funds. Rate of interest is, thus, the price paid for loanable funds. The rate of interest and the demand for loanable funds are inversely related in the sense that higher the rate of interest, lower will be the demand for loanable funds and *vice versa.* The demand for loanable funds for investment purposes is interest-elastic and the investment demand curve for loanable funds slopes downward to the right. In Figure 5.7 the curve 'I' represents the investment demand for loanable funds.

The second constituent of demand for loanable funds is consumption. Individuals or households borrow money for consumption purposes when they wish to purchase in excess of their current incomes. Generally loans are demanded for purchasing durable goods like radio sets, refrigerators, motor bikes, etc. Lower rates of interest will tend to purchase commodities on hire purchase schemes. In Figure 5.7 the curve 'C' represents the consumption demand for loanable funds.

Lastly, loanable funds are demanded for the purpose of hoarding. Hoarding implies people's desire to hold money as idle cash balances. Demand for hoarding is shown by the curve 'H' in Figure 5.7.

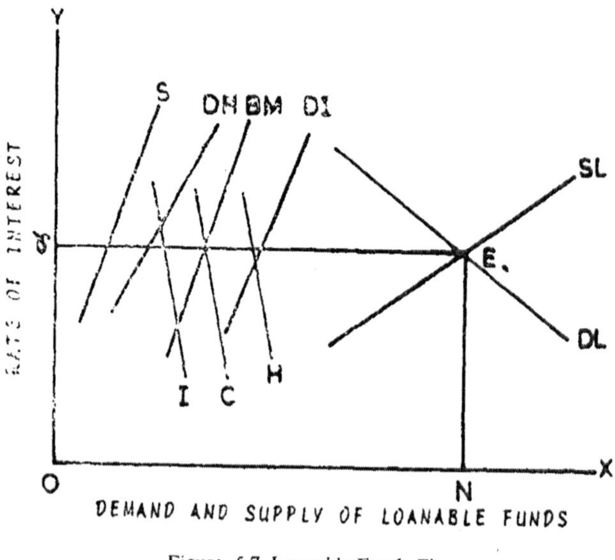

Figure. 5.7 Loanable Funds Theory

The supply of loanable funds, on the otherhand, derives from four important sources viz ; savings, dishoarding, bank credit and disinvestment.

Individuals and households save money out of their current income which constitute an important source of loanable funds.

Savings done by individuals or households primarily depend upon the size of their income. But, given the level of income, savings vary with the rate of interest. Higher rate of interest will tend to increase savings and lower rate of interest will reduce the level of savings. In technical terms, the supply curve of savings is sloped positively as shown by the curve 'S' in the Figure 5.7.

Dishoarding constitutes another source of loanable funds. Dishoarding implies bringing out hoarded money into use. This idle cash balances in the previous period become active cash balances in the present time and are available as loanable funds. At a low rate of interest people dishoard less amount of money and at a higher rate of interest more amount of money will be dishoarded. As the market rate of interest rises, people are tended to dishoard more and more idle cash balances. Dishoarding is represented by the curve 'DH' in the given figure.

The commercial banks in a country also provide a third source of loanable funds. Banks create credit to provide loans. The supply curve 'BM' of bank credit is also seen interest-elastic which is represented by 'BM' in our given figure.

Disinvestment, which is the last constituent of the supply of loanable funds, takes place when the existing capital equipments are allowed to wear out without being replaced during which part of the revenue from the sale of products flows into the market for loanable funds instead of going into capital replacement. Disinvestment is represented by the curve 'DI' in the adjoining figure.

By the lateral summation of the supply curve viz. ; savings (s) dishoarding (DH) bank credit (BM) and disinvestment (DI), we get the total supply curve of loanable funds 'SL'. On the demand side, we get the total demand curve of loanable funds 'DL' by the summation of the demand curves representing investment demand, consumption demand and hoarding.

The rate of interest, accoording to loanable funds theory, is determined by the interaction of demand curve for loanable funds and supply of loanable funds as shown in Figure 5.7. The demand curve for loanable funds 'DL' and the supply curve of loanable funds 'SL' intersect at Point E where the rate of interest 'Or' is determined at ON quantity of loanable funds supplied and demanded.

The loanable funds theory of interest has been severely criticised by Keynes and a host of others. They pointed out that loanable funds theory is a variant of the classical theory of interest.

The classical theory asserts that interest is the payment made for the use of saving while the loanable funds theory considers interest as the price of loanable funds. There is not much difference between classical theory of the rate of interest and the loanable funds theory. The only difference between these two is regarding the meaning of saving. In the former analysis savings meant savings out of current income, while in the latter it implies savings out of the previous income. As per the loanable funds theory, loanable funds are constituted by bank credit and activated idle cash balances in addition to savings out of the previous periods income. In classical theory, savings out of current income may well exceed the savings of loanable funds theory since current income increases by bank credit or dishoardings. Thus, the supply schedule of savings of classical theory is identical with the supply schedule of loanable funds theory.

3. Liquidity Preference Theory of Interest

Lord keynes formulated a new theory of interest commonly referred to as liquidity preference theory of interest. Keynes considers interest as purely a monetary phenomenon. According to him "interest is the reward for parting with liquidity".

According to this theory, interest is determined by demand for money in relation to its supply.

The demand for money is demand for liquidity preference. A man with a given income confronts with the fundamental problem : how much to consume and how much to save. The decision regarding former depends upon propensity to consume while the latter decision depends on "liquidity preference."

Liquidity preference means desire to hold idle cash balances. Everyone likes to have some amounts of money for meeting a large number of purposes. This constitutes the demand for money.

The demand for money arises from three important motives, viz. ; Transaction motive, precautionary motive and speculative motive.

Transaction Motive: People need to keep a certain amount of money to meet day-to-day expenses since they get wages/salaries periodically. That is, to bridge the gap between receipt of income and its expenditure, we desire to keep some amount of money as idle cash balances. This is referred to as transactions demand for money. As A.H. Hanson points out, "the transactions motive relates to the need for cash for the current transactions of personal and business exchanges."

Precautionary Motive : People desire to hold idle cash balances to meet unforeseen contingencies. People hold some amount of money to provide for sickness, and other uncertain perils. This constitutes the precautionary demand for money.

Speculative Motive

Specultive motive relates to the desire to hold one's own cash resources with a view to obtaining profits by taking advantages of future changes in the rate of interest in the capital market. This constitutes the anticipatory demand for money which is commonly referred to as 'speculative demand for money'.

Liquidity preference for speculative motive depends upon the rate of interest while the former two motives mainly depend upon the level of income. The speculative demand for money and the rate of interest is inversely related. The higher the rate of interest lower will be the demand for money for speculatives and *vice versa*.

Another determining factor of the rate of interest is the supply of money which is automously determined by the monetary authority. It includes coins, currency notes and demand deposits with the commercial banks. Keynes, assumes that the supply of money is more or less fixed. Hence, the supply curve of

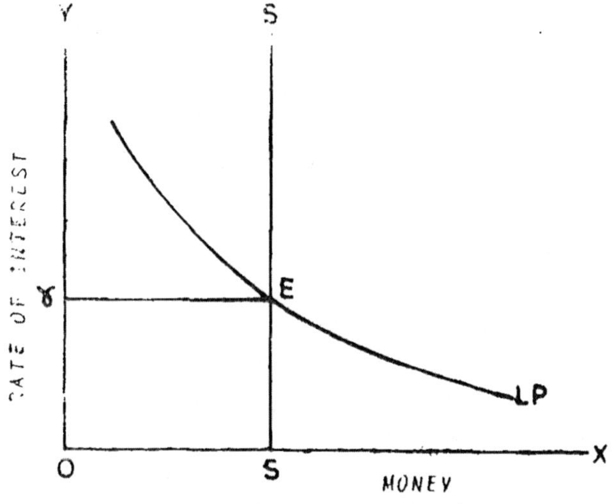

Figure 5.8 Liquidity Preference Theory of Interest.

money is perfectly inelastic as shown in Figure 5.8. We may repeat that the rate of interest is determined by the inter-action of demand for and supply of money. This is illustrated in Figure 5.8. SS is shown as the supply curve of money and the curve LP represents the liquidity preference for speculative motive. The two curves intersect at Point E where the equilibrium rate interest 'Or' is determined.

The liquidity preference theory reiterates the monetary aspect. According to this theory the rate of interest is the price which equilibriates the desire to hold cash balances and the supply of money determined by monetary authorities.

PROFIT

Profit is the reward of the enterpreneur. It is the residual income of the organiser which is the difference between total revenue and total cost. During a given period of time, a firm gets certain revenue from the sale of its products. To produce a given product, a firm has to pay for the hired labour, raw materials, rent for land and interest on borrowed capital. In addition to these, it has also to pay for wear and tear which is called depreciation charges. The excess of the revenue over these various payments and charges is called gross profit. In technical terms, Gross Profit=Total Revenue—Explicit Costs.

Gross profit includes the reward for the factors of production supplied by entrepreneur himself. The reward for the self-owned factors of production is called implicit costs. Implicit costs consist of the payment made to the entrepreneur for his managerial service, rent for his own land and interest for his own capital. When we deduct implicit costs from gross profit we get net profit or pure profit. That is,

Net Profit=Gross Profit—Implicit Costs.

THEORIES OF PROFIT

1. Risk-bearing Theory of Profit

The risk-bearting theory of profit is associated with the American economist F.B. Hawley. He regarded profit as the reward for risks and responsibilities undertaken by the entrepreneur. Every business involves risk and profit is paid to the entrepreneur for this risk. A producer produces goods in anticipation of demand. If demand shrinks. entrepreneur will incur loss; and he will receive profit if demand for products is higher. Profit is, therefore, a reward for risk-taking.

The risk-bearing theory of profit is not free from serious criticisms. It has been pointed out by critics that there exists hardly any relationship between risk and profit. Profits are influenced by many other factors rather than risks. Though business involves some sort of risks, the high profits enjoyed by the entrepreneur cannot entirely be attributed to the element of risk. Profits are not in any proportion to risk undertaken by the entrepreneur. Carver has pointed out that profits arise not because risks are borne but because risks are reduced.

Prof. F.H. Knight has made a distinction between risk and uncertainty. He maintains that profit arises because of uncertainty.

2. Uncertainty-bearing Theory of Profit

Prof. F.H. Knight, an American economist has formulated the uncertainty bearing theory of profit. According to him, an important function of the entrepreneur is uncertainty bearing rather than risk-taking. He considers profit as the reward for uncertainty bearing rather than for risk-taking. We may note that certain risks are foreseen and provided against. Risks of death accidents like fire, etc. are insurable and the insurance companies undertake these risks in return to premia paid to them. The entrepreneurs get no profit on account of these risks. Hence, we conclude that risk-taking is the function of the insurance companies and not of the entrepreneur.

Insurable risks are, then, measurable and insured against. But there are genuine economic risks which are caused by uncertainties. The risks arisen by uncertainties are non-insurable and are not to be covered by the insurance companies. For undertaking these non-insurable risks the entrepreneur is to be rewarded. This reward is called profit. Hence, knight concludes that profit is the reward for uncertainty bearing not for risk-taking.

The theory of uncertainty bearing has been criticised on the following grounds.

1. Uncertainty bearing is not the only function of the entrepreneur and profit is not the only reward for uncertainty-bearing. Profit i also considered as the reward for other services that he undertakes such as initiating, co-ordinating, etc.

2. It is impossible to measure the uncertainties exactly and, therefore, exact amount of profits cannot be determined.

3. Profits also arise on account of monopoly conditions existing in the market. A monopolist can earn higher profits without bearing any uncertainties.

3. Dynamic Theory of Profit

Prof. J.B. clark has evolved the dynamic theory of profit. He maintains that profit is a dynamic surplus. He states that profits arise only in a dynamic society. In a static society, on the other-hand, there would be no profit since cost is always equal to the selling price. Profit, in the strict sense, represents the difference between cost and selling price. It is a surplus over and above the costs of production. But in a static society, under the force of stiff competition, this surplus will disappear. As F.H. Knight points out, "in the static state each factor secures what it produces, and since cost and selling prices are always equal, there can be no profits beyond wages for the routine work of supervision."

We are living in a dynamic world where everything changes. In a dynamic society changes occur in any or all of the factors such as population, consumer behaviour, capital stock, technique of production, innovation, forms of industrial establishments, etc. In such a society there exists difference between price and cost due to certain dynamic changes. Thus, profits arise out of changes. In a 'static world there would be no changes and hence no profits. In a dynamic economy everything changes and hence profit arises.

Prof. Knight has made a frontal attack on dynamic theory of profit. and disagrees with J.B. Clark. He is of the opinion that only such changes which cannot be foreseen and cannot be provided for in advance would yield profit and not others. In the words of Prof. Knight, "it cannot, then be change, which is the cause of profit since if the law of change is known, as infact is largely the case, no profits can arise. Change may cause a situation out of which profit will be made, if it brings about ignorance of the future".

4. Innovation Theory of Profit

Prof. J.A. Schumpeter has formulated the innovation theory of profit. He is of the opinion that profit arises due to economic innovation. Innovation takes place when a firm introduces a new product, or new substitute, or new method of production, or it opens a new market or develops a new source of raw material or new forms of business organisation.

When a firm introduces new technique of production, it would be able to produce more efficiently which would reduce cost of production. Reduced cost of production would necessarily raise profit and innovation thus becomes the source of profit.

According to Schumpeter, the innovation is the main function of the entrepreneur. Hence, profit is to be paid as the reward for his innovation. He emphatically points out that "innovation is the source of profits."

Though it is a great step towards the formulation of a satisfactory theory of profit the innovation theory lacks realism. It completely ignores the importances of risk and uncertainty. Innovation itself involves risk. The entrepreneur has, therefore, to calculate risk and then to undertake innovation. It means that a theory of profit which ignores the possibility of risk is incomplete.

NOTES AND REFERENCES

1. J. L. Hanson : A Text Book of Economics, Seveth Edition, p. 299.
2. Ferguson and Kreps : Principles of Economics, Second Edition oxford & IBH, 1972, p. 664.
3. George J. Stigler : The theory of price third Edition (colleir Macmillan) p. 250.
4. Edward T. Nevin : A Text Book of Economic Analysis, Fourth Edition (Macmillan Education, 1979) p. 259.
5. George J. Stigler, ibid, p. 275.
6. Paish & Culyer : Benhams Economics, nineth Edition, 1973, p. 386.
7. Dudley Dillard : The Economics of J. M. Keynes, p. 162.

1. Ferguson and Kreps, Principles of Economics, oxford & IBH, 1972.
2. Emil Kauder, A History of Marginal Utility Theory, Princeton, New Jesey, 1965.
3. Mrs Joan Robinson, Economic Philosophy.
4. Alfred Marshall, Principles of Economics.
5. Stonier & Hague, A Text Book of Economic Theory, 1953.
6. Edward T Nevin, A Text-book of Economic Analysis, Mac-: millan Education Ltd, 1976.
7. A. Asimakopulos, An Introduction to Economic Theory Micro-economics, Oxford University Press 1979.

8. Donald S. Watson, Price Theory and its uses, Scientific Book Agency, Calcutta, 1970.
9. George J. Stigler, The Theory of Price, Macmillan Publishing Co. Inc. 1966.
10. T. Majumdar, Measurement of utility.
11. J.R. Hicks, Revision of Demand Theory, 1956.
12. F. Benham, Economics.
13. American Economic Review, Vol. 49. June 1959.
14. E.H. Chamberlin, the Theory of Monopolistic Competition.
15. Richard Leftwich, Introduction to Micro Economics, Subject Publications, 1978,
16. J.L. Hanson, A Text-book of Economics, Macdonald and Evans, 1977.
17. Paish & Culyer, Benham's Economics, Pitman, 1973.
18. Dudley Dillard, The Economics of J.M. Keynes, Groshy lock-wood, 1966.
19. Edwin G. Dalan, Basic Economics, The dryden press, Illions, 1977.
20. Frederick L. Gollady, Economics, problems, Principles & Priorities. The Benjamin/Cummings Publishing Company, Inc. 1978.